THE ECCENTRIC
ENTREPRENEUR

THE ECCENTRIC
ENTREPRENEUR

SIR JULIEN CAHN
Businessman, Philanthropist,
Magician & Cricket-Lover

MIRANDA RIJKS

The
History
Press

'The opportunity of a lifetime should be seized in the lifetime of the opportunity.'

Sir Julien Cahn Bt.

First published 2008
This edition published 2011

The History Press
The Mill, Brimscombe Port
Stroud, Gloucestershire, GL5 2QG
www.thehistorypress.co.uk

British Library Cataloguing in Publication Data.
A catalogue record for this book is available from the British Library.

ISBN 978 0 7524 5924 0

Typesetting and origination by The History Press
Manufacturing managed by Jellyfish Print Solutions Ltd.
Printed in India

Contents

1

A Precocious Child

On the afternoon of 20 October 1890, a day before his eighth birthday, Julien Cahn was walking along Waverley Street, Nottingham, with his governess. A horse and carriage swept past, the rush of air rustling the austere governess' skirts, the whiff of horse dung pungent to her nostrils. She stopped abruptly and turned to her diminutive charge.

'Julien – you are a young man now. You should stand on the outside of the pavement and I should stand on the inside.'

Julien queried why.

'The man should always protect the lady from passing carriages,' she explained.

Julien thought for a moment. 'No, that can not be right!' He paused. 'We can always get another governess but there is only one Julien!'

A small boy with dark hair and hazel eyes, Julien was the son of Albert and Matilda Cahn. His heritage was typical of the émigré Jew. Albert Cahn was born in 1856 in Russheim Germersheim, Rheinpflaz, a small village near Mannheim in the Rhineland area of Germany, reasonably close to the border of France. For several generations, Albert's family had played a prominent role in the tiny Jewish community. During the 1860s and 1870s, Germersheim became an uncomfortable place for a young ambitious Jew. Prompted by the indigenous anti-Semitism in Germany, young Albert decided to emigrate to England, leaving his family behind. Over the years, Albert never forgot his origins or his faith, and when he eventually died, he left money to maintain his parents and grandparents' graves. There are no records indicating when Albert moved to England, but by 1881 he was employed as a provision merchant and lodging at 26 Edward Street, Cardiff.

On 4 January 1882, Albert married Matilda Lewis, the eldest daughter of Dr Sigismund Lewis of 155 Duke Street, Liverpool, in an orthodox

Jewish ceremony under a simple chuppah at her parents' house. He married well. Sigismund Lewis had studied medicine in Berlin and practised in Hamburg before settling in Liverpool during the 1850s. He was an eminent, erudite and kindly doctor, single-handedly providing health services to the Liverpool Jewish community and later appointed honorary medical officer to most of the community's welfare institutions and schools. He was also medical officer to Cunard and various other steamship companies for forty years. His good works towards the poor and the Jewish community were well recognised both in Liverpool and in Berlin. Sigismund married Eliza Goldstucker and they had seven children: two boys and five girls, one girl dying in infancy.

The Lewis family lived well. When the children were still young they moved to Duke Street, an area that had been home to the first merchants of Liverpool. By the mid to late 1800s many of the wealthiest merchants had moved to more salubrious areas further up the hill, leaving behind the large terraced houses for the newer middle classes. In the 1860s 153–155 Duke Street had been Mrs Blodget's guest house. When she sold up, Dr Lewis purchased number 155, a handsome, wide, three-storey brick terraced house.

It is not known whether Matilda had a good relationship with her parents, or whether they were pleased with her marriage to Albert Cahn. However Sigismund must have been closer to his daughter Gertrude, for when he retired he moved to Southampton to live with her, eventually dying there in 1899.

Albert and Matilda set up home in Cardiff to allow Albert to continue his employment as a grocer. Exactly nine months after their wedding, following an extremely difficult birth, their only son, Julien, was born. It was thanks to the doctoring skills of her father that Matilda survived the birth. However, much to their chagrin there were to be no more children.

Albert Cahn was ambitious. He did not see his future in the greengrocery trade. He wanted a business that he could grow and leave as a legacy for his son. In 1885, he decided to set up a furniture business. Unconstrained by geography, he selected Nottingham as the ideal location, for being in the centre of the British Isles, it provided him with the widest possible distribution for his future sales. He moved his small family into a modest detached house at 12 Clipston Avenue, Nottingham.

Upon arriving in Nottingham, Albert was given the opportunity to run a cycle manufacturing business, C. Battersley & Sons. But he was not to be distracted from his main ambition and soon established his own, new business called the Nottingham Furnishing Company alongside Battersley's. Success came quickly and by the mid-1890s Albert moved his family to the more grandiose surroundings of 11 Waverley Street, Nottingham, a large imposing house located on a wealthy residential street close to the centre of Nottingham. This was an area the Cahns felt comfortable in, surrounded by their middle-class Jewish friends. By 1899, Albert was only involved in furniture and was the proud owner of the thriving Nottingham Furnishing Company and the Derby Bank of Furniture. A contemporary described Albert Cahn as, 'A man with extraordinary brainpower that astounded one very often'. Many years later such words were also uttered to describe his son.

Religion became the cornerstone of Albert and Matilda's life together, both at home and in the wider Jewish community where the couple played an important role. Young Julien could not escape from an upbringing fully immersed in Judaism.

Immediately upon arriving in Nottingham in 1883, Albert Cahn sought out the thriving Jewish community. Within a year, he had become President of the newly formed, Nottingham-based Hebrew Philanthropic Society. There were a number of Hebrew Philanthropic Societies located regionally around the country. Albert had been inspired by the Liverpool Hebrew Philanthropic Society, an organisation that had been successfully assisting the Jewish poor, sick and needy since 1811.

A devout and charitable man, Albert was a natural organiser and leader and became a highly respected member of the community. By 1889 he was elected President of the small Nottingham Synagogue. His greatest input was as Chairman of the Building Committee formed to oversee the construction of a permanent, modern synagogue on Chaucer Street, the premises having been bought for £1,000.

In spring 1889, the foundation stone was laid for the Chaucer Street Synagogue. Albert Cahn presented a silver trowel to Mr Samuel, who laid the first stone with the ritual formalities. A vote of thanks was passed to Mr Cahn the President.

The synagogue was opened on 30 July 1890. The ceremony was beautifully described in *Eight Hundred Years – The Story of Nottingham's Jews* by Nelson Fisher:

On a glorious summer day, three open carriages came into view. Rev Dr Hermann Adler (acting chief rabbi for his father) and Rev A Schloss sat in the first carriage each holding a scroll of law. Mr Albert Cahn and Mr Theobald Alexander, President & Treasurer also each holding a scroll sat in the second carriage. The synagogue was Moorish in design, seats in the body for 180 and 100 in the gallery. On behalf of the subscribers, Mr J Samuel presented a golden key to Mr Cahn with which to open the synagogue. Of handsome design, the key was inscribed with the initial words of the Ten Commandments in Hebrew, whilst in English there was a brief inscription setting forth the occasion of the presentation. Mr Cahn, in response, acknowledged the great kindness of his gift and his thanks that he had been spared to witness the accomplishment of their labours that day. He trusted that blessings would be showered on all connected with the Synagogue, which he concluded in formally declaring open.

Similar to his son, Albert Cahn was not only generous with his time, but also with his money. After the ceremony a reception was held by Mr and Mrs Cahn at the Masonic Hall, Goldsmith Street.

In 1892, Cahn became Chairman of the newly formed Chovevi Zion Association, a rapidly growing European Zionist organisation. This movement, which was the predecessor of political Zionism, was sponsored by Jews living in Europe and the USA, whose common interest in Jewish life, stimulated by the persecution of the Jews in Romania and Russia, led them to believe that it may be a good idea to create a Jewish country. The principal ideas were to foster the 'national idea' in Israel, promote the colonisation of Palestine and assist those already established, to make people aware that Hebrew was a living language and to better the moral, intellectual and material status of Israel. Critically, members of the association pledged themselves to 'render cheerful obedience to the laws of the lands in which they live, and as good citizens to promote their welfare as far as lies in their power'. Although Albert may have wished for a secure country for Jews at large, he was utterly loyal and grateful to England, his adopted homeland.

Albert and Matilda kept a strictly kosher home, where milk was separated from meat and the Sabbath and all Jewish holidays were stringently adhered to. Albert did not dress in the garbs of the Orthodoxy as he wished to assimilate in England, but the beliefs and rituals in the home were never forgotten. As a child, Julien had no choice but to conform to his parents' expectations and behaviour. He dutifully sat through the Friday night Sabbath meals, chanting his prayers in Hebrew. He attended Saturday services at the synagogue and Sunday morning cheder classes where the children were taught all about the religion and studied Hebrew. But from a very young age he began to question it.

Julien and his mother adored each other, but such adoration did not make for an easy childhood. Matilda smothered her only child with affection, indulging his whims and inadvertently encouraging his eccentricities. She was undeniably a rather strange woman. When guests came to her house in Waverley Street she would lock the door of the downstairs cloakroom so that they were unable to use the facilities. She had an obsession with health and cleanliness and did not want other people using her toilet. Matilda was viewed by many (particularly the servants who cared for her in her latter years) as a miserable woman who spent most of her days complaining and bossing staff around.

Julien's childhood was uneventful and provided no precursory suggestions as to the successes he would achieve in adulthood. He attended a small private school in Nottingham for a few years, with the future Sir Harold Bowden, but thereafter was educated privately by a succession of governesses and tutors. Julien and Harold (of Raleigh Bicycles) became lifelong friends, bonded initially by being joint bottom of their class. In their adult years the men would spend happy hours fishing together on the lakes at Cahn's future home, Stanford Hall. How ironic to consider that they were both to become the leading businessmen of their era. Bowden was sent to Clifton College to complete his education, but Matilda preferred to keep her son nearby. For the rest of his childhood Julien was tutored at home.

Home education allowed him plenty of time to indulge in his hobbies, childhood hobbies that were to mature into lifelong passions. Hours were spent reading *The Boy's Own Annuals* and magazines, gaining inspiration for the magic tricks that he tested out on his mother. Magic was a common interest for young boys growing up in the latter decades of the nineteenth century. The popularity of amateur conjuring can largely be attributed to Professor Hoffmann, who published a book called *Modern Magic* that was serialised in the pages of *Every Boy's Magazine* from 1876 onwards. Julien read each edition avidly. Every month he would wait in eager anticipation to find out the latest secrets of the professional tricks exposed by Hoffmann. Many of these were tricks performed by the world-famous Maskelyne and Devant. John Neville Maskelyne, born in 1839, is considered to be the founding father of the modern British magician. He was a prolific inventor of magic tricks and presented his illusions as magical sketches. By 1893, he was joined by David Devant. Maskelyne and Devant's, just north of Oxford Circus, became the place for family entertainment. Between them they presented many famous illusions. Albert and Matilda took Julien to visit a Maskelyne and Devant show for his tenth birthday. The experience had a profound influence on him. He watched in amazement as the magicians took seemingly endless supplies of eggs out of an empty hat and passed them to the children to hold. His mouth fell open as a lady mysteriously walked through a wall and a donkey simply vanished in mid-air. For weeks afterwards Julien tried to work out how the magicians extracated themselves from a secure wooden box. Many of the illusions presented by these masters were to form the foundation of tricks that Julien performed thirty years later. As a young boy, whenever he had any spare pocket money, Julien would buy apparatus from the local magic shop and practise the magic tricks, patiently and diligently until they were almost perfect. But it was the grand illusions performed by Maskelyne and Devant that mesmerised him the most.

As he became older, Julien's interest in magic diminished and was replaced by a passion for the game of cricket. When he was old enough to slip out of the house unnoticed, he would spend happy afternoons sitting under Parr's Tree at Trent Bridge (an ancient elm named after George Parr, a famous Nottingham cricketer who regularly hit the ball into the tree) listening to the observations of his hero, Arthur Shrewsbury, and watching him play. Julien adored everything about the game. It is not known how or when he began playing himself. But he must have practised the rudiments of the game as a boy, for when he launched his own team in 1902, he included himself as one of the key players.

In the 1901 census, Julien Cahn, then aged 19, listed his profession as 'Clerk to Piano Importer'. His father had every intention of employing his son in due course, but first he wanted him to gain experience in the 'real world', starting in a lowly employed position and working his way up. When Charles Foulds, owner of Foulds Music – a highly respected chain of music shops selling instruments and music – offered to employ Julien, Albert was delighted. Julien could learn the rudiments of retail and salesmanship and then, when he had proven himself to an objective outsider, Albert would welcome him into the Cahn family business, the Nottingham Furnishing Company. In fact, Charles Foulds was to become a firm friend, mentor and business associate to Julien. When Foulds Music teetered on the brink of collapse during the inter-war years, Julien came to the rescue, recalling with fondness the experience he had gained in his early years. He set up a piano division within Jays and Campbells, installing Charles Foulds and his son Arthur on the top floor of Talbot House to manage it along with the single Foulds music shop that still remains as a successful family enterprise today. Charles was heavily involved in music promotion and Julien was to become a key benefactor.

A love of music sustained Julien throughout his life. The first record of his involvement can be seen in Allen's *Nottingham Red Book* of 1903, an annual book that lists all civic information, where it is noted that Julien Cahn was the Treasurer and Secretary of the Nottingham Aeolian Society, set up for the cultivation of the mandoline. No one recalls him playing the mandoline, although he did play the viola, badly. Some years later, he even had four songs published by Cary & Co., highly reputed music publishers. Julien composed the music and his friend Harry Farnsworth wrote the words, giving the pieces sentimental titles such as 'England, Dear England' and 'My Heart is Faithful'. They did not become memorable hits, but do still lie in a published tome within the archives of the British Library.

Many years later, Julien Cahn talked about his early career with his eldest son, Albert Junior. 'I had to sell pianos once. It doesn't matter what you sell, if you can sell, you can sell.'

In 1902, Albert decided that it was time to offer his son a job. Julien had shown a particular aptitude for figures, and Albert needed someone to keep a discrete eye on his bookkeeper. Officially, Julien joined his father's business as a junior furniture salesman, but it wasn't long before he was spending all day on commercial rather than direct-sales activities. In fact, Julien had no particular desire to work for his father, but there was one significant advantage of working at Nottingham Furnishing Company versus Foulds Music. At the furniture business he could get hold of his father's workers.

In the late eighteenth and early nineteenth centuries it was commonplace for businesses employing a dozen or more workers to assemble their own cricket team. Play normally took place in the afternoon of an early closing day. This was particularly so in cricket-obsessed Nottingham. One of the big attractions for joining his father's furniture firm was the chance to organise a group of men into a cricket team. At the tender age of 19, Julien Cahn cajoled sixteen of the Nottingham Furnishing Company's staff to come together to play for the newly formed Nottingham Furnishing Company Eleven. During that initial year of 1902, the team enjoyed just two matches. Playing against the Liverpool Victoria Friendly Society on 21 August on the YMCA ground in Nottingham, they lost their first match. But a week later they played their second game on the Forest ground against a team put together by the Nottingham provision merchants, Furley's. Cahn's team scored their very first win.

Buoyed up by the success of his second game, Julien spent the next few months refining the team. He culled half of the 1902 players and went on an active recruitment campaign to find better cricketers to improve the chances of his XI in 1903. Not wanting to limit himself to the employees of the Nottingham Furnishing Company, he poached players from elsewhere. By the next season he had a posse of thirty-five men to call upon. As the team no longer comprised just Nottingham Furnishing Company employees, he was obliged to change the name of the team and so the players now found themselves part of the newly formed Notts Ramblers. Between 21 May and 3 September 1903, the Notts Ramblers played eight games, winning four and losing four. They played a number of local teams including Notts Unity 'A' team. This team comprised the founding members of the Nottinghamshire Cricket Association, one of the oldest cricket clubs in the country and still in existence today. Unsurprisingly, Cahn's team lost.

Even in those early years, Julien Cahn's personal averages were poor. In fact, in 1903 his averages were the worst in the whole of his team. But his inability to play well did not deter the young Julien. Intensely competitive by nature, his ambitions were clear from the outset. He wanted to have an outstanding team. Year after year he was determined to increase the number of matches played, attract better players and play against stronger sides. In 1904 the Ramblers played fifteen matches, winning nine, losing four and drawing two. This was a particularly auspicious year, for it was the first year that a member of the Vaulkhard family was to join the team. W.H. Vaulkhard was to become a firm friend and cricketing confidant, and it is believed that he was the man who originally suggested that Cahn should run his own cricket side. Later on, during the 1920s, recognising the cricketing talent of Vaulkhard's four sons, Cahn was to mentor the boys and groom them for his team.

The Notts Ramblers grew rapidly in size year on year. In 1905 they won eleven of the fourteen matches they played, losing one game and drawing two. By 1907, they were playing against recognised teams and travelling around the country for games. Cahn had some notable players, including Goodall, a famous local architect, and Stapleton, the Nottingham reserve wicket-keeper. In 1907, the Nottingham Furnishing Company team was resurrected and they played a single game against Lenton United. The Furnishing team was, for that year only, Julien's second team. By 1908, they were relegated to Cahn's third team – for this was the year that the Julien Cahn's XI was born. The Ramblers played nine games, Nottingham Furnishing played one game and Julien Cahn's XI played one game against J. Holroyd's XI.

Although the team created in his name lost their first game, this did not deter Julien. He concentrated on accumulating a smaller, more select group of players. The occasional friend or relation appears in the players list, such as B. Serabski in 1908 (one of Julien's closest lifelong friends), but this was rare. Julien wanted only the best players. In 1910, the Ramblers played sixteen games, Julien Cahn's XI played three games and the Furnishing XI just one. His players were now regularly scoring centuries. There were impressive performances against impressive teams. Matches took place against teams from Lincoln, Buxton, Uppingham, Spalding, Sheffield, Eastbourne and North Warwickshire, to name but a few. Over the next couple of years, Cahn's teams travelled as far afield as Folkestone.

By 1911, cricket was the most significant part of Cahn's life. He personally played twenty-five games and Vaulkhard played twenty-one. Cricket certainly seemed to be more important than work. Bearing in mind that some of these fixtures were two-day matches, Julien must have been out of the business and playing cricket for over six weeks.

During these years Albert was subtly encouraging Julien to become more involved in the business, take more decisions and be responsible for its growth. Julien rose to the challenges offered by his father and began to enjoy business life. He spotted an enormous opportunity in the development of hire purchase and persuaded his father to allow him to create credit terms for the business. He took control of the advertising and promotions of the company. Most significantly, he encouraged his father to begin acquiring other furniture businesses, the largest and most important being Jays. As long ago as 1910, as was evidenced in a typical advertisement carried in the *News of the World*, Jays were promoting themselves as 'England's largest and best credit furnishers'. By our modern standards, the adverts were polite and quite charming. They went on to state, 'We have furnished over 250,000 homes on our famous system. May we furnish yours? Our furniture will give you pleasure and comfort for a lifetime.' The Cahns' furniture business was growing fast and by 1914 was one of only nine multiple-shop firms in existence in the UK.

The start of the First World War resulted in the instant demise of Julien Cahn's cricket teams but business activities were deftly positioned to fill the void.

By his early thirties, Julien had taken over the reins of the Nottingham Furnishing Company but he was still living at home with his parents at 11 Waverley Street. While it was not uncommon to remain at home until marriage, Julien was certainly no young groom. Even Matilda recognised that it was time for her son to wed. The Cahns employed the services of a traditional Jewish matchmaker and before long Julien had been introduced to the young and exuberant Phyllis Wolfe.

Julien Cahn married Phyllis Wolfe on 11 July 1916 in the Bournemouth Synagogue. Phyllis was the daughter of Abraham Wolfe, who was born in Sunderland, Durham, in 1865. In 1881, he had been a boarder at 20 Alexandra Grove, Headingly Cum Burley, York, and was employed as a clerk in a loan office. Abraham Wolfe had three brothers, Jonas, Walter and Alec Wolfe. After marriage and the birth of four children (Jonas, George, Phyllis and Roland, the latter who died in childhood), the Wolfes moved to Bournemouth. When she married, aged 20, Phyllis had also been living at home with her parents at 61 Wellington Road, Bournemouth. Youthful and naïve, she had no idea that she was to embark on a life of wealth, status and excitement.

2

The Power of Philanthropy

Julien and Phyllis began married life at Papplewick Grange, a grand house for newly weds, situated in the delightful village of Papplewick, near Hucknall. It was a large and comfortable family house, with eight bedrooms and five bathrooms, a 30ft entrance hall, drawing room, dining room, study and library. The first few years of their marriage were happy and rather uneventful.

But by the early 1920s things were to change. Julien was to experience emotional turbulence such as he had never known.

After five years of marriage, Phyllis gave birth to their first son. Tragedy was to beset them during those late winter months of 1921. The baby died at birth. The infant's name was never officially registered, but he was referred to as Roland, named after Phyllis' younger brother who had died before his fifth birthday. Julien was particularly devastated by the death. Here was a man who had escaped the First World War unscathed, a man who had an easy life and was in command of every aspect of it. For the first time he was faced with an event over which he had absolutely no control. The repercussions of Roland's death would affect him in both positive and negative ways for the rest of his life. While it propelled him to take a deep interest in infant mortality and to spend considerable sums of his fortune on improving conditions in childbirth, it also had a negative effect on his relationship with his future sons. He never became emotionally close to the boys.

Later that year, on 8 June 1921, aged just 66, his father, Albert Cahn, died suddenly of a heart attack. Matilda and Julien were devastated. The wealth he left them did nothing to appease their grief. By the time of his death, Albert was a rich man, leaving an estate of £260,397 gross (equivalent to £7 million today), net £189,505. The *Nottingham Guardian* carried the headlines: 'Over a quarter million left by Jewish merchant!' Although the financial legacy he left to his son was considerable, so was the responsibility. Julien was now solely in charge of one of the largest businesses in Nottingham. In previous years, he had always discussed his problems with his father, and was grateful for the wisdom and insight Albert provided. With the loss of his father, Julien's life had, quite suddenly, become serious.

During these difficult years Julien Cahn's bizarre habits became increasingly evident. As his wealth and status increased, so he began to care less about hiding his eccentricities. The most obvious was a compulsion to turn around in a full circle whenever he walked through a doorway. The reasoning behind this was never known. While many believed such behaviour was due to superstition, Julien was much too rational to be superstitious. This behaviour must have been a form of obsessive compulsive disorder. It caused various problems, most commonly when the person walking behind Cahn inadvertently found themselves walking straight into him, nose to nose. He even turned around 360 degrees when he got out of the rear of a car, typically leaning back in to pick up his *Financial Times* as he did so, in order to disguise the habit.

Eager to comfort her bereaved husband, Phyllis quickly became pregnant again and in February 1922 gave birth to the simply named Patience Cahn. Julien was to fall deeply in love with his daughter, a girl who inherited his dark features, a child whom he overly indulged for the rest of his life. Meanwhile, the pressures in Julien's life continued to mount. He had moved his mother from her home in Waverley Street to Papplewick Grange.

Matilda Cahn was a demanding woman, controlling of all those around her. While most observant Jews didn't work on Saturdays, they nevertheless visited the synagogue, said their prayers and socialised with friends and family. But Matilda refused even to get out of bed on Saturdays, announcing that it was the Holy Day, the day of rest – a commandment she took quite literally. Servants were expected to bring her food and drink in bed. Despite her difficult manner, Matilda had been devoted to her husband. After his death she lost interest in life. Within a year she was seriously ill and by the middle of 1923 it became apparent that she was dying of cancer. Towards the end of her life, she was so mean and bitter towards her carers that the regular nurses refused to help her and instead Julien found some nuns to administer to her needs during her final weeks. For a woman who professed to be so committed to Judaism, this was tragically ironic. She died at Papplewick on 1 December 1923, aged 63.

Phyllis' life became easier after the death of her mother-in-law. She was now the lady of the house, a young woman with a zest for life. The staff adored her. She loved horse riding and the outdoors and had a coterie of young female friends with whom she played raucous games of bridge. She rarely interfered with the workings of the house and left all domestic decisions to the butler, an attitude that had been frowned upon by her late mother-in-law. She was loud and fun with a mischievous sense of humour that shone through, despite her deference to her older husband.

Julien had married well. Such willingness was important to him for he had a plan, and Phyllis' compliance with it was essential for its success. In the years following his father's death, Julien Cahn laid down the foundations for his climb up society's ladder. His strategy was multi-stranded. It included the obvious – using his wealth to achieve recognition – and the less obvious – indulging in the 'right' pursuits. Hunting, philanthropy and the development of certain critical friendships were key ingredients. That he and Phyllis actually enjoyed these activities simply added to the rapid achievement of his aims.

Phyllis and Julien shared a passion for fox hunting. The Cahns were fortunate to be living in Leicestershire, the home of some of the best hunting territory in the country.

After the birth of Albert Jonas in June 1924, Phyllis was eager to return to horse riding and was thrilled when her husband was appointed Joint Master of the Craven Hunt based in Berkshire. This was the first time that Julien had used his money to buy himself status, but it was a subtly undertaken move, quite acceptable to his contemporaries. The hunt wanted a Master with funds and they wanted a Master who respected the ways of the countryside. Julien fulfilled both criteria and he rapidly garnered a good reputation among his hunting colleagues. The annual hunt ball was held at the Corn Exchange in Newbury. It was a fine occasion for the Cahns to show off their wealth and status. However, the location was far from convenient for the Leicestershire-based Cahns and Julien wanted to impress those closer to his home.

For several hundred years hunting was an integral and important part of social and rural life in Great Britain. In the late 1800s an estimated 50,000 people were involved in fox hunting, with about 150 people attending each meet. Whatever your opinion of hunting today, in the early twentieth century hunting was considered the natural and most humane method of managing and controlling foxes, hares, deer and mink in the countryside, and it was often the method particularly favoured by farmers. Hunting created a social mesh, bringing together communities and classes. It was considered such an important part of life that all of the local papers reported upon the local hunt's activities. The weekly *Loughborough Echo* carried at least a paragraph or so on its local hunt, the Quorn. A change of Masters was deemed sufficiently newsworthy to be noted in the national papers. Each time Cahn took up a new Mastership it was reported in *The Times*. In light of this, it would be dangerous to judge the Cahns and their hunting compatriots by the standards of today.

During the first half of the twentieth century, to put the letters 'MFH' (Master of Fox Hounds) after one's name provided immediate elevation in society. Only those who were truly the 'pillars of society' were Masters and upon attainment of such an honour, doors opened among the upper classes. A prerequisite for being an MFH was wealth. Perhaps the title could have stood for 'Money Forthcoming Here!', for that was what the Masters were required to do – fund the hunt.

There was never a shortage of candidates for vacant Masterships. So how did Julien Cahn, a little-known Jewish retailer, become a Master? The hunt committees sought gentlemen (or women, although there were few female Masters) of sophistication, possessing considerable intelligence, great tact and diplomacy – gentlemen who wanted to carry on the 'Englishman's best tradition'. If they lacked kennel experience or did not live in the county of the hunt (both categories into which Julien fell), they had to be 'inspired by real keenness and enthusiasm, impelled by public-spirited anxiety to further the interest of sport and possess . . . an abiding love of the fox-hound'. It was his personality and commercial skills that endeared Julien to the hunt committees. He was gifted with all the attributes that Lord Willoughby de Broke considered a Master should have. Julien had tact, administrative talent, the 'power of penetrating character', the desire to take on responsibility and all other attributes that 'form the essential equipment of a successful public man'. Skill in public relations was essential for the role, as the Master needed to gain the allegiance of landowners, great and small, to gain permission for riding over their land. Although most Masters were expected to have been 'reared in the atmosphere and tradition of country life', Julien must have managed to persuade the committees that he had a passion for the sport and while he was not brought up in the country ways, he had fully adopted them in adult life. He was certainly persuasive and deeply competitive. Another key attribute of the Master was 'thick skin'. This Cahn seemed to have in abundance. Superficially at least, he cared little what others thought of him.

Mr Bromley Davenport, himself an MFH and MP, wrote:

> No position, except perhaps a Member of Parliament's entails so much hard work accompanied by so little thanks as that of a Master of Fox-hounds. A fierce light inseparable from his semi-regality beats on him; his every act is scrutinised by eyes and tongues ever ready to mark and proclaim what is done amiss. Very difficult is it for him to do right.

The hunts were run as businesses, therefore commercial acumen in the Master was much sought after. Masters of the hunts would take on all financial responsibility and management. Should the hunt have any outstanding debts, the Master would have the responsibility for settling them. He also undertook financing and managing the breeding and rearing of hounds and keeping a stable of horses. The annual cost of running the hunt was considerable as it included payment of servants, horses, kennels-men, whippers-in and horses. It has been said that Sir Julien spent up to £50,000 per year on hunting in today's money. Rather a large sum for a sporadic hobby.

Fortunately for Cahn, by 1925 the Burton Hunt was struggling. Based in Lincolnshire, which was somewhat nearer to their home, Papplewick Grange, the Burton Hunt's subscriptions were down, the sport was bad and the Master, William Barr Danby, had resigned due to old age. So, when the committee learned that Julien Cahn was interested in the Mastership there was universal relief. Although he was yet to achieve his knighthood and subsequent elevation in society, Julien's financial wealth and astute business acumen were renowned and he was welcomed with open arms. As is recalled in *A History of the Burton Hunt – the first 300 years*: 'For nine seasons he used this income to the benefit of the Burton, but in return ran it as he wished.'

A considerable part of Julien's enjoyment of fox hunting came from the dressing up. As fox hunting became fashionable, so the traditional hunting costumes became all the rage: a red coat, traditionally called 'pink', tight pants and riding boots. Dapper as always, Julien had all the necessary accoutrements. His tailors were engaged to produce his outfits and his boots, saddles and bridles were made to order, the leather buffed to a mirror-like sheen before every meet. In later years, Charlie Rodgers, Julien's head groom, assisted by Wallace Addy, an assistant groom and great favourite with the housemaids, was responsible for ensuring that spurs and tack were polished, coats cleaned, hats brushed and smoothed. Everything had to be spotless, although five minutes into the hunt all was mud-splattered and filthy. Nevertheless, the dressing up and accessories added much charm to the whole exercise. Cahn frequently chose to be photographed in his hunting pink and the only portraits of him that exist today are of him in his hunting attire.

Phyllis Cahn, in her long skirts, was a confident horsewoman. She enjoyed riding, was proficient and, as was the custom at the time, rode sidesaddle.

In 1926, the year before their youngest child, Richard, was born, Julien Cahn, the Burton Hunt's new Master, was received with 'rapture', his wealth, cricket and philanthropy preceding him. The previous Master introduced him as: 'A Master who knew exactly how things should be done and intended to do them.'

Although the hunt was in financial difficulties, this did not deter Cahn. He was confident that, financially, he could turn the Burton Hunt around. He had sufficient funds to indulge in the hunt and right from the beginning intended to be its benefactor. Upon joining the Burton Hunt, he asked for a Master's guarantee of £500. The Master's guarantee was the sum of money that the Master expected to receive in return for running the hunt. Should the cost of running the hunt exceed that sum, the Master was personally required to foot the difference. For the first time, the Burton Hunt had asked tenant farmers and others whose land they hunted over for a subscription. Nevertheless, the money raised was £600 down on the previous year and a loan of £200 had to be taken out. On receiving his guarantee, rather than pocketing it, as was common practice, Cahn returned it to start a wire fund.

The wire fund was established to mitigate the dangerous effects of wire fences that were being erected across the countryside. As large estates were cut up, farms were purchased by tenants and smallholdings increased, so fields were divided by wire rather than the traditionally expensive to maintain wooden fences or hedges. Understandably, it was deemed more economically viable by many farmers to use wire.

Of course, wire fences were of great danger to the huntsman and it was in their interest for the wire to be removed. Julien described barbed wire as 'a death trap'. Having put his guarantee of £500 towards the wire fund, he then gave another £150 in 1930. The money was used to cover the expense of removing wire at the beginning of the season, replacing it with rails or fences and then reinstating the wire at the end of the season. He used his administrative skills and powers of persuasion to set up a Wire Committee. Each member looked after two parishes and purchased the necessary timber for fencing. Julien was vociferous in his complaints if wire was left up. So as to encourage the growth and maintenance of hedges, in line with many hunts, the Burton Hunt instigated hedge-trimming competitions, with prizes being given to farms with the best-kept hedges.

While Julien claimed to enjoy the thrill of hunting, this was not strictly true. In fact, he was profoundly nervous of the pursuit. In a similar vein to his concern over getting hit by the cricket ball, he mitigated his risks of injury when hunting by employing a groom who would ride in front of him, warning of difficult places and cutting down branches if required. When they approached a difficult ditch, Julien would dismount, the groom would jump the horse over and Julien would remount on the other side. It has been commented that Cahn paid a great deal of cash not to jump fences in some of the best hunting counties in England. While his riding skills must have been mocked, few would have been openly critical for he spent a fortune 'subsidising everyone else's fun'.

Hunting was one tactic Cahn pursued for social acceptance; another method was philanthropy – a gesture altogether more flamboyant and instant in its results. Although he was a ruthless businessman, Cahn was also a generous benefactor. And he quickly realised that giving things away had other more important consequences over and above the feel-good factor. It brought him public gratitude, publicity and respect among the great and the good.

Over the years, many of Cahn's philanthropic gestures were of a medical nature. His first public donation was not. It was the construction and donation of some almshouses in Hucknall, provided as homes of rest for elderly industrial workers. It is likely that Cahn gave these as much for the benefit of the local community as for the benefit of his friend, Sir Harold Bowden. On 10 February 1926, the Duke of York visited Nottingham as President of the Industrial Welfare Society. He was shown around the Raleigh Cycle Company's works by Sir Harold Bowden. Afterwards he took lunch with the Bowdens and the Cahns and then visited the Hucknall almshouses donated by

Julien. This was an enlightening experience for Cahn. He was invited to hobnob with one of the most important people in the country thanks to a donation.

Cahn's second act of public philanthropy was medical in nature. Dr Henry Jaffé was Julien Cahn's doctor and a close friend. From 1921, he and his colleague Rupert Allen specialised in caring for children with rickets, working in light treatment clinics in Nottingham. The UV rays emitted by the quartz lamps were believed to cure many skin conditions and be beneficial in cases of nervous excitability, sleeplessness and loss of appetite. A leaflet about the Hanovia Quartz Lamp (a typical lamp found in sun-ray clinics) explained that 'irradiation simultaneously stimulated all the defensive processes of the body'. It was believed that the body was strengthened and so energised by the light that it was able to throw off the disease. As such, people believed that the light cured numerous illnesses, from gangrene and tuberculosis to rickets and anaemia. The medical profession and Cahn alike genuinely believed in the health-enhancing properties of this equipment.

During the mid-1920s, Cahn funded Jaffé and Allen to run a sun-ray clinic at 32 Heathcote Street, Nottingham. The services were offered at very low prices and sometimes free to those in need. However, in 1927 Cahn decided to withdraw his patronage, due partly to increased expenditure and partly because he wished to give his money to other causes. This was not a popular move. In a letter to the Mayor of Nottingham, the Revd Henry Canon Hunt of Nottingham Cathedral wrote that Cahn had received so many appeals asking him not to withdraw his support that he consented to keep the clinic running and had offered to hand over the apparatus to anyone who would carry on the good work. In March 1928, Julien Cahn gave over his clinic at 32 Heathcote Street to Nottingham City Council as a gift, on condition that the treatment was made fully available to poor people. Cahn equipped the clinic with the necessary apparatus and refurbished it with new furniture. Julien Cahn received much positive publicity and accolades about his donation in the local Nottingham and Leicestershire press.

After the deaths of his parents and firstborn son, Julien felt the need to resurrect his hobby of cricket to relieve some of the pressures of his daily life. Hunting was sporadic and occurred only in the winter months. The First World War was over and he had the money, even if he didn't necessarily have the time, so in 1923 cricket began to feature once more in Cahn's life.

While the Notts Ramblers and the Nottingham Furnishing Company teams were never to play again, the Julien Cahn XI was reborn in the summer of 1923, initially in a modest way. That first year they played only four mediocre matches. However, the numbers of matches played and the calibre of the players increased rapidly year on year. In 1924 they played twelve games, in 1925 twenty-one games and in 1926 thirty-four games. By 1927, the Cahn XI comprised outstanding individuals, playing an ambitious programme of fixtures around the country.

It seems extraordinary that a man could have such passion for his sports, participate in them, but show no skill or talent for them. Most incompetent players would accept their inability and minimise their participation to that of a spectator – but not Julien Cahn. A nervous horseman, he was nevertheless Master of the Hunt. An unskilled cricketer, he captained the leading private team of the twentieth century.

From these early years, Julien Cahn had ambitions to be part of the powerhouse of cricket, first in Nottingham and then at the Marylebone Cricket Club, Lords. By the mid-1920s he was already recognised as a man of stature, a major Nottingham employer and a donator of philanthropic gifts. On 18 February 1925, he was made a member of the Nottinghamshire County Cricket Club Committee, most probably elected by Mr Swain and Mr Goodall, two committee members who had played against his team in earlier years.

That same year Cahn bestowed his first considerable gift to Trent Bridge. The small scoring board was taken down and a new, up-to-date one was erected, paid for by Cahn. A year later his gift was much bigger. Trent Bridge, the home of Nottinghamshire County Cricket Club, was of considerable national importance. A vast number of wooden stands, a reporter's box and a ring of covered seats going all the way around the ground had been built in 1899, the year that Trent Bridge hosted its first test match. Test matches were played against the Australians every four years and the next one was due in 1926. The wooden stands had degenerated and it was decided that new stands should be built in time for the match. Modern concrete stands were erected, costing in the region of £5,000, largely financed by Cahn. Although the concrete stands have lasted well to this day, the pressure to get them built ready for the 1926 test match was, disappointingly, all for nothing – only 50 minutes of play took place due to rain. Cahn was sanguine; his gift would last for years to come.

The following year it was declared that the old practice building at Trent Bridge had become unsafe, so it was demolished. A new practice hall was constructed at a cost of £1,700, half of which was contributed by Cahn. Designed by H.H. Goodall, it was perceived as the best in the country. It was officially declared open on 17 January 1927 and still stands today.

There are numerous descriptions of Julien Cahn's cricket playing, unanimously uncomplimentary. Although Cahn supported some of the very best cricketers of the 1920s and 1930s, he was really most unsuited to be a hands-on captain. He had a profound theoretical knowledge of cricket but, as Jim Swanton, the cricket writer and BBC commentator, kindly observed, 'he was unblessed with natural ability in the game'.

Cahn loved to bowl, throwing the ball high in the air and relying on athletic fielders to take boundary catches. J.M. Barrie (author of *Peter Pan*) used to say that Cahn's bowling was so slow that if he didn't like a particular delivery he could run after it and fetch it back. There were many similarities between Barrie and Cahn. Barrie had had his own team (the Allahakbarries – Arabic for 'God help us!') before the First World War and had, for a short time, worked as a journalist on Nottingham newspapers. His playing was equally poor, although he similarly knew everything about the theory of cricket. Other contemporaries described Cahn's bowling as 'inordinately slow' and 'quite without intrinsic merit'. Benny Green, the jazz musician, broadcaster and cricket writer, noted that he bowled 'not so much up and down as to and fro'.

Over the years, rather cruelly, if any schoolboy got two or three quick wickets and started to boast about his ability as a bowler, his friends would immediately holler, 'Bowler? Call yourself a bowler? You couldn't bowl Julien Cahn out!' Those youngsters, most now deceased or in very old age, eventually learned to appreciate all the things that Cahn did for cricket and Nottingham cricket in particular. Mr D.E. Williamson, one of those Nottingham schoolboys who uttered such comments, stated in the late 1980s, 'Come back Sir Julien, cricket could do with you again!'

Cahn did get the occasional wicket, although surprise was probably his main weapon. Perhaps it was Cahn's fielding that was the most excruciating and, on plenty an occasion, embarrassing. When fielding he wore shin guards and had to be placed in a sheltered position. This was usually deep mid-on, sometimes mid-off with a further fielder stationed several yards behind him in a direct line so that whenever the ball was hit with any force in the captain's direction, Cahn would step to one side and let the man behind him pick it up.

There was many an occasion when a dolly catch was coming his way at mid-on, and he cowered away from the ball covering his head with both hands. He was inclined to ignore catches, exclaiming, 'Nowhere near me!' He was good-natured over this and even the odd laugh from the crowd passed without unduly upsetting him. A leisurely single, off a stroke played gently towards a less than athletic fieldsman, was for many years known in local Nottingham cricket circles as 'One to Sir Julien'! Of course, in later years those youngsters appreciated the irony, or tragedy, of such a dedicated cricket-lover being so totally inadequate on the field.

Various commentators have suggested that Cahn's inadequacy in the field and sometimes glaringly obvious abject fear of the ball were due to brittle bones or even haemophilia. In fact, these were kindly but quite inaccurate observations. The reality was that he had no sporting prowess, ability or agility and he didn't want to get hurt! One of his secretaries, a Miss Lane, commented that he probably lacked stamina as he never moved very fast.

The *Cricketer*, of September 1997, summed up Cahn succinctly. It described Sir Julien as, 'At once the most prolific patron of cricket between the wars and comfortably the worst ever first-class cricketer'.

Julien had learned much about business from his father and many of the mottos by which he lived his life originated from philosophies expounded by his wise father. April Sebag Montefiore, daughter of Cahn's great friend Dr Henry Jaffé, recalls a number of Julien's aphorisms. The first one relates to personal self-development and was strictly adhered to by Julien. 'Others value you as you value yourself' emphasised his conviction that in order to succeed in life one should have self-belief and never underestimate oneself. Indeed, such self-confidence was never in short supply. The next two relate to business success. 'When negotiating a deal, don't be greedy – let the other side feel as if they are getting a bargain', and, 'Only ask advice from those who are successful in life'. The final statement of 'Don't set the world to rights' is more general and reflects his growing cynicism. While he was an ardent believer in doing good, he despised proselytising and interfering do-gooders.

These convictions were put into practice, particularly during the first half of the 1920s, when, after the death of his father, he launched a programme of dramatic growth for the Nottingham Furnishing Company.

Cahn went on an ambitious acquisition trail buying up local furniture shops in towns all across the country. These shops were rarely rebranded, and normally kept their original names. The initial tentacles of that life-changing method of retailing, hire purchase, were beginning truly to take hold. Cahn could see that his innovative business ideas were working. The tills were ringing faster and faster and Cahn's personal bank balance was growing daily by quite unprecedented amounts. He had the money to do whatever he wanted.

And what he wanted went beyond just having a superb team in his name. As a young boy, he had dreamed of having his very own cricket ground. Prior to the First World War, and then between 1923 and 1926, Cahn's teams played on the old YMCA ground, the site of the current Nottingham County Hall. But this wasn't good enough for Julien Cahn. He wanted his own ground, and now he had the money he intended to create one.

In 1926, Cahn built his own cricket ground at West Bridgford, Nottingham, on a 9-acre site adjacent to Loughborough Road, at an estimated cost of £12,000. The site was originally owned by W.H. Vaulkhard's father, William Gillespie, and the sale of the ground was negotiated by W.H. Vaulkhard. The pavilion that Julien built was described in the local newspapers as 'delightful'; it was designed by C.L.A. Sutton. Cahn had been impressed by Sutton in their previous meetings – the most memorable occasion being on 10 June 1926 when Cahn's side played against RAF Cadets, a key member of their team being the architect.

All was done to exacting and modern standards; the outfield and square were perfectly maintained. The pavilion included baths, dining and dressing rooms and an up-to-date score box. Inside, the interior could be used as a hard tennis court. Also in the pavilion was a fabulous collection of cricket bats, referred to by Julien as 'famous bits of wood', today housed at the Nottinghamshire Club. Amusement was gained from the collection of uncannily accurate caricatures of many of the famous players who played for the team.

On the balcony at West Bridgford (often called 'Loughborough Road' by locals) Cahn had three wicker chairs, as large as sentry boxes but extremely comfortable. These special chairs were for Julien and his privileged guests, and he spent the little free time he had sitting there, watching any games in which he wasn't playing and smoking his large cigars. Work was never far from Cahn's mind. He was known to dictate his business affairs to his secretary while Robson, his chauffeur, prepared him for an innings or a session in the nets.

The atmosphere at Loughborough Road was quite different from the hullabaloo of Trent Bridge. Here it was quiet, almost reverential. Grahame Booker, a local man, explained that the crowds, 'infected perhaps by the peaceful atmosphere, were very subdued and well behaved'.

As this was Cahn's private ground, he rarely charged spectators. Consequently, with the exception of an ice-cream seller who toured the ground on big match days, there were no concessions or commercial activities. Occasionally, for important matches, a band played popular marches and other tunes. Fixture cards were printed on silk, octagonal in shape and entirely covered in broad stripes of black, pink and light blue. If gate money was taken, the collections were either given to charity or to cricketers' benefit funds.

A 6ft boarded fence enclosed the ground around three-quarters of the circumference. A single row of backless benches lined the inside of the fence. More benches were brought in for tourist and other major games. The rest of the ground was taken up by the tidy black-and-white pavilion that was surrounded by perfectly tended bedding plants. Cahn's pink, light-blue and black flags fluttering from the pavilion created an additional splash of colour.

The enclosure was opened on 4 June 1926 with a match between a Notts eleven and 'sixteen amateurs of the county captained by Mr Cahn'. The players wore caps of navy blue with a badge depicting a fox's head and cable-stitched sweaters sporting black, pink and pale blue – the Cahn colours. Initially, their blazers were striped in these colours, but this was then changed to navy blue blazers edged with the diagonal Cahn colours and a pink fox's head on the breast pocket. Two ties were worn – the playing tie had broad diagonal stripes of black, pink and pale blue; the winter tie had thin pink and pale-blue diagonal stripes on a black background. Julien always wore at least one white cardigan buttoned down the front. He felt the cold, and it was easier to layer his clothes wearing a combination of sweaters and cardigans.

Ginty Lush recalls playing a game in Walsall against the Woodpeckers, a team for whom the great English bowler 'Tich' Freeman played.

When Sir Julien stepped out of his Rolls Royce he was resplendent in the most perfectly fitted blue suit from Savile Row. All the boys commented on the suit, which in those days must have cost £200. He tossed for choice of innings, lost and then went into the pavilion to change on that very, very raw morning. Just before lunch Sir Julien decided he would have a bowl, and after peeling off his sweater and two or three of his cardigans, he sent down (or rather, up) three of the worst possible deliveries. Then he turned to me at mid-off and said, 'I know what's wrong, I've still got my braces on.' He had pulled on his cricket gear over the pants and vest of that beautiful suit.

Reflecting his love and ambitions for hunting, the fox was Cahn's mascot. He had a wooden fox made, with moveable head, legs and a brush tail. This sat on top of a stake that was pushed into the ground near the pavilion. Generally, the fox's tail would reflect how well the side was playing. If things were going well, the tail would be raised, if play was poor, the tail would be lowered. On occasion, if Cahn expected an immediate improvement in his players, he would personally go over to the wooden fox and raise its brush tail to the vertical. A silent but instantly understood gesture that indicated to his team they were required to up their game.

After that first match on the West Bridgford ground on 4 June 1926, the Cahn XI continued its excellent form, winning seventeen games and losing just three. Centuries were scored by C.E. James, A. Newman, F.C.W. Newman, J.F. Bishop, C.A.L. Sutton and W. Vaulkhard. There was excellent bowling by John Gunn, A.O. Ashley, C.H. Parkin, W. Hickling and T.L. Richmond. Larwood played for the side in September at Skegness. Cecil Parkin played fairly regularly, as did G.F.H. Heane and S.D. Rhodes.

Cahn's cricket was the epitome of 'country house cricket', although considerably more ambitious and competitive than any country house cricket seen up until then. Sir Pelham Warner, the great cricketer, once remarked of Cahn, 'this is indeed cricket de luxe'. The play was outstanding on a perfect ground. The food and wine were sumptuous. Perhaps the only blight was the playing of the captain, the very person who made it all possible.

Most of the matches were open to the general public, whom were allowed into the ground free of charge. Unfortunately, there was many an occasion when the crowd got bored of watching Julien Cahn's long hops and full tosses. Unforgiving spectators yelled 'take him off', or 'take yourself off', or 'get yourself a coach Julien', or 'wait for it, there'll be snow on this one when it comes down'. After a minute or two of this verbal abuse, Cahn would turn to the pavilion, clap his hands and his secretary or manager would run out to the wicket. Within a few moments the ground staff would assemble and usher every single spectator out of the ground. For the remainder of the day the game would continue in silence except for the occasional polite applause from the pavilion. The hecklers and locked-out crowd were in no position to complain as they had not been charged for admission.

Nevertheless, this did not discourage Cahn from allowing the public to enjoy his ground and it certainly did not deter his enthusiasm for cricket or his own personal involvement in the matches.

The bad weather of 1927 resulted in many drawn games but no matches were lost despite strong opposition. One of the key games of that season was against the Craven Gentlemen, who comprised many famous players. Cahn's success was often credited to Captain F.W.H. Nicholas (who had played previously for the Army and Essex), a good hard-hitting batsman and efficient wicket-keeper who formed a formidable and fast-scoring partnership with Newman, too good for most of the opposition. 'Lofty' Newman joined Cahn as his private secretary for cricket in 1926, having played a few games for Surrey. He was his right-hand man in cricket, even after Newman relinquished the official role of secretary to Cyril Goodway years later. Newman went on to play in nearly every game from 1926, scoring 15,000 runs and about 37 centuries over the years. He also became an invaluable member of Cahn's business empire.

Occasionally, the stage in the game was reached when Sir Julien decided that he would prefer to manoeuvre for a draw rather than face the possible ignominy of defeat. The customary 40-minute luncheon interval would then be stretched by the addition of an extra course, an inexplicable delay over coffee or even the appearance of a bottle of port followed by cigars. Eventually, the visiting captain would lead a bewildered and befuddled side back on to the field, very much later than the time laid down by the MCC or any other cricketing body. Although the opposing team would have been overfed and watered, Cahn kept a strict eye on his own team, who were strictly rationed to ensure they did not imbibe too much alcohol.

Julien's fear of the ball led him to take some outrageous measures of self-protection. Cahn's outsize leg guards were infamous and a cause of great hilarity. The pneumatic batting pads were inflatable and had to be blown up to approximately 23lb pressure all around. This task was given to Robson, his trusted chauffeur, before Cahn went into bat. When getting ready to bat, Cahn would always put on the right pad first. This was just one of his many idiosyncratic habits.

Philip Snow recalls playing for the Leicestershire Gentlemen at West Bridgford on an occasion when Cahn's pads deflated. 'He'd no sooner come out to bat when there was a loud hissing noise. I liked him, but he was a real autocrat, a martinet. He stalked off the pitch, in his trim, short steps, swinging his bat furiously, disappeared into the marquee, sacked his chauffeur on the spot and declared the innings.'

Snow's tale has almost certainly been embellished by the addition of the sacking of the chauffeur, as the only chauffeur who was fired by Sir Julien was Tacey, who was dismissed in the late 1930s due to an unfortunate incident between the cricket bus and a gatepost.

Seemingly, Cahn's pads were of some use to his team, for when he played a defensive straight bat, he could 'enjoy the benefit of the minutest doubts in the case of leg-before-wicket', and was on occasion surprisingly difficult to dislodge. However, after a few mild complaints these batting pads were eventually discarded.

They were replaced by a pair of especially reinforced batting pads, made with a steel framework. As well as playing against Cahn, Joseph Shrewsbury was a director of the Nottingham sports firm Shaw and Shrewsbury which was commissioned to make them. Occasionally, his company was asked to supply various items of cricket equipment to the Loughborough Road ground. Normally, these were a couple of dozen balls or half a dozen bats.

Shrewsbury recalled that the batting pads were a difficult contract to carry out, but nevertheless the pads were eventually made and became a subject of much amusement among the staff. A typically caustic comment from Joseph Shrewsbury was, 'Julien doesn't score many runs but with these round his legs he'll score a damn sight less.'

Shrewsbury's recollections of Cahn are tinged with bitterness. In a letter written many decades later reminiscing upon his dealings with Cahn, he remembers that there was never any mention of payment and, in fact, it was only after several reminders spread over many months that Cahn was 'persuaded to cough up'. Shrewsbury commented that Cahn could afford to be generous to large organisations but was strangely reluctant to settle small business debts.

In the most important matches Cahn usually batted at number eleven and frequently finished unbeaten. Grahame Booker recalls applauding the batsmen in at the end of yet another massive score and Cahn, probably not out one or two, remarking to the little knot of spectators around the pavilion, 'they couldn't get me out!'

Of course, it wasn't done to get Julien Cahn out. Woe betide the bowler who appealed for LBW or a catch at the wicket. Cahn was the generous benefactor of high-class cricket and unrivalled hospitality and no one wished to offend him. Fortunately, the umpires, John Gunn in particular, knew their role. Cahn was never given LBW and, keen to retain their fixtures with the Cahn XI, neither did opposition umpires.

Typical was a scenario recalled by F.E. Moore, who opened bowling for the Leicestershire Club and Ground XI in the late 1920s against Cahn's team. Despite the fact that the team contained excellent players, Cahn decided not only to open the innings but also to take the bowling. John Gunn whispered to Moore, 'Let him have one to get off the mark!' Consequently, Moore bowled a couple of innocuous deliveries, neither of which produced any contact with the bat. As a somewhat young and impatient bowler, he then bowled a very good ball that Cahn promptly edged for four runs between the wicket-keeper and first slip.

'Excellent,' muttered John, 'now we can all sit back and enjoy the rest of the day's cricket!'

The reality was that in every match played in which Julien operated as captain, the Cahn XI played with ten men. All members of the team had to be cricketing stuntsmen, performing extraordinary feats of cricket. Interestingly, when the team played against national first-class visiting sides, such as West Indies or South Africa, Cahn did not play because deep down he did recognise his lack of skill.

D.M. Dunning, who played for the Old Worksopian XI against Cahn's team at West Bridgford, recalls an occasion when Julien missed a simple catch. (Cahn did a great deal for cricket at Worksop College, paying for the re-laying of the square on the cricket field and the erection of a fine score board and box.) A section of the spectators in the covered stand jeered. Cahn strode over to the stand, starting at one point and pacing to another, and shouted, 'From here to here, get out!'

Dunning recalls how the hospitality at Cahn's cricket matches was legendary. He remembers having to sign for drinks on a chit. Although the visiting sides were permitted to consume as much as they liked (and often encouraged to do so), the signing of chits was a new phenomenon that had arisen due to various unworthy guests taking blatant advantage of the Cahn hospitality. At the end of the match, Julien asked the team where they would be eating that evening. They told him that they had fixed up dinner at the Black Boy Hotel in Nottingham. At the end of their dinner, when they had finished their large steaks, they asked for the bill. To their amazement and delight they were told that the meal had all been paid for by Julien Cahn.

3

Luck, Largesse & Laughter

The atmosphere at Papplewick Grange was light-hearted and joyful. To everyone's delight, Julien's loud and highly infectious laugh could be heard most evenings. How different it was to the morose mood of just a few years earlier following the deaths of his parents.

On 15 December 1927, Phyllis gave birth at home. The pregnancy was unplanned and had come as rather a shock. With two healthy children, she had not wished to go through a fourth pregnancy. To everyone's relief, the birth was easy. Little Richard was scrawny and pale, so different to his dark-haired siblings. A few of the staff gossiped among themselves about the new baby's fair hair and complexion – was he really Julien's child? Unbeknown to Richard, the rumours surrounding his heritage perpetuated for the next two decades, until it became more than obvious that he had inherited his father's stature, intellect and idiosyncrasies.

In the months leading up to Richard's birth, Julien had been actively seeking a new home. He instructed his friend and land agent Guy German to find him an estate in the locality – not an easy undertaking as large mansions rarely came on to the market. The rooms at Papplewick Grange were plentiful but not grand. The principal rooms were too small to host large parties; the kitchens were modest but most importantly the grounds were insufficiently extensive to accommodate a cricket pitch. Even though Julien now owned his own ground at West Bridgford, Loughborough Road, he wanted another pitch in his back garden, a pitch where he could practice and play matches on Sundays, a day when no one else played the game.

In November 1927, a month before the birth of Richard, Julien Cahn purchased Stanford Hall in a private sale. German could not believe his luck that such a suitable estate had come on to the market. It was local and the obvious choice for the Cahns. Best of all, it was in the heart of the finest hunting territory, straddling Leicestershire and Nottinghamshire, and abutting land hunted by the leading hunt in England, the Quorn. Phyllis Cahn had little to do with the decision. Thirteen years younger than her husband and always unworldly, she had no input into the major decisions of their married life. Her aspirations were modest and she was overwhelmed by the prospect of their new home.

Described in *The Times*, of 1927, as a 'stately Georgian mansion embodying a great deal of fine decorative work of the Adam type', it comprised nine reception rooms and thirty-five bedrooms, together with an estate of 3,000 acres. It was not an attractive house, but it was very large and both German and Cahn recognised its enormous potential and heritage.

The history of the Stanford estate can be traced back to 9 November 1558, eight days before the death of Queen Mary, when she granted 1,200 acres to her goldsmith, Robert Raynes. In 1641, his grandson built a stone house on a hill a mile to the north of the village of Stanford. This was the first Stanford Hall. It is not known why it was pulled down and rebuilt in 1774 for Charles Vere Dashwood, Sheriff of Nottingham. Only the central portion of that building now remains and is identified by the older brickwork and the dogtooth decoration below the roof eaves. Later generations of the Dashwood family extended the house by adding two low-level wings.

In 1887, the Ratcliffe family, who were well-known brewers from Burton, took over the hall and estate and made considerable alterations. They added another floor to the two wings, built the main staircase and laid out the gardens and terraces. They built the stable block and also rebuilt and renovated a number of farm dwellings and cottages on the estate and in the village.

However, the renovations were modest by Cahn's standards. Julien promptly set about converting the hall from an unpretentious country home into something much grander in style. As neither he nor Phyllis had any experience, or indeed great interest in interior decoration, the whole project was handed over to White Allom Ltd – the preferred decorators of Queen Mary, William Randolph Hearst and other famous and wealthy individuals. Their commissions included refitting the grand cruise liners the *Queen Mary* and the *Queen Elizabeth* during their heyday. Sir Charles Allom was fêted as the leader in all aspects of design and decoration, and as architectural decorator to the Queen he had a number of Royal Warrants. His right-hand man was Joe Redding, and it was Mr Redding who oversaw the Stanford Hall project.

The 1920s were a particularly exciting era for interior design. Significant developments and ingenuity, especially in bathrooms, were taking place. The design industry was heavily influenced by the Paris exhibition of 'Arts Decoratives', and White Allom were excited to be able to develop these ideas at Stanford Hall. In 1925, the 'Exposition Internationale des Arts Décoratifs' – an international exhibition of decorative arts – was held in the centre of Paris, a convenient location for Sir Julien, who visited it as inspiration for his furniture business and where he was to gain ideas for his future home. Nearly 6 million people attended this world fair, which showed off the opulent decorations of the era produced by the famous houses such as Lalique, Brandt and Dunand. The leading Parisian department stores, such as the Galeries Lafayette and Au Bon Marché, displayed their wares in exhibition halls providing inspiration to the masses.

At the Place des Invalides, twenty-five rooms were individually themed, designed, furnished and decorated by the leading French artists. Themes included a room for 'Monsieur', a room for 'Madame', a working office-library and a special chamber for music. Each space was crammed full of works of art and crafts, mostly in the modern art deco style. White Allom gained much inspiration.

'Stanford Hall is a bizarre eclectic mix of styles, revolving around Cahn's eccentricity. Either he set out to create pastiches in each room, or he just had no bloody taste.'

This amusing statement was made by Mervyn Wilson, Chief Executive and Principal of the Co-op College, and printed in the *Sunday Times* in April 2001 upon the sale of Stanford Hall.

Although White Allom Ltd, still in existence today, may baulk at the description, Wilson was correct. Stanford Hall, in Loughborough, is an eclectic mix of late eighteenth-century architecture, mock Tudor and art deco. But it wasn't always that way – the 'eclectic mix' was the creation of Cahn.

White Allom was at the epicentre of the avant-garde and new design of the early twentieth century. For them, Stanford Hall was a dream project. They were instructed to gut the centre of the building, change the shape and size of the rooms and reconstruct them in a combination of imitation period and modern styles, having almost free reign to decorate and furnish as they saw fit. They were given a massive budget of £100,000, equivalent to about £4 million in today's currency. The rooms reflected different periods and styles, including the latest French and English 'moderne'. Sourced from the Continent, every room and piece of furnishing was profusely and richly decorated in period style. While Cahn was less than interested in choosing the fixtures and fittings in the first place, he became almost pedantic in his desire to ensure every last detail was historically correct. Rooms included the Spanish Room, the Italian Room, the Charles II Room and the Louise XV Room. Most major rooms, including bedrooms, had decorative cornices, panelled dados and decorative marble. A number of rooms had intricate ceilings and ornate shaped doorways. Julien's study was panelled with 22-carat-gold gilt decoration. Some other rooms were enriched with silver. In 1945, when the Co-op announced the purchase of Stanford Hall, the *Co-operative Review* wrote, 'It is a large building and no one apparently has tried to count all of the rooms, so numerous are they.'

That is not strictly true, as in 1938 Cahn commissioned the Nottingham-based firm of auctioneers Place and Kirk to undertake an inventory of all fixtures and fittings for the purposes of fire insurance. This exercise took two people over one year to complete and at the end they produced a book 350 pages long, itemising every single chattel within the building. There were 27 bathrooms, many more WCs, 43 bedrooms and approximately 170 rooms in total.

During 1928, as the building work was taking place, Julien began to plan how he would use Stanford Hall. To their delight, the Papplewick Grange staff were all promised jobs in the Cahn's new home. Cahn realised that with the size of his new abode and the opulent entertaining that he was planning, he would need more staff. Within months of their relocation to Stanford Hall the Cahns employed a retinue of over sixty to maintain the house, grounds and personal needs of the family of five. A staggering thirty-two employees worked in the house alone.

Julien himself spent more time overseeing the re-laying of the cricket pitch and improvements of the outfield at Stanford Hall than he did supervising the refurbishments of the house. Similar to the pitch at Loughborough Road, this cricket pitch was maintained to the highest of standards. The excellent wickets were of a curious light colour due to the very close cutting of the grass. Another pitch, known as the practice ground, was located in the park some distance from the house. It was not maintained to the same standard as the main ground, and was used for both recreational purposes by the staff and for local teams to play their matches.

S. Perbedy was friends with many of the children of the Stanford Hall staff, in particular Ken Robson, the head chauffeur's son. During the summer holidays the children went daisy gathering on the second cricket pitch. They were supplied with kneeling mats and daisy-grabbing tools and weeded the whole pitch this way. With a wage of £2 10s (£2.50) a week, the proud 12-year-olds felt like millionaires.

Cahn was excited about his new home. He planned to show it off to those wealthy landowners who had peered at him down their long aristocratic beaks, preferring to take note of Cahn's Jewish looks rather than listen to his deep, crystal-cut voice. Stanford Hall fitted in perfectly with his plans for elevation and acceptance in society. Although by the late 1920s he was well on his way to cultivating the right friendships and putting down his philanthropic building blocks, he still had work to do. Julien had studied the system, and realised that if he wished to elevate himself in society successfully, the quickest way to do this was to obtain a title.

In some respects little has changed during the last century. Honours oiled the political cogs in the early 1920s in the same way that they appear to do today. By the time he accepted the position of Vice-chairman of the Nottingham Conservative Association, Cahn had studied politics in depth. An avid and quick reader, he preferred fact to fiction. He read all of the national newspapers and whichever international publications he could get hold of. His voracious thirst for knowledge was always put to good use and this time he intended to utilise the system to his own benefit in the way that so many others had before him.

Cahn fully understood the machinations of political wheeler-dealings. He had read about Lloyd George and he sat up with interest whenever the purchasing of honours was debated in the newspapers. Little did he realise that he was to become instrumental in saving the Government from the greatest honours-fixing scandal of the century. As Cahn mused over how he could obtain his own title, he recalled the furore Lloyd George had caused. Prime Minister Lloyd George had realised that if he was to retain political power after the war he would need to found a party of his own and such a party needed funds. An effective way to do this was to appoint men of means. Lloyd George added ninety-one new peers to the House of Lords in six years, a 50 per cent increase over the record rate established by Campbell-Bannerman and Asquith. The Birthday Honours List of June 1922 proved explosive. It included three barons who were considered most unsuitable for peerage. The matter was widely debated and figures were bandied around. It was quoted that £10–12,000 could buy a knighthood and £35–40,000 a baronetcy. After much embarrassment to the Government, a Royal Commission was set up to advise on the honours' procedures and a bill was introduced in 1925. After the introduction of this bill there were only the occasional allegations about the sale of political honours and it really passed out of public interest until the proceedings against Gregory in 1933. However, this is not to say that it was not going on – far from it, and Cahn knew it.

Key to the acquisition of titles under both the Conservative and Labour Governments was an unsavoury character called Maundy Gregory, a man whom Julien Cahn met initially at the Carlton Club in the mid-1920s. Founded in 1832 by a number of Tory MPs, the club was, and still is, the club of the Conservative Party. Members met there to discuss the problems of the day and after any big event at Westminster the leaders of the Conservative Party went there to hear the views of their followers. Many men who lived in the country used it as their London base, Cahn included. It was an ideal venue for the avid capitalist Julien Cahn to meet like-minded individuals. However, it wasn't until 1930 that Julien was elected a member of the Carlton Club. This in itself was no small achievement; during the years 1919 to 1939 there were only twenty-six Jews elected to membership. Every member had to be proposed and seconded by existing members.

Julien took a suite at the Carlton Club, located at 7 Carlton Gardens. Whenever he stayed in London, at least once or twice a week, he stayed in his rooms there and was able to entertain guests. The food, service and rooms were of the very highest standard. Evening dress was compulsory for dinner. In his book *Jews and the Carlton Club*, Michael Jolles describes how one night the Baldwins entered in day clothes and sat down to dinner. When the steward made them aware of the dress code, Stanley Baldwin went to every occupied table in the room apologising for his unorthodox attire, excusing himself on the grounds that 10 Downing Street was closed and that he was himself only passing through London. There were many taboos in the club. For instance, a new member was advised not to sit in the window of the smoking room until he had been elected for at least two years and he should eschew tables near the fire in the coffee room until he was a Privy Councillor or Under-Secretary. On the other hand, Jolles explains that to sit at one of the tables along the wall was a confession of failure; this area was called Brook Street because no one knew the people who lived there. In theory there was no snobbery in the club itself. Once elected, a member was treated as an equal by fellow members – this was particularly attractive to the etiquette-savvy Gregory.

Maundy Gregory had elevated himself from a 'nobody' to a leading figure in society, largely through deception. In August 1919, he produced the first issue of the *Whitehall Gazette*, an expensively produced monthly with the appearance of an official publication that was circulated freely among the gentlemen's clubs of London. Most of its articles were signed with *noms de plume*. In fact, they were written by Gregory himself. The articles detailed affairs of the Court, current events concerning the Empire and embassies, and commented upon the functions of the leading London clubs. Events held at the Ambassador Club were covered particularly favourably. It seems extraordinary that no one at the time made the connection; Gregory himself owned the Ambassador Club.

Two features that provided much of the financial backing and rationale for the *Whitehall Gazette* were entitled 'British Enterprise' and 'Officials I have Met'. These were extremely flattering profiles of individuals, normally accompanied by a fabulous picture of the person concerned. Notable individuals featured included the Prince of Wales, European dignitaries such as Prince Peter of Montenegro (who supposedly stayed at Stanford Hall), Imperial and non-European dignitaries and individuals who, it is believed, paid up to £500 to be well advertised among British society. According to John Walker, author of *The Queen has been Pleased*, this last category of individuals comprised 'unexceptional British businessmen'. By positively profiling them, Gregory used the *Whitehall Gazette* to get potential honours prospects higher recognition among those that mattered. It is said that Gregory charged £25,000 for the acquisition of a baronetcy and £10,000 for a plain Knight Bachelor.

The list of men who were profiled was long. John Walker lists various examples, such as a Mr Calder, landowner and distiller, who four months after his profile was published was awarded a knighthood; Edward Edgar, a merchant banker and financier, received a baronetcy within the year; Edmund Buckley, a cotton merchant, was awarded a knighthood – and the list goes on and on. Unsurprisingly, Julien Cahn was profiled in the *Whitehall Gazette* in February 1927 under the heading 'Master of the Hunt'. The large double-page spread included a full-page picture of Cahn in his hunting pinks, dapper but rather more puffed up in the cheeks than is evident in photographs. It is interesting how society at the time afforded such importance to the pursuit of hunting; cricket was a poor second. Many paragraphs were accredited to Cahn's involvement in these activities, some coverage was given to his philanthropy involving the sun-ray clinic, homes of rest and the proposed orthopaedic hospital for crippled children, while his business involvement was summed up as 'Chairman of a company owning the largest number of retail furniture establishments in the world'. John Walker notes the irony of the article's last sentence: 'Mr Cahn has not, until now, participated actively in the political world, but as vice-chairman of the finance committee of the Nottingham Conservative Association, he has started on the tortuous road of politics, which may lead him who knows where.'

The Ambassador Club, in Conduit Street, was an inspired tool for Maundy Gregory's trade. It permitted him to entertain in great style; from 1928 until 1933, the annual pinnacle was the grand Derby Eve Dinner. Founded by the late Colonel Walter Faber, the event had previously been held at the Carlton Club. However, Gregory had engineered the venue change to his Ambassador Club. This dinner was attended by many distinguished men, including the Prince of Wales, Winston Churchill, the Duke of Westminster and, of course, Julien Cahn, who attended every annual Derby Dinner from 1927 through to 1933. The vast majority of guests had titles, including dukes, earls, marquises, viscounts, barons and knights. There were no ladies present.

Gregory described the Ambassador Club in the *Whitehall Gazette*: 'Primarily a luncheon, dining and supper club, with all the adjuncts of music, dancing and lighter entertainment, it affords a rendezvous alike for the Diplomat, the man about town, the Society dame and the country resident.' He goes on to describe it as having

comfortable entrance lounges and staircases, where hangs a unique collection of forty-eight hand-done portraits upon vellum of the notables and dignitaries who attended the Coronation of King George the IV, a collection quite unique which originally belonged to the Duke of York, the restaurant itself with its marble columns, its scheme of Rose du

Barry, and its effect of sunlight streaming through the glass roof whether the month is June or foggy November; the Restaurant Balcony, where evening dress is not indispensable, and from which in the evenings, as in the Restaurant below, the exquisite tones of Jack Hylton's band does not drown comfortable conversation; the richly appointed Grill Room and American Bar, a mighty change from the crude and garish refreshment rooms of our ancestors; the oak panelled Reading Room with its stained glass windows, where not a sound can be heard, with its regally bound copies of Punch dating from January 1883 counterbalanced by a voluminous collection of Hansard's Parliamentary Debates; one and all have to be seen rather than learnt of by proxy.

Maundy Gregory was a superb actor and managed to build a web of falsities around himself. When he moved his home address to 10 Hyde Park Terrace he told his staff to tell anyone who called his office to say that he was 'over at number 10'!

He befriended the good and the great, including the Duke of York and the King of Greece, both of whom were to stay at Stanford Hall, as well as all the senior members of the Lloyd George Coalition.

Two years after Cahn's coverage in the *Whitehall Gazette*, he was knighted. It is naïve to believe that Cahn would have had the coverage in the *Gazette* without some financial consideration. Whether Gregory really was instrumental in Cahn acquiring his knighthood is debatable. It is most probable that while Cahn was actively cultivating relations with Gregory as a backup, in fact he didn't need him. Maundy Gregory may have been influential but having a direct link to the Prime Minister was more efficient. By 1929, Julien Cahn was firm friends with Stanley Baldwin's wife, Lucy Baldwin (known to her friends as Cissie). Her dedication to raising awareness of and providing maternity care was close to the Cahns' hearts. Through her, Julien had a direct link to the Prime Minister.

For a number of years Julien Cahn had been quietly undertaking philanthropic acts, including funding the sun-ray clinic in Nottingham, an orthopaedic clinic and almshouses for retired workers in Hucknall. Up until 1928, the projects had been local to the Nottingham area, however in 1929, Cahn's largesse rose to a national level. Julien Cahn's self-confidence had grown considerably of late. He was now beginning to be accepted within the upper echelons of society. If he decided he wanted to meet someone, he would sit at his oval walnut writing table in his study – known to all as 'the Library'–

and gaining inspiration from the finely panelled walnut walls, carved and embellished with gilt architraves and mouldings, he would pen his letter, inviting his hitherto unknown guest to a weekend of country sports at Stanford Hall. While most people would be far too inhibited to approach the rich and the famous without proper introduction, Cahn felt that he had nothing to lose. Curiosity normally prevailed, and the strangers invariably accepted these invitations.

The Cahns had met the Baldwins on a number of occasions and when Julien learned that Lucy Baldwin was particularly interested in maternity welfare, he realised that here was a cause they could develop together. The Cahns had lost their first son, Roland, at birth. The Baldwins' first child had also been stillborn. Lucy Baldwin was an eloquent spokesperson and, as the wife of the Prime Minister, had a high profile that would propel any cause dear to her into the forefront of the public eye. Julien had the money, she had the connections and the time. And they both shared a passion for cricket.

In 1929, Cahn put forward an estimated £10,000 for the creation of the Lucy Baldwin Maternity Hospital in the Baldwins' home town of Stourport-on-Severn, Worcestershire. This was the first maternity hospital of its kind and considered pioneering. Cahn's act of philanthropy thrust his name into the public domain. Up until this time, he had been mentioned on a few occasions in *The Times* newspaper, but all references were related to his cricketing activities or attendance at social events.

The Times of 17 April 1929 records Baldwin's lengthy speech at the opening of the hospital.

> There are few subjects in which I and my distinguished friend Neville Chamberlain are more interested than those combined questions of maternity and infant welfare, because on them are built up the health and strength of the nation.

While infant mortality had been reduced in the UK, maternal mortality rates were still worryingly high, worse than many other European countries. The timing of the opening of the hospital was disappointing for Cahn, who arrived back at Southampton from his tour of Jamaica just two days later, so was not able to attend the ceremony. Nevertheless, the Cahn public-relations machine was fully operational and his name was mentioned many times by all of the dignitaries present.

On 18 April 1929, Stanley Baldwin composed a handwritten letter to Julien Cahn from 10 Downing Street, Whitehall. It read:

> Dear Mr Cahn,
>
> I still find it extremely difficult to thank you adequately for what you have done. You have made many happy and I believe your gift will be a source of blessing and of inspiration for many years to come. Thank you again. Believe me to remain,
>
> Sincerely yours, Stanley Baldwin

This letter, and the fact that Cahn had been fêted a cricketing hero abroad, almost made up for the disappointment of being unable to attend the opening ceremony of the hospital.

The Cahn XI enjoyed a brilliant season in 1928. The only match they lost was against the West Indies team, which came to Cahn's West Bridgford ground in early September. After such a good year, all was set for the biggest cricketing event in the history of the Sir Julien Cahn's XI – their first overseas trip, planned for January, February and March of 1929. Jamaica was the chosen destination – a country known for its cricketing prowess. With the exception of missing the opening ceremony of the hospital, the timing was excellent, for the tour took place during the three months prior to the Cahn family's relocation to their new home, Stanford Hall. The key structural changes had been made to the hall which allowed the finishing touches to be completed while the Cahns were abroad.

The team (including Lord Tennyson, E.W. Dawson, F.W.H. Nicholas, A.L. Hilder, F.C.W. Newman and W.H. Vaulkhard) sailed on the RMS *Mauretania* from Southampton to New York and then on to Jamaica, arriving on 14 February 1929. Also aboard were Julien and Phyllis Cahn, their two elder children, Patience and Albert, Phyllis' parents, Abe and Cissy Wolfe, and a few staff. With the exception of Captain Nicholas, who was accompanied by his wife, all of the cricketers were young, single men travelling alone, enjoying the luxuries of travel beyond their wildest dreams.

The recently refurbished RMS *Mauretania* was renowned for its opulence and speed, crossing the Atlantic faster than any other vessel at that time. The cabins were large and luxurious, the state rooms were ornately decorated with a great deal of fine wood panelling. As would be expected, the Cahn party had a huge amount of luggage, but this was bolstered by many large hampers of food from Fortnum & Mason in anticipation of mediocre food at their destination.

It was in Kingston, Jamaica, where Cahn, at the age of forty-six, made his first-class debut, captaining a team that included eight test cricketers. This was quite extraordinary, for Cahn was most unsuited to be a playing captain.

In Jamaica the important task of blowing up Cahn's inflatable leg guards was handed to John Gunn, Cahn's chief cricket advisor, sometime umpire and coach. Gunn remembered to hand Cahn his right pad first; the right-hand pad had to go on before the left-hand one – another of Cahn's bizarre idiosyncrasies. Even though everything was completed in the correct order, Julien did not have a good game.

As was customary, Cahn batted at eleven. Unfortunately for him, but fortunately for the rest of the team, he broke his thumb in the first match when hit by a fast rising ball and was bowled for nought. He was livid, particularly as his team lost that first match. The throbbing pain and large bandage prevented him from any further play, so reluctantly he handed over the captainship to Lord Tennyson, the cricketing grandson of the great poet. Fortunately for all, they then drew the second match against the Jamaicans but lost the third against a West Indian team. The Jamaicans met Cahn's XI for a final five-day fixture game in Kingston, from 12 to 17 March. Over 8,000 spectators watched the game each day. The atmosphere was exhilarating; the crowds cheered both sides and the scenes of welcome were overwhelming. Julien found it difficult to remain irritated. Although he rarely drank alcohol, he made an exception for the excellent Jamaican rum that eased both his physical pain and his annoyance.

Julien was deeply competitive, to the extent that the purpose of any game played was to win. This applied equally to games played in the nursery with his children, on the cricket pitch against international teams and in the boardroom. In every arena, because his tentacles of control stretched so far, the odds were normally stacked in his favour, but he was never prepared to play for the sake of playing – winning was always paramount. In the nursery his children could never hope to outwit their brilliant father; in the boardroom his purchasing power was so vast that smaller adversaries had no hope; on the cricket pitch he was able to buy the very best players and win matches by huge margins. His players were not permitted to even countenance defeat. The team realised that their poor playing against the Jamaicans was not acceptable. Their captain was sour-faced and moody, regardless of the fact that they were playing against a national team of great ability. In the coming years and for future tours, the pressure of winning was increased and it paid off. And if the rules had to be bent a little to achieve a win, so be it. No one was going to object.

If the players realised that their boss was unhappy, the Jamaicans had no idea. They were most taken with the debonair British captain, transfixed by his clipped vowels, hearty laugh and convoluted vocabulary that they rarely understood. At the end of the final match Sir William Morrison (President of the Jamaican Board of Control) presented Cahn and Lord Tennyson with souvenirs and commemorative bats for the players on both sides. Morrison announced that the tour was considered a tremendous success and that 'Jamaica was deeply indebted to Mr Cahn'.

When his grandson, also called Julien Cahn, visited Jamaica some sixty years later, he was introduced to an elderly Jamaican who as a boy had carried Cahn's bags. The Jamaican had been so impressed by Cahn that he had changed his name by deed poll to 'Julien Cahn'.

On their return from Jamaica in early April, the Cahn party stopped off at Cuba. Julien Cahn and Lord Tennyson were met by Sir John Broderick, British Envoy to Cuba. (This was prior to the introduction of ambassadors, but Broderick held the equivalent position.) A keen supporter of cricket, he, along with other leading lights in Cuban cricket, approached Cahn and asked him to present a cup. Cahn readily agreed to do so, but commented that the Cubans really needed to get themselves a good ground.

In anticipation of the cup being sent from England, the five clubs in Havana City got together and called themselves the Metropolitan League. As instructed by Cahn, Broderick found an excellent ground shortly thereafter and encouraged the local teams to study cricket and put into practice the instructions in *The Boy's Book of Cricket* by F.A.H. Henley. They arranged a series of matches called the 'Sir Julien Cahn's Cricket Competition'. While the competition was in full swing, word was received from Sir John Broderick that the cup promised by Cahn had arrived. As the silver loving cup was especially for the promotion of cricket in Cuba, it was decided that it should be known as 'Sir Julien Cahn's Cricket Challenge Cup'. It was competed for on an annual basis by those clubs that complied with the laws of the Cuban Board of Control. The name of the winning club was engraved on the cup at the end of each season. To this day, both

Broderick and Cahn are recognised as playing instrumental roles in the promotion of Cuban cricket.

Cahn's cricketing largesse continued at home. That same year Cahn promised to be responsible for the cost of Nottinghamshire County Cricket Club's new open concrete stand adjoining Fox Road and to pay for a new office for the Secretary and staff room. This cost Cahn £2,345 and was completed in time for the test match of 1930.

Phyllis, Julien, Patience and Albert disembarked at Southampton on 19 April 1929 following their trip to Jamaica. After a weekend in London to collect 16-month-old Richard, who had been left in the care of the Norland Home for children during his parents' three-month absence, the family were driven north to their new home. Phyllis had been excited to see her youngest child. It was customary for children to be brought up by nannies and governesses, but she had still missed her baby. However, little Richard stared at his mother with big eyes and showed not the slightest hint of recognition. Phyllis felt as if a large dagger had been thrust through her stomach but she could tell no one. She picked up the toddler and hugged him, an action that provoked a wail followed by inconsolable crying. Reluctantly and privately ashamed, she handed him back to his nanny. It was not done to miss one's children, and in the society they now mixed in, parents had little hands-on involvement with the rearing of their offspring. There was nothing she could do.

On Monday 22 April, the Cahns received a welcome from about fifty tenants and employees of the Stanford Hall estate. Representing the tenants of the estate, James Gibson congratulated Julien on his safe return, and went on to say, 'We at Stanford Hall yield to no one in our admiration, loyalty and respect for you both. We extend you a most hearty welcome and sincerely hope you and in due course your children's families may be blessed with health and happiness and success.'

Julien was deeply touched by Gibson's words and the warm smiles of the tenants and staff. In response he replied that he had never experienced such an unexpected, spontaneous and warm welcome. He commented on the immaculate cricket pitch, one of the principal *raisons d'être* for the purchase of the estate, and, referring to his bandaged thumb that had been broken in the cricket game in Jamaica, noted that he didn't think his thumb would get broken on his new ground. Cahn went on to say, 'I don't want people to look upon me as a squire, but as a friend . . . I will do all that I can to assist you'.

42

While he never exactly had an 'open-door' policy, and many would have been too intimidated to approach him directly, he did wherever possible go far out of his way to ensure the well-being of all his staff. After a toast to good health, some of the tenants were entertained to dinner. It was an auspicious beginning.

Not so for Papplewick Grange. The departure of the Cahns was its demise. With no interested purchasers, the house stood empty until 1932 when it was offered for sale at auction. Bidding started at £500 but only advanced to £657, whereupon it was withdrawn. The estate was expected to make £2,000. Sadly, this was the beginning of the era when large houses were simply a financial burden upon their owners. Like so many homes of its generation, eventually the best fixtures and fittings were removed and Papplewick Grange was demolished.

That first night as she lay in bed in their new house, Phyllis Cahn was quite overcome by the grandeur of it all. Their bedroom was perhaps the finest room in the whole mansion. The walls were panelled in blue and silver Louis XVI silk, made especially by a firm in Lyons. Long blue and silver silk curtains lined the windows, falling heavily onto the heavy pile, cream fitted Axminster carpet. The chimneypiece had a carved Louis XVI frieze, while the hearth was constructed from *brèche violette* – a white marble with mauve-coloured veins. A two-tiered gilt light fitting with crystal lustre drops and silk shades hung from the centre of the ceiling, gently lighting the room with its twelve candle bulbs.

The 5ft 6in bedstead, small by today's standards, had a carved painted frame. Above the bed was a painted canopy from which draped blue satin descended in manicured folds. This was complemented by a blue-and-gold-figured silk bedspread. The bedroom furniture was particularly beautiful and all acquired to fit the room. While Phyllis appreciated the magnificence, she lay in the new bed wondering how long it would take to feel like home. She had had little input into the décor, and Stanford Hall felt to her like the most grandiose of hotels. Most of the furniture in the bedroom was made from mahogany inlaid with kingwood and tulipwood, accessorised with ormolu feet and handles. One of the most valuable pieces of furniture was an inlaid Louis XV chest of drawers with shaped rouge marble tops. But other notable pieces included a French ormolu writing table, Poudresse table, armoire and many other pieces. Chaise longues and other chairs decorated in grey-and-rose-trellis-design silk taffeta provided comfortable seating, rarely used.

Unlike in other rooms, the Cahns had a three-way, silver-metal bell press for their butler, maid and valet. Whenever they needed anything at all, however small the request, the appropriate button was depressed and the appropriate servant would come running. Initially, Phyllis enjoyed her new toy, but quickly began to feel sympathy for the poor maids who had to hurry along the long corridors to attend to her every need. Stanford Hall's telephone exchange was permanently manned, so whether Julien or Phyllis wished to call someone internally or place an external call, they could do so instantaneously. Nothing was wanting. White Allom had attended to every last detail. In Julien and Phyllis' bedroom, there were numerous ornaments ranging from a gilt elephant with electric light-bulb attachment to a Wayfarer portable wireless set. It was beautiful but was it really a home? The sums spent on the room were extraordinary. When the inventory was prepared in 1938, the Cahns' bedroom alone was valued at £160,000 in today's money. Phyllis took pleasure in her fine things, but was it really worth it? Even she was prone to wondering.

Attached to their bedroom were Phyllis' bathroom and Julien's dressing room and bathroom. His bathroom was fitted out in a severe Roman style. His dressing room had wall-to-wall cupboards designed especially to house his elaborate wardrobe of 120 suits. It is estimated that each bathroom alone cost between £5–7,000 in 1930s currency.

Phyllis' dressing room was opposite her bathroom. It wasn't until 1937 that this room was transformed into the most magnificent octagonal boudoir. That summer the Cahns visited the Paris Exhibition and were inspired to purchase the various components. Each wall, and even the door, was panelled with a mirror. A large circular mirror surrounded by decorative metal work and painted flowers took up most of the ceiling. Lighting was concealed behind various panels to create a fabulously bright room full of optical illusion. A circular carpet lay on the floor, mirroring the circle of the ceiling.

Less than two weeks after the Cahns moved into Stanford Hall, the general election held on 30 May 1929 resulted in a hung Parliament. Labour won 288 seats to the Conservatives' 260, with the 59 Liberals under Lloyd George holding the balance of power. Stanley Baldwin resigned and Ramsay MacDonald formed a minority Government, supported by Lloyd George. While in the longer term this was bad news for Julien Cahn, as his friend was no longer Prime Minister, in the short term it offered up an opportunity – the Resignation Honours List.

The months of June and July 1929 were particular highlights in Julien Cahn's life. They represented public recognition of years of hard work and a bout of great fortune. The latter was thanks to Sheba Chapman, Phyllis Cahn's aunt.

A warm-hearted lady with bright-red hair, somewhat over-enhanced by the use of a bottle, Aunt Sheba was the family's favourite relation. Widowed tragically early, she was exceptionally gentle in manner. Julien was particularly fond of her, as she had so many of the qualities that had been missing in his own mother. Some weeks earlier, Sheba had purchased a ticket for the London Stock Exchange Sweep Stake on the Derby. The Epsom Derby was one of the most famous races, largely because so many people placed bets upon it.

Describing the unfolding of events to a journalist, Julien explained that Aunt Sheba came to lunch one day after the announcement of the draw had been made. He congratulated her on her luck in drawing the horse Trigo. In response, she mentioned that she wished she could find someone to buy half her share. Without giving the matter serious thought, Cahn offered to purchase half the ticket for £500 and thus the deal was quickly concluded over the luncheon table. And it was forgotten about.

Trigo, ridden by apprentice jockey Joseph Marshall, won the 1929 Derby at odds of 33/1. Julien Cahn and Sheba Chapman each won an extraordinary £63,000, equivalent to £2.3 million in today's money. Trigo, a handsome bay, had been a successful juvenile horse in Ireland, but in England had performed very badly in the 2000 Guineas for no apparent reason and was sent off at 33/1. Aunt Sheba, who watched the race at Epsom on that rain-swept afternoon of Wednesday 5 June, couldn't contain her delight upon seeing her horse win by 1½ lengths. When Trigo crossed the finish line there was absolute silence, broken only by a shriek of delight from Sheba Chapman. Crowds of men besuited in grey top hats and bookies with chequered vests trained their binoculars upon the slight, flame-haired lady jumping up and down with joy. As soon as she could, Aunt Sheba wired over her congratulations to the Cahns.

After the race Julien Cahn's win attracted a great deal of media interest, with the story being reported all across the world, from *Time* magazine to *The Times*. In an interview with a journalist, Cahn explained, 'I hardly gave the matter any thought until today. I can honestly say that this win is unexpected. I know nothing about flat racing and take very little interest in it, although as MFH (Master of the Fox Hounds) here I run the horses over the sticks pretty often.'

In fact, Cahn never backed horses and despised all forms of gambling, considering it a form of weakness. Needless to say, he didn't mention this to the curious press. Instead, he went on to explain how the winnings would benefit his cricket team. 'The other day I mentioned my half share and they asked to be allowed to participate. So they bought a £1 share each and now there will be almost £1,000 to be distributed amongst them.'

When asked what he would do with the money, he stated, 'I haven't much idea. I suppose I shall give it away as I have the rest of my money.'

Indeed, this was not a flippant remark. Although this was a phenomenal win, it represented only a small amount of the money that Julien donated to philanthropic causes during the 1920s and 1930s.

That night Cahn attended the Derby Dinner at the Ambassador Club. He was in an ebullient mood, dapper in his new morning suit, collected earlier in the evening from his tailors on Savile Row. News of his win spread fast. Many of the high-powered men, such as the Duke of Westminster, the Earl of Birkenhead and Winston Churchill, had not heard of Julien Cahn before that evening. By the end of the night most had shaken his hand, eager for a little of his good fortune to rub off upon them. It was fortunate indeed that he shot to fame on the very day of the first Derby Dinner he was to attend.

Just two weeks after the phenomenal win on Trigo and the status-enhancing Derby Dinner, Julien Cahn received the official letter he had been secretly hoping for. Julien was overjoyed. Dated 21 June 1929 it read:

Sir,

I have the honour to inform you that I intend in connection with my Resignation Honours List, to submit your name to the King with a recommendation that he may be graciously pleased to approve that the honour of Knighthood be conferred upon you. Before doing so, however, I should be glad to know that this mark of His Majesty's favour would be agreeable to you, and I would therefore ask you to be good enough to communicate with me accordingly at your earliest convenience. I am,

Yours very truly, Stanley Baldwin.

On the morning of Wednesday 10 July, Julien and Phyllis Cahn were driven by their chauffeur in their Rolls Royce to St James's Palace. They were accompanied by Julien's childhood friend Sir Harold and Lady Bowden of Raleigh bicycle fame, Sir Harold having been awarded a CBE for philanthropic and public services during the same dissolution honours ceremony. Both Julien and Harold were dressed in their ceremonial garbs. The jacket and matching plus-fours were made from the softest of navy blue silk velvet, highlighted with large, white-gold buttons running down the jacket with identical buttons on the plus-fours. The jacket was worn over a white dinner shirt, white silk bow tie and silk waistcoat. He wore thick, black tights under the plus-fours and black leather pumps bedecked with large golden buckles. They looked dapper if rather antiquated. Unfortunately, the King was absent so the ceremony was conducted by the Prince of Wales.

The Prince of Wales entered the gold-encrusted Throne Room accompanied by the Secretary of State for the Home Department and took his place on the magnificent throne. There were various Gurkhas, ushers and Yeomen of the Guard present, taking care of the guests. After the national anthem, the Secretary of State announced the name of each of the recipients, along with the achievement for which they were being decorated. *Sotto voce*, the Equerry to the Prince of Wales gave a brief background to the Prince as each recipient approached the throne.

'Julien Cahn, philanthropy and public services. Paid for the Lucy Baldwin Maternity Hospital and various other good causes. Master of the Hunt, very successful businessman with retail furniture shops.'

Julien Cahn's calm approach belied his nerves. He knelt in front of the Prince on the investiture stool to receive his accolade. After the sword lightly touched both his shoulders, he rose, with knees trembling, and bent his head to receive the medals.

The months following the receipt of his knighthood were crammed full of social engagements in the company of the great and the good. Typical was the evening of Thursday 18 July 1929, when Sir Julien was the guest of Mr Eveleigh Nash, a famous publisher, at the Wellington Club. He was in fine company. Other invitees included Prince George of Russia, Lady Norah Spencer-Churchill and the Earl and Countess of Cardigan. A couple of months later, on Wednesday 16 October 1929, Sir Julien was elected a member of the Imperial Society of Knights Bachelor during a ceremony at Ciro's Club in London. Each person that received the official knighthood was accepted into the society, which as a charity was formed to uphold the dignity of knights and advise its members.

Cahn had always cared about his appearance and personal grooming, but now he was almost fanatical about it. He knew first impressions counted and he wanted his presence to be felt the moment he entered a room. A good shave came at the top of his daily personal ablutions. With his black hair, he quickly gained a dark shadow on his face, giving him a menacing look that he vehemently disliked. He would have preferred to have no moustache but as it was de rigueur in the 1920s, he ensured his small moustache was kept neatly trimmed. Every single day during the 1920s he visited a barber's shop adjacent to Midland station in Nottingham on his way to work. Some years later, when he built his offices at Talbot Street, he included his own barber's room in the development. His first personal barber was a Russian called Louis Dubnikov. Louis was a small, portly man, who, unfortunately for a barber, was completely bald. To alleviate this misfortune he wore a toupee. Louis shaved Julien every single day until his retirement in 1939. Louis' job took him wherever Sir Julien went. He accompanied him on world tours, to London and to Europe.

Similar to his grooming, Cahn's clothes were an essential part of himself and they had to be perfect. He had two tailors on Savile Row, London, one of whom was called Johnson and made his exquisitely tailored suits and monogrammed silk shirts, embroidered with the newly formed Cahn crest. As was typical, the tailor's name and the date that the suit was made were embroidered on the inside of the jackets. For each of his 120 suit jackets, Julien had two pairs of trousers made. He insisted upon razor-sharp creases down the front, changing trousers should the creases fall out. While Julien did not create fashion, he was very aware of it and ensured that he kept abreast of all emerging trends. At the same time, he could not afford to be too avant-garde as he had to keep up with the Joneses of the aristocracy, and the upper class were never ahead of the game in the fashion stakes. Julien managed to tread the fine line of being absolutely correct in his dress code (and behaviour) while also being subtly ahead of the masses. As was typical for the time, he changed into black tie for dinner every night and Phyllis Cahn into evening dress.

Julien had all of the finest garbs for his various sporting activities in addition to some rather extraordinary garments especially commissioned. These included the well-documented inflatable pads that he wore when playing cricket. Less known was the inflatable swimming costume. What a strange sight he must have been bobbing up and down in the pool, a slender man suddenly made fat! While the costume would have ensured Sir Julien didn't sink, it cannot have made for easy swimming. No one seems to know whether this outfit was designed as a buoyancy aid for a weak swimmer or as insulation for a man who felt the cold.

Unsurprisingly, Lady Cahn also wore the very finest clothes and gowns, the majority designed especially for her. Her jewellery was equally spectacular. She favoured large pieces. When she was presented at Court, along with her Prince of Wales feathers, Lady Cahn wore an elaborate ruby and diamond necklace with matching earrings and bracelet. Shortly afterwards it was deemed too large and overly ornate so it was broken up and crafted into smaller pieces.

Stanford Hall was fully fitted out when the family moved in; there were beautiful artefacts and antiques in every room and the very finest paintings hanging on the walls. However, White Allom had been told not to spend any money on paintings and that Julien Cahn would organise this himself. Joe Redding, the project manager, had been surprised. He had not expected Cahn to be an art connoisseur. In fact, he was right.

Within weeks of taking up residence, the walls of Stanford Hall were bedecked with the very finest of paintings. In the summer of 1929, the *Nottingham Journal* reported that two important paintings by Arthur Spooner (1873–1961), *The Goose Fair* and *Nottingham Old Market*, had been 'purchased by a gentleman prominent in Nottingham'. Both the paintings were considered to be among the finest achievements of the artist. Some locals had tried to encourage the city authorities to buy the paintings as a permanent record of these two distinctive and historical events, but to no avail. Although Julien publicly stated that the pictures would be made available for exhibition, both were to remain at the hall, hanging on the main staircase until they were finally sold off by the Co-operative Society in the 1960s. The paintings were never put on public display. In fact, the real reason why the Stanford Hall paintings could never be shown to the public was due to a potentially embarrassing secret. A secret that was in jeopardy following the death of the 10th Earl of Harrington a few months after the Cahns moved into Stanford Hall.

The art hanging on Stanford Hall's walls were national treasures, the finest of paintings by the likes of Van Dyck, Rembrandt, Gainsborough and Lely, paintings that today hang in Windsor Castle as part of the

Royal Collection and on the walls of the National Portrait Gallery. However, other than the Spooner paintings, Julien did not invest in art. He preferred more modest collecting for his hobbies – cricket and magic, and eventually had the finest cricket library of all times. Nevertheless, he knew that fine art was essential for a country house. So, he developed a private, rather innovative scheme that he ran with the Earls of Harrington. This was kept utterly secret as it would have been a potential source of embarrassment to both parties.

Charles Stanhope, the Earl of Harrington, lived at Elvaston Castle in Derbyshire. The building was and is quite beautiful, however, it was the grounds of Elvaston that were truly spectacular, famous for the long avenues, serpentine lake, a Moorish temple and golden gates. The Earl had inherited a glorious seat, and while he was asset rich, he was distinctly cash poor. Julien wanted to fill Stanford Hall with beautiful things, quickly. He didn't have the time or the inclination to scour galleries and auction rooms. So he put a proposition to the Earl of Harrington to rent some of his art. This suggestion was received warmly and within days over twenty stunning, world-renowned paintings by leading artists were hanging on the walls of Stanford Hall. In return, the Earl had a tidy sum of annual cash handy to boost his income.

The fabulous paintings sent to Stanford Hall included *Tangier* by Sir Peter Lavery, *The Children of Charles I* by Sir Anthony Van Dyck, painted in 1634 and currently hanging in the Galleria Sabauda in Turin, a self-portrait of Peter Paul Rubens, painted in 1628 now in the Kunsthistorisches Museum in Vienna, and a portrait of the Duchess of Cleveland by Sir Godfrey Kneller, painted in 1705 and currently displayed in the Primary Collection at the National Portrait Gallery, London. The Stanford Hall dining room was home to eleven portraits, including one of Queen Henrietta Maria, Queen of Charles I, by Sir Anthony Van Dyck, painted in 1633 and currently hanging in the National Gallery of Art in Washington DC, a self-portrait of Rubens, now part of the Royal Collection at Windsor Castle, a portrait of Charles II, Duke of Grafton, by Sir Joshua Reynolds, a portrait of a lady in a ruff holding a glove by Hendrik van der Vliet, a portrait of a gentleman in a lace collar by Cornelius Johnson, painted in 1625, and a portrait of Lady Stanhope as *Contemplation* by Sir Joshua Reynolds. Together these formed quite a line-up of masterpieces.

Fortunately for Julien, the executors of Harrington's estate were pleased to continue the scheme after his death; it carried on under the supervision of the young 11th Earl of Harrington and only ceased upon Sir Julien's death in 1944, when the paintings were quietly returned to Elvaston Castle. If any discerning guest recognised the art hanging on Sir Julien's walls, they were certainly too discreet to say anything.

During the latter half of 1929, the Cahn family settled into their new home. Julien was away much of the time. Phyllis began, slowly, to get used to her increased retinue of staff.

At the top of the staff hierarchy, sat the butler. As was typical for any large country house, the butler was in charge of everything and everybody. He ran the house, organised rotas and oversaw every aspect of care for the Cahn family, their guests and the house itself. The previous butler, Victor Campbell, had proved to be dishonest, and Phyllis was eager to ensure that they did not have similar problems with the new butler. An article from the *Hucknall Dispatch*, of December 1926, explains how Campbell had a lapse of honesty. The court was told that Campbell had stolen banknotes from his employer, Mr Julien Cahn of Papplewick Grange. The notes were missed by Mr Cahn and others substituted, their numbers having first been noted. Campbell denied taking £40 (equivalent to £1,500 today) but admitted to a £10 note and two £5 notes. He was bound over for the sum of £100 for twelve months and ordered to repay the money within a fortnight or go to prison for two months.

Dressed in his uniform of morning suit, Dutton, the butler, had an onerous, all-consuming job. Often up at 5 a.m. to rally his staff and set them their daily tasks, he would be on duty day and night at the beck and call of the family. When guests came to stay, a footman or housemaid would be assigned to look after all the needs of each individual guest. This involved unpacking their suitcases upon arrival, turning down beds, running baths, cleaning shoes, delivering food or drink to bedrooms and any other personal requirements that the guest might have had. If there were any problems, the butler would have had to deal with them. The more generous guests left substantial tips for the staff. Apparently, when he visited in 1931, the Greek premier Venizelos was particularly munificent, enabling the staff to have a fabulous night out on the town after he left.

The servants all lived at Stanford Hall. More senior staff with families were assigned apartments, some within the hall itself, others in adjacent buildings, and some were given houses or cottages on the estate. The single staff, such as the footmen Langsdale and Cover, and the young housemaids, such as the Walton sisters, lived in the hall. The single female staff lived on the top floor of the hall above a wing. The men lived on the lower ground floor. Unusually for many grand houses of the era, the servants each had their own room, regardless of how junior they were. Although simply furnished, the rooms were comfortable and all the facilities were to a high standard with a basin in each bedroom. The footmen's rooms had dark-green cork carpet-tiles on the floor, covered with hearth rugs, and cream linen blinds and floral chintz curtains at the windows. Typically, each room had a 6ft wardrobe, a chest or dressing table, a chair and a single bed with feather pillows and quilts covered in printed satin. Most of the maids and footmen's bedrooms were accessorised with linen baskets, occasional tables, china lamps, vases, medicine cabinets and electric radiators. While the rooms were compact, they were homely and care was taken to ensure that the staff had privacy and comfort.

Life was good for the staff. Time and time again they have described themselves as 'One big happy family!' Mabel Thomson, a senior housemaid, made contact with Bill Robson, the son of Thomas Robson the head chauffeur, some forty years after they all left Stanford Hall. She states in a letter to Bill that the eight years she lived at Stanford Hall were 'the happiest and most carefree days of my life'. She reminisced about, as she called them, 'such privileges' when the family were not in residence – the use of the swimming pool, tennis courts, golf course, staff cricket pitch and so on. Her particular favourite was the annual day out for staff on the River Trent with Lady Cahn's motor launch and the annual staff trip to the seaside, usually a visit to Skegness. These people did not have the aspirations and expectations of today's youngsters. They were content with their lot in life, accepting of their position. Society owed them nothing. If they were to achieve anything it was by hard work and good fortune. And they certainly believed that working and living at Stanford Hall was their good fortune.

While her husband was at work or socialising in London, Phyllis Cahn filled her days with sport. Although Julien was comically inept at all sport – with perhaps the exception of table tennis – Phyllis was a competent sportswoman. Stanford Hall was a veritable sporting emporium. The grounds housed two fabulous cricket pitches, a swimming pool (which was to be built in the early 1930s), a nine-hole golf course, croquet lawn, bowling green, short tennis court, two hard tennis courts and two grass courts. There were numerous guns and rifles for shooting – and even an antique Arab rifle. Phyllis played tennis and golf, was a strong swimmer (after her husband's death she swam daily in the English Channel) and a good shot. Unfortunately, she did not share her husband's passion for cricket or fishing.

One of Julien's favourite pursuits, for which he now had little time, was fishing. While living at Papplewick Grange, Cahn had spent many a summer's evening with Hollywell, the village miller, standing together on the bridge over the River Lean, fly-fishing into the river. Disenchanted by the lack of fish, Cahn arranged to have the river stocked with brown trout. Nearly a hundred years later, the trout are still caught today and fried up by the local Papplewick boys.

In March 1928, prior to moving into Stanford Hall, Cahn ordered the hall's lake area to be drained and enhanced. The lake was extended and the stream diverted. It was at about this time that Bob Mason saw the advert for water bailiff at Stanford Hall. Bob had been working for Lord and Lady Hereford in Leominster and was looking for a change. The position at Stanford Hall was ideal for Bob and he stayed there for many happy years. He was responsible for the coarse fish being taken out of the lake and restocking with trout that were bred on the estate. Brown trout were kept in the bottom lake and rainbow trout in the top lake. When Julien or guests wanted to fish, Mason was responsible for looking after them. He would change the flies and help them land a fish.

One day young Albert Cahn decided he wanted to have a go at fishing. He approached Mason and eagerly grabbed his rod. To their mutual horror the hook flew back and caught in Bob Mason's ear, leaving him with a neat hole in his lobe. As pierced ears were most certainly not in vogue for men during the 1930s, Bob suffered with a hole in his ear for the rest of his life. And Albert never held a fishing rod again! It was to be another ten years before Mason really came into his own and assumed what was possibly the most interesting and unusual position among all the staff of Stanford Hall.

On hot summer afternoons, the staff would collect small rowing boats from one of the two boathouses and row out onto the lake alongside the graceful swans. Every winter these same lakes would freeze over and were used by the Cahn children and the staff for skating.

The interior sporting facilities were equally magnificent. The ground floor of the west wing had been converted into a badminton court and ballroom, over the top of which was a gymnasium that was later converted to a squash court. At the back a small balcony was built so that select guests could sit and sip drinks while watching a game. The badminton hall had hand-painted walls depicting garden scenes and lattice decoration and full-length glass doors that opened up onto the Italian Piazza. This was one of the few facilities used with great regularity by the whole Cahn family. Every Sunday afternoon the Cahns had a private tea party, to which their best friends were invited, normally the Newmans and the Solbys. As they grew older, this event was also attended by the Cahn children. Before tea the adults partook in a game of badminton. Albert loved playing badminton but he never dared to ask if he could join in. Instead, the children sat on the wicker chairs and watched. Children were only to speak when spoken to and were to be on their best behaviour whenever surrounded by adults.

Strangely, Julien did not expect such strict standards from other people's children, many of whom found him more accessible than his own children did. Gabriel Jaffé, son of the Cahns' friends Dr and Mrs Jaffé, remembers how Julien regularly visited their home, The Hollies on Derby Road, Nottingham, and frequently offered to play ping-pong with him. Despite being rather a good table-tennis player for a 10-year-old, Gabriel was consistently beaten by Julien, whose speciality shot was a 'devastating little drop shot' that just tumbled over the net after a serve. April Jaffé, whose parents named her Phyllis April out of affection for Lady Cahn, recalls Julien listening to her play 'Chopsticks' on the piano. He gave the young girl his total attention and uttered such warm words of approval one would have assumed she was a serious performer. While Julien took the time to engage with other children, sadly he seemed less inclined to spend time playing with Pat, Albert and Richard.

The gymnasium was fitted out with the very latest keep-fit equipment, mainly used by Phyllis Cahn in her eternal quest to stay slim. There was a rowing exercise machine with a sliding seat on rollers with sculls. The 'Battle Creek' health builder mounted on an iron frame with an electric motor, canvas belt and chart was, with hindsight, the most amusing of machines. This contraption was developed by Dr John Harvey Kellogg, brother of Will Kellogg, the man responsible for inventing breakfast cereals. Dr Kellogg owned the Battle Creek Sanatorium, in Michigan, where he offered a number of health treatments, including the health builder which was based upon a form of vibratory massage. Straps were placed around the user's waist, or other body part they wanted to reduce in size, and the rapid vibration of the straps supposedly worked the body to reduce the fat. While this was obviously the precursor of such modern-day devices as Slendertone, it did little other than severely chaff the user. Nevertheless, it was used with great regularity by Phyllis, along with an electric rotating machine.

When she wasn't engaged in sport, Phyllis found herself chatting to Mrs Bentley. Mrs Bentley was the head chef and the kitchen was her empire. She had joined the Cahns when they were living at Papplewick Grange. Her cooking skills and organisation of the kitchen impressed her employers greatly. When she married and had her two daughters, Muriel and Barbara, she left her job. However, her marriage broke up and the Cahns asked her to return to their employment at Stanford Hall. The Bentleys lived in a cottage on the estate but the girls spent most of their time in the kitchens of Stanford Hall, listening to the gossip of Dutton the butler, Chesham the engineer and Alice, Lady Cahn's maid. In recognition of the high esteem in which he held Mrs Bentley, Julien Cahn agreed to pay for Muriel and Barbara's education as weekly boarders at Loughborough Girls High School. This placed the Bentley family on a higher social stratum than any of the other staff. Julien was so impressed by Mrs Bentley's cooking and genuinely thrilled to have her back, he decided to invest in her training. To her delight, she was sent to the best hotels in New York, Paris and Brussels to learn the tricks of the culinary trade. This was an extraordinary gesture and a fabulous opportunity for the young lady, an experience that she appreciated for the rest of her life.

The kitchen was the hub of Stanford Hall's activity. At the centre stood an 11ft beech kitchen table. As with everything else in the house, the equipment was of the very highest standard. There was a modern range with three ovens from France, another kitchen range from the USA, an electric dishwasher also imported from the USA, an electric cake maker and a 3ft Frigidaire ice-cream maker. The scullery housed an electric dishwasher, another range cooker, the vegetable larder, a couple of fridges and three enormous fridge meat safes – one was 10ft wide and the other two nearly 4ft wide each.

While everyone else in the kitchen was called by their first names, Mrs Bentley was always called 'Mrs Bentley', even by Phyllis Cahn. There was one exception: Julien called her 'Lizzie'! Mrs Bentley had a large retinue of kitchen staff. She was responsible not only for the day-to-day food of the family, but the day-to-day food of all the staff and the sophisticated catering required for visiting guests, dinner parties, cricketing parties, dances and charity functions held at or in the grounds of Stanford Hall. When the Cahns were entertaining, the menus for the events were discussed and agreed between Mrs Bentley and Julien. On non-entertaining days the menus were agreed with Phyllis. One of their favourites was the 'green meal'. This consisted of green pasta as a starter, an all-green main course and dessert with green beer to drink.

Christmas 1929 was a quiet affair. The children awoke to find large pillowcases stuffed full of presents at the ends of their beds; the fruits, nuts and gifts were selected largely by their nanny. Although both Julien and Phyllis had been brought up in traditional Jewish homes, their own kitchen was not kosher and they did not adhere to a kosher diet. Christmas was a strange combination of English customs in a Jewish home. Mezuzahs adorned each doorway but beautifully decorated Christmas trees stood within the rooms. Turkey was cooked, but never served with bacon.

When at home alone, the Cahns ate simply, preferring fish such as sole and plaice to red meat, followed by the likes of orange soufflé. Muriel Bentley, Mrs Bentley's eldest daughter, recalled that Julien Cahn's favourite was stuffed eggplant and what was referred to by all as 'Jew pancake', and appeared to her young eyes much like a cluster of worms with powdered sugar on top.

The Cahns saw in the new decade with a few of their closest friends. At dinner they were amazed by Mrs Bentley's new *pièce de résistance* – a fabulously elaborate dessert made in the shape of a swan. Home-made vanilla ice-cream was put in a bombe and then gently removed and placed in a mist of spun sugar that lay on a large silver salver.

'Sir Julien wants that damn swan again!' Mrs Bentley would mutter whenever it was requested, which it was many times over the next ten years. Particularly fiddly to make, its slender neck was subject to breaking when removed from the caste and on more than one occasion had to be remade. But on 31 December 1929 it was quite perfect.

At the end of dinner, Sir Julien raised his crystal-cut glass of champagne and took a customary modest sip: 'Health and happiness and to another great decade!'

4

Seizing Opportunities

The new decade began in style with a ball. The Cahns attended the Lincolnshire Stuff Ball on 6 January 1930 at the County Assembly Rooms in Lincoln. An important society event, this ball had been fundraising for the textile trade for more than fifty years. Ladies were expected to wear a different coloured dress every year, to encourage the regular purchase of fabric. This was the first year that the Cahns had attended since the receipt of Julien's knighthood. The new Lady Cahn dressed in opulent style in a full-length, deep-maroon velvet dress, with long black gloves and a mink stole. Rubies dripped from her neck and wrists. Her contemporaries stared at her jewels with little concealed envy; her friends took pleasure from the simple joy that flowed through Phyllis as she spoke admiringly about her husband's success and their exciting new lifestyle. But most of the talk centred on the Cahns' forthcoming tour. Within their group of friends, no one had ventured as far as South America and the Cahns' excitement was tangible.

The Cahn XI cricketing tour to Jamaica had been such a success and so enjoyable for all concerned that Sir Julien decided to escape Britain for another winter. Once again the team was to cross the Atlantic, but this time the Argentine was their destination. They sailed from Tilbury on the *Avila Star* of the Blue Star Line on 20 February, bound for Buenos Aires.

The full party included Sir Julien as Captain and Lady Cahn, F.W.H. Nicholas, F.C.W. Newman, T. Arnott, L. Green, P.T. Eckersley, H.R. Munt, R.W.V. Robins, H.R.S. Critchley-Salmonson, G.F.H. Heane, S.D. Rhodes, C.W. Flood, C.A. Rowland, J.R. Gunn, T.L. Richmond and H.D. Swan. Although John Gunn was in attendance as the umpire, he actually played in two of the matches. G. Shaw, the dressing-room attendant at Trent Bridge, accompanied the side as 'Chef de Baggage'.

The team's manager was H.D. Swan. A cricket-obsessed, rotund, pipe-smoking man, during his career he served on the committee of the MCC and managed more matches for premier clubs than anyone else. They were also accompanied by a number of the Cahn family as well as Alice, Lady Cahn's personal maid, and Louis Dubnikov, Sir Julien's personal barber. The total party numbered about thirty.

Lady Cahn's maid, Alice, had one of the most important and trusted jobs among the Cahns' personal staff. She was responsible for all of Lady Cahn's belongings, her jewellery and clothes. Her skills lay in sewing, which she undertook in her own workroom at Stanford Hall located next to her bedroom. On one side of the room were seven large wardrobe cupboards filled to the brim with Lady Cahn's occasional wear, evening gowns and the like. Over the years, Alice was given the use of a modern Singer and a state-of-the-art electric iron and ironing board. Lady Cahn gave her an electric mains wireless set and HMV table gramophone so she was able to listen to music as she worked. Although she was thrilled to be accompanying her mistress on such a lengthy cruise to an exotic location, her job was onerous. The Cahns travelled with a phenomenal wardrobe; they changed clothes several times each day, culminating in the finest ball gowns and evening wear for dinner with Captain Vernon most nights. Alice had to make sure that everything was perfect.

The Atlantic crossing was smooth with delightful weather. They were lucky. On that outward voyage there were not many passengers on board, so the Cahn party figured prominently in the various sports and games that were organised. The officers enjoyed caring for the players, a lively bunch of men supported by their patron Sir Julien, who tipped most generously. While crossing the 'Line' (as the equator is proverbially known), many of the cricketers had to pay the usual tribute to Father Neptune, their immersion in a large tank of water causing much amusement. This traditional ceremony still takes place today for equator-crossing virgins. The captain, or another member of the crew, becomes King Neptune, in beard and costume, and as passengers come up to meet him they are dunked by crew-members, some in fancy dress, in a large vat of water – or nowadays into the on-board swimming pool.

The grand ocean liners hosted many social events to keep their passengers entertained. During this particular crossing the guests enjoyed a fancy dress ball. H.D. Swan, in conjunction with a couple of other members of the team and assisted by a Mr Warren, one of the ship's officers, organised a revue, entitled 'Naughty-calities'. This provided great amusement and appealed to Sir Julien's somewhat coarser sense of humour. Reports of the trip describe F.W.H. Nicholas and H.R. Munt as 'working indefatigably in promoting the sports and amusements on board'.

The first port of call in South America was a night in Rio de Janeiro. Although the heat was oppressive for the British travellers, they were over-awed by the stunning scenery. During their short stay in Rio, Sir Julien and Mr Swan were entertained to lunch at the Jockey Club by Major J.C. Muriel, the President of the Brazilian Cricket Association. They discussed the possibility of a combined Argentine, Brazilian and Chilean team making a tour to England in the near future. Sir Julien made one or two suggestions to enable such a tour to take place. It was thought that 1932 might be a convenient year and H.D. Swan undertook to arrange a fixture list should the idea come to fruition. Indeed the tour did take place.

E.W.S. Thomson (Tommy), the Honorable Secretary of the Argentine Cricket Association, travelled from Buenos Aires to greet Cahn's visiting team in Montevideo, and joined them on the steamer for a trip up the River Plate.

Wherever they travelled, the Cahn team were treated as VIPs and cricket emissaries and greeted by the most senior dignitaries and representatives of the British Empire. It was no different in Buenos Aires when they arrived early in the morning on 13 March. The party was met and welcomed by several well-known supporters of cricket in the Argentine, including Robin Stuart, the President of the Argentine Cricket Association, R.C. Drysdale, G. Drysdale, A.W.F. Hobson, A.H. Isaac (the old Corinthian footballer) and others. Formalities at customs were quickly completed and no time was lost in taking up quarters at the Plaza Hotel, the best hotel in the city, built in 1909. In the afternoon a short spell of net practice was indulged in at the Belgrano ground. In the evening an informal reception was held at the English Club, where a large gathering received the team, including Mr E. Millington Drake, HM Charge d'Affaires, Sir Herbert Gibson and many others.

The following day further practice took place in the morning and afternoon, and in the evening all the team were entertained to a first-class boxing display at the Mission to Seamen's Hall, on the invitation of the Revd Canon W. Brady, the popular padre who specialised in caring for seafarers in South American ports.

The first few days of the tour were extremely hot. Even Sir Julien, who never ventured out without his layers of sweaters, stripped down to his shirt sleeves. Fortunately, after a few days the weather became cooler and the more pleasant conditions made play much easier for the British group.

In all, six matches were played, but the ones of importance were the three tests against Argentina. Some good bowling by Robins (who later played for England and was often consulted by Cahn regarding strategy) gave Cahn a victory in the first test. In the second they were lucky to scrape a draw and the third was also drawn, but in favour of the visitors. Owing to a split finger while practising before the first match of the tour, Rowland was unable to appear in any of the matches. Cahn's XI were impressed by the high standard of cricket in the Argentine and in particular the excellent cricket grounds.

The team was shown great hospitality off the field and some enjoyable functions were arranged in their honour. At Hurlingham and Belgrano they were entertained to dinner dances – high-spirited occasions. A farewell dinner was given at the English Club on the night before they sailed home, when Robin Stuart presided over a large gathering of past and present Argentine cricketers. Sir Julien was presented with a handsome silver salver by the Argentine Cricket Association as a memento of his visit.

Unfortunately for Cahn and the team, as all the fixtures were played on suburban grounds in Buenos Aires there was little time to see anything of country life in the Argentine, but on the days they did not play cricket they visited places of interest in the neighbourhood of the city. A number of the team were invited to make a tour of inspection of the Frigorífico-Anglo under the guidance of Mr Richard Tootell, and were fascinated to see this chilled meat factory, probably the most important factory of its kind in the world. On another occasion some of the party spent a very enjoyable day visiting the Carlos Casares milk and cheese factory and estancia.

On the return journey they docked at the port of Santos. Sir Julien and several members of his team were escorted by Lieutenant-Colonel Johnston (the first patron of the Brazilian Cricket Association) and Major J.C. Muriel on an interesting trip to São Paulo. The outward journey was made by road, an extremely steep, thrilling, winding route that tested their nerves. Pleased to be on terra firma in São Paulo, they were shown around the city, and paid a visit to the cricket ground. Apparently, the guests were particularly intrigued by the huge sight-boards (or billboards as we know them today) that had been erected in order to prevent the stoppage of play by the frequent passing of trains. Afterwards they were the guests of Colonel Johnston and Mr Ernest Cunningham at the Automobile Club. The return journey to Santos was made by train, a steep descent demonstrating an extraordinary feat of railway engineering that was particularly impressive, although less nerve-racking than the outward car journey.

On the last night of the voyage, Sir Julien and Lady Cahn were entertained to a farewell dinner, over which H.D. Swan presided. In the course of a short speech he expressed the thanks of all the team to Sir Julien and Lady Cahn for all their kindness during the tour and on behalf of the players presented their captain with a silver cigarette box bearing all the autographs engraved on the lid, and to Lady Cahn he handed a silver flower vase, also inscribed. The weather was rough in the Bay of Biscay and the Cahns were pleased to land at Plymouth on 23 April.

Having been away from his business for so many weeks, Julien threw himself back into his commercial affairs. The trip to South America had allowed him time to think and he had written down copious notes on innovative retailing ideas, penned in green ink as normal.

During the inter-war years, Cahn's furniture business spearheaded the most significant changes in retailing – hire purchase, mass appeal, promotions and customer service. Julien was never short of interesting ideas.

Around the turn of the century, less expensive and less lasting furniture began to appear in significant quantities. The output of low-priced furniture for the working and middle-class markets was made possible by improvements in the methods of production, which transformed the industry from one based on handicrafts to one based on factories and machines. The better-off sections of the working classes were shunning second-hand furniture or the making of their own and buying suites of matching furniture such as tables, chests of drawers, chairs and chiffoniers.

Eric Pensen worked for the firm of accountants that audited the books of furniture-makers Bottomore, Day & Co., of Haydn Road, Nottingham, suppliers to Sir Julien's chain of retail furniture shops. He was surprised by the process the furniture was put through. In a large upstairs room a number of employees wearing masks and protective clothing applied stains to the whitewood wardrobes, turning them into walnut, oak or mahogany, depending upon the liquid applied.

By the inter-war period there were opportunities galore for the furnishings trade – opportunities that Sir Julien grasped. One of his favourite mottos was 'the opportunity of a lifetime should be seized in the lifetime of the opportunity'. He certainly did that in his business life.

The rapid rise in the number of houses built, particularly after 1931, and the increase in the number of households at a rate faster than the increase in population, was key to the furniture trade's dramatic success. But perhaps the greatest importance in relation to working and middle-class demand was the spread of the hire-purchase method of trading.

Hire purchase was much the same in the 1920s and 1930s as it is today. When goods were sold, the buyer had to pay an initial deposit, normally about 15 per cent, followed by a number of equal installments paid over a specified period. Over the years, as competition increased, this initial installment was used as a competitive advantage and increasingly reduced until sometimes no initial deposit was required at all. The legal ownership of the goods did not pass to the buyer (or hirer as they were officially called) until the payment of the final installment. This meant that if someone defaulted upon the payment under the hire-purchase agreement, the goods would be re-taken by the owner and all the payments already made were forfeited. This Draconian agreement did not deter customers, and by 1932 it was believed that there were 5 million hire-purchase transactions carried out each week.

The public enjoyed many advantages from hire purchase. The ordinary man in the street could purchase goods that had previously been beyond his reach. He had the pleasure of using the furniture while paying for it. In general, hire purchase raised the standard of living of the working classes, increased employment, savings remained intact, periodical payments were considered convenient and the budgeting necessary to meet these payments was generally considered to encourage thrift.

Of course, there was the negative side of hire purchase. Credit agreements were bitterly harsh. If a hirer could not afford to repay, the goods were repossessed even if the majority of the payment had been made. Sir Julien reckoned that 50 to 60 per cent tried to do the right thing and made their payments with little correspondence. But 30 per cent required a scare before they were prepared to pay and a good 10 per cent could not be forced to pay. This of course meant that the credit losses were passed on to those who did pay.

Hire purchase presented the retailer with a huge amount of clerical work and bookkeeping, but this was considered well worthwhile due to the extra amount of profit obtained on the transaction. Most stores added about 10 per cent onto the cash price of an article when credit was required. Shops that offered both cash and hire purchase tended to mark goods at a price whereby they could deduct 10 per cent for a cash customer and add 10 per cent for customers wanting to pay on credit. This 20 per cent easily covered the extra cost of short-term transactions. As installments had to keep pace with the depreciation of goods, most furniture agreements were spread over three to four years. Many stores tried to encourage customers to pay weekly in cash at the store, this also gave shop staff the opportunity to build up relationships with their customers whom they saw on a regular basis, encouraging them to purchase more. Cahn employed a team of enquiry men on his staff who collected information from customers and then verified it.

A whole new arm of the insurance industry was spawned as a result of hire purchase, as most traders involved in hire purchase insured the risks. Jays was instrumental in developing insurance packages for its customers, to cover them should they default on future payments. Insurance was used as an additional enticement to encourage prospective buyers. By the mid to late 1930s some cynics believed that the selling of insurance became the primary generator of funds, with the sale of furniture being of secondary importance.

The multiple-shop retailers recognised the need to appeal to every sector of the market. Initially, Jays and Campbells had offered low-priced furniture with no frills to the working classes. Now, Sir Julien recognised that his margins would increase if he could also sell to the more wealthy sectors of society. And thus he introduced service alongside price; he differentiated his shops so that Jays would sell the cheaper, utilitarian furniture, while the Nottingham Furnishing Company would sell the more expensive furniture accompanied by a higher level of service. Some shops would offer furniture only on hire-purchase terms, another shop in the same town, also owned by Sir Julien, would offer cash terms. The large shop on Derby Road, Nottingham, catered for the middle classes, unlike the shop opposite that sold cheaper, basic furniture. Both stores were owned by Sir Julien but the general public thought the stores were in competition with each other. The shops he took over rarely changed their names. So it would be normal to find a Jays on one side of the street and a Gosford Furnishing or Smart and Brown on the other side of the street. The more upmarket shop displayed burr-walnut suites in the ground-floor window and expensive bedroom furniture.

The profit margins were extremely high and the prices were very much geared up for the hire-purchase system. Salesmen were trained to discuss the furniture in terms of its weekly value. In his book of memoirs, the cricketer Tommy Reddick described his typical sales patter.

> Now sit in this beautifully sprung easy chair, Madam, and relax . . . and to think that you could enjoy such luxurious comfort, Madam, for the rest of your life for the expenditure of only one and nine pence a week.

An unfortunate young novice salesman, working in the large Jays store on Derby Road, failed to grasp the strategy. He recalled Sir Julien entering the shop just as he was completing the sale of a three-piece suite. The middle-aged couple handed the salesman the full price in cash and with a handshake left the store with smiles on their faces, delighted with the purchases that were to be delivered the next day. The young man turned towards Sir Julien expecting praise for the quick and efficient sale. To his dismay, Sir Julien had a scowl on his face.

'I don't make money by selling goods to customers who pay the full amount immediately!' he uttered witheringly, clearly annoyed that the young salesman had little grasp of the foundations upon which Sir Julien made his fortune – hire purchase.

When a new cream rubber floor with a red pathway was laid on the ground floor of the Derby Road store, the staff were told that it was especially for Sir Julien to walk along. It had to be kept immaculate. The scope of responsibility for shop managers increased, as did the numbers of staff they employed. In the 1930s most of Cahn's stores employed between eight and twelve people, with the larger emporiums employing over eighteen salesmen, all competing for commission. By the end of that decade, he was employing well over 4,000 staff. Managers were instructed to consider the attractiveness, layout and siting of their branches; greater numbers of ranges were held in store, designed to appeal to many different sectors of the market. Furniture retailing was becoming both an art and a science.

The location of the shops became critical and, for the first time, furniture shops could be found in the main streets of all the major towns in the UK. The shops became larger, brighter and cleaner, with more elaborate fittings. Service and choice were better. Firms gave home delivery and free credit. Key to the success of Jays and Campbells was the ability to centralise and standardise property acquisition, shop layouts, fittings and decoration, purchasing, stock control, transport, credit and promotion policies. Head office, directed by Julien Cahn and his right-hand man and lawyer, Sir Robert Doncaster, controlled every element of every store. The savings made from economies of scale were considerable; the controls on each element of the business were impressive.

Cahn particularly enjoyed coming up with innovative marketing ideas – although of course they were not defined as that in the 1930s. He introduced free gifts, elaborate window displays and the liberal distribution of catalogues. Typical was a coffee table positioned attractively in front of a sofa and armchairs; the coffee table would be given for free upon the purchase of the suite. Jays and Campbells undertook extensive newspaper advertising all across the country in regional and national press. The adverts were not subtle. An advertisement carried in *The Times*, of March 1930, screamed out in bold type: 'Jays' Terms Stand Out as the World's Best – Sound Quality! Best Value! Easiest Terms! Place your order with the firm of 75 years standing. Write for bargain catalogue post free.'

Most of Cahn's retail success was due to the hire-purchase system applied to the majority of the goods stocked. At times, 90 per cent of the retail sales were on such terms. Of course, the hire-purchase system was open to abuse and considered by many to be unethical. Hired articles were 'snatched back' when payments were defaulted upon, sometimes when over three-quarters of the payments for the item had been made. This pressure led to some of the worst sections of the system being removed under the Hire Purchase Act of 1938. Hire-purchase trading added considerably to the staff required to conduct a retail business. Contracts had to be drawn up, accurate records of purchases, payments made and payments due over long periods of time had to be kept. This was one of the reasons so many were employed at Cahn's head office. Outside staff was required by most firms to collect the instalments due and if necessary handle the delicate business of recovery of property in the cases of default.

Collecting outstanding debts was a huge part of Cahn's business. It was harsh and unpleasant and a job that Cahn was all too happy to hive off to others. The man who was responsible for the team of bailiffs and all of Cahn's other 'dirty work' was Frank Merchant Wolfe, no relation to Phyllis Cahn. He was a secretive, mysterious little man, officially describing himself as a bookkeeper, but in reality employed as Cahn's private detective. If Sir Julien wanted to find something out, it was Merchant Wolfe who was called for. No one knew exactly what he did, and most realised it was in their best interests not to probe too deeply. In fact, Frank M. Wolfe was one of the witnesses to Sir Julien's final will and testament, signing his name and describing his occupation as 'Manufacturer's Agent'.

Glenis Rhinds recalls how her grandfather, Arthur Partridge, was employed as an apprentice in the Nottingham Furnishing Company in the 1920s, progressing to the position of manager with bailiff duties some ten years later. Thursdays were half-day closing and during these afternoons he was expected to play cricket or at least watch the games. Fridays and Saturdays were designated as the money collecting days. He would visit customers' houses armed with a hardwood walking stick. Typically, customers who were keen to avoid the bailiff would send their children to answer the door, so he developed a canny technique whereby he would push the stick firmly into the bottom of the door as it opened to prevent it from being slammed in his face. Clearly, it was a difficult job. On one occasion he had to revisit an elderly lady who offered an aspidistra plant adorned with pictures of deceased people attached to the leaves as an alarming substitution for the money she owed. Most stores employed their own debt collectors, invariably ex-police sergeants, but ultimately it was down to the store manager to ensure all debts were collected.

Julien Cahn's greatest skill was in the selection and retention of the finest staff. He was forced to delegate; the business was too big and he had too many other interests beyond his furnishing empire. And he delegated extremely well. The most important member of the team was Sir Robert Doncaster, an accountant by trade and a highly astute and successful businessman in his own right. The key man on the 'shop floor' was William Yarnall. Described as a 'Furniture Sales Man' on his marriage certificate of 1909, he worked for Cahn for most of his adult life, progressing rapidly through the ranks until 1939 when he retired in considerable comfort in his mid-fifties, having fulfilled the most senior management position within Cahn's business. Wherever the Nottingham Furnishing Company expanded, Yarnall went. His work relocated him from Nottingham to Blackpool, Scarborough to Llandudno, Bournemouth to Norwich. Utterly loyal to Cahn, he enjoyed a successful career at the business he fondly nicknamed 'the Furno'. Cahn's good living had enormous influence upon Yarnall, who emulated his boss in every possible aspect of life, from the crocodile-skin briefcase and tailored suits, to the open-top cars and burgeoning property portfolio. Felicity Eggins' father, owner of Taylor's Veterinary Service on Waverley Street, died when she was very young and so her uncle, William Yarnall, became her mentor. In fact, her family held the Cahns in such high esteem that she was christened Phyllis, supposedly after Phyllis Cahn (similar to April Jaffé), although she later changed her name to Felicity. She recalls how all of Cahn's key values became Yarnall's key values – education and charity were healthy obsessions.

As the money poured in, Julien began to turn his thoughts to what he could do with all of the cash. His philanthropic donations had had the required effect in the late 1920s when he received his knighthood. It was time to get involved in more charity.

On 9 May 1930, Sir Julien accepted the chairmanship of the National Birthday Trust – a charity he became increasingly passionate about, and an organisation through which he made numerous invaluable contacts and friendships. Not least it fermented his friendship with the future Lady Baldwin.

Two years previously, in 1928, Queen Mary had made a public announcement regarding her concern about the continued high rate of mortality. This speech influenced Lady George Cholmondeley, along with her friend the Marchioness of Londonderry, to set up the Birthday Fund, a charitable foundation that was to address the high incidence of maternal mortality, support maternity hospitals and the development of midwifery. An early recruit was Mrs Lucy Baldwin, who cared passionately about maternal welfare. Soon, the fund was joined by many other titled ladies and a few gentlemen from British high society, including the Marchioness of Londonderry, Lady George Cholmondeley, the Marchioness of Cholmondeley, Viscountess Bearsted, the Countess of Bessborough, Lady Ebbisham and her husband (who was President of the Federation of British Industries and Treasurer of the Conservative Party), Lord and Lady Melchett (the former being the creator of ICI and a prominent politician) and Lord Strathcona and Mount Royal (parliamentary Under-Secretary of State for War until 1939). Julien Cahn's association with the Trust enabled him to build up friendships with plenty of important people. The Stanford Hall visitors' book mentions Lady Melchett, the Dalrymple-

Champneys, Lord Ebbisham, Neville Chamberlain and Lucy Baldwin. There is an uncomfortable photograph showing the Cahns seated next to the Dukes of Gloucester, Norfolk and Kent at Stanford Hall. While they all accepted Sir Julien's hospitality, the expressions on their faces portray an unpleasant distaste for their host.

It was Lucy Baldwin who proposed Julien Cahn as a suitable Chairman of the National Birthday Trust, and when the other ladies met the dark, enigmatic and most charming Sir Julien they were eager to welcome him to their cause. They were impressed by his generosity in funding the Lucy Baldwin Maternity Hospital and they were entranced by his deep voice spouting forth long, complicated words that they pretended to understand but had never heard before.

Julien Cahn accepted the chairmanship in a handwritten letter to Lady Cholmondeley dated 6 May 1930. She replied by saying that '[We] feel certain the Fund will make vast and rapid advances under such able guidance'.

Over the forthcoming years, most of the charity's funds came from a few major benefactors, of whom Sir Julien was the most important.

The name of the fund was a hindrance to its success as most people assumed it was something to do with birthdays. Julien thought it was an 'asinine title' and complained that 'a quick glance at the heading gives me the idea that the Trust is founded to give us presents on our birthday!'

Many years later, he made a request to the Charities Commission to change the name to the 'National Maternity Services Trust', but this was not approved.

The first official meeting he attended was on 28 May 1930. He wrote to Lady Cholmondeley prior to the meeting.

> If by chance, you happen to be at liberty, I should be glad if you would take lunch with me, as it seems to me that there may be many points which it would be advantageous for us to discuss privately, after the meeting.

This was to be the first of many meetings with Lady Cholmondeley, during which time they developed a firm friendship based upon mutual respect.

During the first couple of years he was Chairman, Julien's main role was to oversee fundraising activities. Most of the fundraising was achieved through the organisation of large charity balls with unusual themes. It proved a highly proficient way of raising money. In a letter to Lady Cholmondeley, Julien wrote, 'I had one or two big schemes in mind, but I am one of those who do not like to rush matters.' Indeed, Julien's actions were always carefully considered; he rarely, if ever, lost his temper. On many an occasion, if someone posed him a question they would begin to wonder if he had heard the question or had even fallen asleep. The long pauses as he mulled over his answer invariably caused discomfort to the questioner. His answers were always worth waiting for, well thought out, articulate and pumped full of common sense.

As the months and years progressed and Julien's medical knowledge increased, so he began to pioneer the introduction of medical care that was to change the face of maternity provision forever.

However, back in 1930, Julien's ambitions could have been perceived as less altruistic. On one of the many occasions Sir Julien met Stanley Baldwin, late in 1930, he enquired, none too subtly, 'So my good man! Do you think I may be due a baronetcy?'

'I think you've done quite well already, haven't you?' stated Baldwin, trying to deflect the question.

'Up to a point, up to a point!' mused Cahn.

He considered his schemes of abundant philanthropy. Was Baldwin implying that they were not quite sufficient to warrant a baronetcy, the next accolade that Cahn so desired? A baronetcy would be passed down through the generations, remembering Sir Julien for centuries to come. A baronetcy would elevate him to the next rung of the British society ladder. A baronetcy would be quite a remarkable accolade for a self-made Jewish entrepreneur. But how was he going to achieve it? Perhaps a bit of philanthropy could work again.

Just weeks later another opportunity presented itself. Newstead Abbey was Lord Byron's ancestral home, a fabulous, romantic stately pile located between Mansfield and Hucknall, just down the road from Papplewick Grange. It was owned by Charles Ian Fraser, inherited through his mother's family. Fraser lived in Scotland and had little interest in the property. He had sold off much of the land to Nottingham City Council during the 1920s. In 1930, he converted the habitable part of the abbey into three flats but he did not know what to do with the historic, public rooms. Harry German, Cahn's friend, was appointed to sort out this problem. His solution was to ask Cahn for help.

In the years after the centenary of Lord Byron's death, Sir Julien had publicly expressed a desire to erect a commemoration to the great poet, possibly a statue. However, he was now presented with a much better opportunity. Originally, Cahn offered to spend £2,500 on buying some of the remaining rooms. In July 1930 he agreed a deal with Fraser to buy the property. Over the next few months, Cahn offered to give the rooms to the National Trust. They were indifferent; they did not take an interest in buildings until 1933. He approached Nottingham City Council, which was interested. In return for agreeing to care for Newstead Abbey in perpetuity, the council persuaded Cahn to buy and donate all of the outstanding land as well, including 12 acres and two lakes for a total of £3,900, approximately £187,000 in today's money.

The Newstead Abbey deal shows Cahn at his very shrewdest. He did not sign any documents with Fraser until 12 February 1931, ensuring that he did not have to part with his cash until it was absolutely necessary. At this time, Sir Julien was most popular indeed with the Corporation of Nottingham. Just two days earlier he had presented the Spirit of Welcome statue to the city to adorn the new Council House. The bronze statue of a woman sculpted wearing Nottingham lace by Mr Reid Dick, RA still stands there today and was erroneously believed to be modelled on Phyllis Cahn. Sir Julien also paid for the demonic lion statues that stood outside 'guarding' the Council House. Some time later, Cahn also gave a bronze bust of Lord Beaconsfield to the Nottingham Constitutional Club.

Although Charles Fraser of Newstead Abbey proceeded to donate invaluable relics to Nottingham, including a large quantity of Byron's furniture and portraits and swathes of land, it was Cahn who got most of the publicity, managing to garner maximum prestige for minimum investment. The gift generated reams of newspaper coverage – much more than his previous benefactions achieved, donations that were considerably greater in value. Three-quarters of a century later, Cahn is still credited for saving Newstead Abbey, although it is inconceivable to imagine that Newstead Abbey would have been knocked down if Cahn had not bought it.

During the summer months of 1930, cricket was once again high on the Cahn agenda. By the early 1930s the Sir Julien Cahn XI had attracted some of the best players of the era and was widely recognised to be one of the leading teams in the world. Between 1923 and 1939 the team played 621 matches, of which they won 299 and lost only 19 – just 3 per cent of all the games they played. They played the national teams from India, New Zealand, South Africa,

South America and the West Indies. Surely, such extraordinary success has never again been matched.

While Julien and his cricket team were busy playing a highly successful season, there were changes afoot at home.

When he had undertaken the extensive renovations of Stanford Hall, Cahn had linked all the premises on the estate to the Loughborough water mains. To mitigate the considerable cost of having piped water, Sir Julien struck a deal with Loughborough Council so that the estate was free of water rates for ten years. Originally, water had been stored in various reservoirs, including a large tank sunk into the ground to the side of the house. In the graveyard of Stanford church lies a tombstone to the memory of an Arthur Page of London, who in 1890 fell into this tank and drowned. At this time the property was owned by the Ratcliffe family and nothing is known as to who this young man was or what he was doing at Stanford Hall.

By 1930 this pool of water was a redundant, stagnant reservoir. Sir Julien had no interest in it, and as he did not particularly enjoy swimming, a pool was not part of his renovation plans. However, the summer of 1930 was warm and various members of the estate staff thought otherwise. They asked Jack Chesham, the estate engineer and the member of staff who was least afraid of Sir Julien, to put the idea to him. Cahn gave permission for the project to go ahead, but made it clear that 'the project is entirely the responsibility of the staff and to be done in their own time'.

The estate team consisted of about twenty workers, gardeners, grooms, chauffeurs and others. When the pool was drained, a revolting, foul-smelling black slime, about 2ft in depth, remained, covering the base of the pool. It had to be removed. Desperately trying not to gag, the dedicated staff shovelled it into buckets, which were hauled up from the bottom and emptied among the bushes and shrubs surrounding the pool. But there was so much of this slime that it was in danger of swamping the greenery. Harry Leatherland, the estate carter from Rempstone, produced an old horse called Blossom and the estate sanitary cart, the vehicle that, prior to the modernisation of the hall, had been used for the emptying of the pan lavatories. Leatherland, otherwise known as 'red-faced Harry', stoically disposed of the remaining sludge. Every night from 6 p.m. until dusk, the estate staff undertook this hard, back-breaking work, until eventually the job was completed.

The interior of the pool was then thoroughly scrubbed out and the brickwork painted. It wasn't until it began to be filled that the staff realised that the whole pool was 7ft 6in deep, ideal for proficient swimmers but much too deep for those who couldn't swim. Bert Firth, the estate carpenter, built wooden steps for each end of the pool and the water level was kept low making it safe for swimmers and non-swimmers alike. The following year Firth constructed a wooden platform that was placed on the floor of the pool, raising that section of the pool to 4ft. A low wooden rail separated it from the deep end. This created a safe area for non-swimmers and the rest of the pool could be filled to its proper level making it safe for those who wished to dive into the pool.

This tank was to become home to the most fabulous lido-style swimming pool, measuring 114ft by 60ft, which was to provide phenomenal pleasure and wonderful memories for all who lived at and visited Stanford Hall.

In the early 1930s, the swimming pool had a parapet edge 18in wide, made from blue brick, while a few feet behind, surrounding the whole area, stood a spiked iron fence with two small iron gates at each end for access. Trees, bushes and shrubs planted behind shielded the pool from the drive.

Lady Cahn, a keen swimmer, became increasingly impressed by the hard work of the volunteers and the result of their labour. Encouraging her husband to inspect the swimming pool, she persuaded him to have the pool upgraded professionally. Of course, it was done to the highest of standards. Over the next three years, a series of major improvements took place. The floor was re-graded and sloped so that the shallow end started at 3ft in depth, sloping downwards to 8ft 6in in the deep end. A heating system was installed, along with underwater lighting. The emergency generating station, located just beyond the swimming pool, housed a chlorination and water-purification system. Although the water was cleaned with chlorine and ammonia, there was no smell. The full capacity of the pool, 196,000 gallons of water, was filtered every six hours. Even so, staff were not permitted to swim for twenty-four hours prior to Sir Julien taking a dip. This meant that the water was filtered four times ensuring it was pristinely clean and unlikely to infect him with anything! Fortunately, his dislike of swimming was such that he very rarely used the pool.

The whole pool area was enclosed in rock walls that contained petrified moss and trees taken from the Via Gellia Valley in Derbyshire.

Beautiful changing cubicles were constructed to look like grottos, and seats faced the extraordinarily coloured sea-blue water. One of the entrances was built into the rock walls and was invisible but for a length of chain. It contained a counter-balanced door of stone weighing 14cwt, apparently inspired by the film *Ali Baba* and built by Jack Chesham. When the chain was pulled, it caused the door to swing slowly open from what was apparently a blank wall. The total bill for creating this wondrous swimming pool was in the region of £60,000.

Glorious evenings were spent frolicking in and around the swimming pool. This enchanting place was beautifully lit and music was piped around the pool. Not surprisingly, the swimming pool became home to infamous parties and clandestine romance. It is said that on occasion the water in the swimming pool was coloured to match the theme of a party or a lady's dress.

The year 1931 was packed to the brim with committee meetings for fundraising events and society balls, predominantly to raise money for the National Birthday Fund. Julien was a master of organisation, every moment of his time accounted for.

In a letter to Miss Manningham-Butler, Secretary of the National Birthday Trust Fund, he wrote, 'May I ask you to be good enough to remember that Mondays and Wednesdays are my hunting days, but I am at liberty any other days – Thursdays for preference.' Indeed, he was in London most Thursdays throughout the 1930s, usually travelling by train from Leicester.

Many wealthy people who had their main residence in the countryside during the 1920s and 1930s also maintained a London house. This arrangement did not appeal to Sir Julien. Instead, he maintained suites at London clubs and hotels. Initially, he had permanent rooms at the Carlton Club and then later on he maintained a suite at Claridge's, known as 'the first hotel of London'. At £3 10s a day, the cost of an apartment at Claridge's was about the same as running a London home.

In the Claridge's book *Celebration of a Century*, a journalist's description of the hotel from an article printed in the late 1920s is quoted. The interior of the hotel is described as 'to be such as one might find in a private home and to have the refinement that one would expect in such a place and which one never seems to meet in public'.

A typical apartment comprised a living room, bedroom, dressing room and bathroom. It incorporated pilasters, cornice and walls grained in a light walnut, had rounded curves and contrasting veneers, Sienna and black marble fireplace surrounds and mirrors made from white slate and peach-coloured glass. The electric lights were typical art deco created from circular dishes of opaque glass. Even the wastepaper baskets, ashtrays and ink stands were designed to match the decorative schemes.

On a few occasions, Albert and Richard stayed in their father's first-floor suite at Claridge's to break up the long journey from Nottingham to their school in Eastbourne. Albert recalls the amazement of watching television in the living room. An hour's worth of black-and-white programming could only be seen in London.

After numerous planning meetings, the first event of the year, the Strauss Ball, took place at the Savoy Hotel in London on 6 January 1931. It was a fabulous occasion, with the ladies' gowns and hairstyles harking back to the days of Old Vienna, and the lilting music sweeping the guests back to an era, not so long past, but largely forgotten.

Johann Strauss III, the nephew of the composer of the great waltzes, conducted the orchestra. It was Sir Julien who had pulled off this coup, by contacting the famous musician in Vienna and persuading him to conduct his orchestra at the ball. Strauss stayed the night with the Cahns at Stanford Hall – the first of many of the world's leading musicians to enjoy Julien and Phyllis' hospitality. Music was a passion for Julien. Although he was particularly keen on opera, he adored the tunes of Strauss, a genre of music that flowed through his veins.

As *The Times* newspaper reported the next day, 'although the room at the Savoy remained obstinately modern, and although many of the dresses were the only compliment that 1931 pays to a former generation, there was, directly the orchestra under the inspiration of Herr Strauss struck up the opening bars of "The Blue Danube", the sensation that time had ceased'. The reporter went on to say that, 'Herr Strauss must have been proud of his name, as he saw for one night, a London ballroom rescued from the paradoxes of Harlem and dedicated to the sense and sensibility of melody.'

It was at the society balls of the 1930s that the divergence between the rich and the poor became most apparent. The Depression of the early 1930s was hitting hard. A typical family lived in two rooms at a rent of 8s 7d per week. The average income per head, exclusive of rent and rates, ranged from 4s 9d for the unemployed to 10s 6d for the employed. This weekly sum had to cover not only food but clothes, heating and lighting. However, the Depression did not threaten the living standards of the very rich. Tickets for the Strauss Ball were 3 guineas to include a sit-down supper, champagne and buffet. The committee were delighted with the funds raised from the Strauss Ball and immediately set about planning their next event, the Lace Ball.

The Lace Ball was another fine feat of organisation. Lady Violet Astor, an outspoken lady whose MP husband owned *The Times*, was the Chairman of the ball that was to be held at the Dorchester Hotel for its grand opening on 21 April 1931. Once again, the theme was devised by Julien, inspired by the Lincolnshire Stuff Ball that he had attended a year earlier. By choosing the theme of lace, it had the dual purpose of raising money for the National Birthday Trust Fund as well as promoting the Nottinghamshire lace industry. Guests were required to wear some piece of historic or modern lace. Sir Julien asked Mr Jefferson Arthur to design a pageant of lace to carry out the theme of the ball. This was 'The Old Garden of Dorchester House' and those taking part had to represent the wall and flowers that grew in the original garden.

All of the bigwigs from Nottingham were invited to the ball, including the Lord Mayor, the Sheriff and other senior dignitaries who were entertained to dinner prior to the ball by Sir Julien and Lady Cahn. The Cahns were then entertained to a supper party at the ball, hosted by Lady Violet Astor, with guests including Lord and Lady Ebbisham, Sir Albert Levy (founder of British American Tobacco), Lord Henry Bentinck and many other famous people from high society. The Duchess of York also attended.

The summer of 1931 was a whirl of social activities. Julien was Honorary Treasurer for the Deptford Fund Ball in aid of the Deptford and Greenwich Babies Hospital, a position that he was to hold for numerous fundraising events over the coming years. Julien enjoyed the company of women and relished the fact that he was one of the few men involved in the charity. They put him on a pedestal, a position he was mostly pleased to assume, but on occasion he despaired at their apparent lack of logic and un-commerciality.

'I am content to leave the decision making to the women,' he declared, after one particularly challenging committee meeting. In a letter to the secretary of the fund, he wrote, 'I do not pretend to understand the psychology of women.'

The Deptford Fund Ball was held on 12 June at the Dorchester Hotel with the guests of honour being Princess Alice, Countess of Athlone and the Earl of Athlone. In addition to the giving of his time as Treasurer, Julien paid for the cost of the programmes that were printed in the colours of the 7th Queen's Own Hussars, the Earl of Athlone's regiment. Oiled by strategically placed cash, the Cahns had well and truly arrived in society. They were included in the party of Princess Alice, whose guests included the Duchess of Somerset, the Earl of Clanwilliam, the Portuguese Ambassador and various other people of great importance.

Less than two weeks later, Julien and Phyllis were back at the Dorchester Hotel for yet another ball – the Famous Beauties Ball in aid of the Papworth Village Settlement for the Tuberculous. The highlight of the evening was a parade of famous beauties throughout the ages, attractive young girls dressed up as the most beautiful women from all time.

On 14 July the Cahns attended a matinee performance in aid of the Marie Curie Hospital for Cancer, at the Cambridge Theatre. The programme was arranged by Miss Olga Lynn, the famous fashion model, and Cecil Beaton, the renowned photographer. There was an extraordinary line-up of famous entertainers, including the cellist Madame Suggia, who was fêted at a time when female cellists were almost unheard of, Harriet Cohen, a pianist particularly known for her fine playing of Bach, Naunton Wayne, a famous actor, the actors Patrick Waddington and Francine Larrimore, as well as members of the Rambert Ballet and many more. A year later, in November 1932, Julien gave £1,000 to Lady Plunkett to name a bed in the Olive Dent Ward of the Marie Curie Hospital for Cancer in memory of his mother, Matilda Cahn, who had died of the disease ten years previously.

On 16 July 1931, Sir Julien was able to bask in the glory of his grandest philanthropic gesture to date. The handover ceremony for Newstead Abbey was attended by the Prime Minister of Greece, M. Venizelos, in honour of Lord Byron who had died at Missolonghi in 1824 fighting for Greek freedom. Having stayed the night at Stanford Hall along with two other Greek ministers of state, Sir Julien asked M. Venizelos to present the deed of the abbey to the Lord Mayor, Alderman A. Pollard. The Greek Prime Minister was met in Hucknall market place by the 750 pupils from the Hucknall National School. A group of boys held aloft banners in the Greek colours of blue and white. Two children presented him with a scroll designed to send greetings to the children of Greece. Later, he laid a wreath on Byron's tomb in Hucknall parish church, formed from scarlet and yellow flowers surrounded by a border of laurel leaves that he claimed he had personally gathered from the banks of the River Ilissus.

Hundreds of guests were entertained in temporary pavilions and marquees around Newstead Abbey, while the Greek dignitaries toured the abbey itself. During the handover ceremony, Sir Julien gave a speech and explained that various suggestions had been put to him for a monument to Byron, none of which met with his approval. And then he hit on the idea of buying the abbey for the city. Of course, it did not happen in this manner, but Cahn was able to slant the story to put himself in the very best light! As part of the ceremony, M. Venizelos bestowed a Greek honour on Sir Julien Cahn – the Greek Night Commander of the Order of the Phoenix. In return, M. Venizelos received a commemorative casket made from a Byron oak that contained a scroll of welcome to the city. Sir Julien presented twelve gold medals especially made for the occasion to guests, including Mr Fraser – the donor of the Byron relics – and the Lord Mayor. It seems a bizarre omission that none of Byron's poetry or great works were recited during the ceremony.

Later, the party was greeted in Nottingham by the City Police Band playing in the market square. More than 3,000 people watched the Greek Prime Minister's arrival for a luncheon in the ballroom of the Council House. Sir Julien Cahn was hailed a hero.

Due in part to the Cahns incessant socialising, there were no grand tours for the cricket team in 1931. The furthest they ventured was to Scotland for a couple of weeks in the latter part of July. The most important match of the year was in September when the Cahn XI played against New Zealand at Loughborough Road, and the game was drawn. That year R.W.V. Robins scored four centuries.

In his book of memoirs, Tommy Reddick recalled a memorable incident involving Robins and Sir Julien. During a game against the West Indians that included George Headley, the West Indian known as the Black Bradman and a great leg-side player and fabulous hooker of the ball, Robins suggested a most unorthodox strategy to his captain.

'Bowl yourself, Sir Julien', he said. 'Play on his strength and concentrate on the leg stump. Place eight men on the leg side and stick Tom Reddick close in at short leg.'

Reddick remembered how the rest of the team tried to laugh it off as an example of Robins' sick humour. To their dismay, Sir Julien took the suggestion seriously. Reddick remembered 'standing in terror 4 yards behind Headley awaiting his personal demise'. He need not have worried, with extraordinary reflexes he 'leaped for the ball, protecting his face with one hand and grabbing the ball with the other'.

For the next two seasons Reddick was positioned there whenever Cahn bowled. As a result, Reddick never quite forgave Robins.

G.F. Summers, from Richmond, was Cahn's most successful batsman (a prodigious hitter who scored over 13,000 runs for Cahn) followed by Newman and Heane. H.S.R. Critchley-Salmonson was top of the bowling. In total they played 37 matches, winning 18, losing 3 and drawing 16. Interestingly, the West Bridgford ground was chosen to host a women's match – quite a novelty, and perhaps prompted by Sir Julien's friendship with Lady Baldwin who was, unlike Lady Cahn, an avid fan of cricket, and in the 1890s belonged to the only women's cricket team in Britain.

Earlier in the year, Cahn had become President of Nottinghamshire County Cricket Club. Presidency was for just a year at a time, but he was re-elected again in 1935 and 1938. In 1935, he was elected President of the club on the nomination of His Grace the Duke of Portland. The Duke commented that Sir Julien 'had been assiduous in performing the duties of the office and had carried on assisting the club in a most generous manner'. That year, after Nottinghamshire lost hundreds of members due to insufficient support for the county's players involved with bodyline, Cahn paid the subscriptions of 800 new members.

When he was not President, he was still an important member of the committee. During that first year of his presidency he gave the club what was minuted as 'a handsome bookcase' to house a set of cricket books given by Mr Shelton, as well as 100 guineas. During the years 1932, 1933 and 1934, Cahn financed the Nottinghamshire County Cricket Club Year Book – a tome that was given to all members, including juniors.

Julien had even managed to fit in engagements on behalf of the Notts Club in between his social activities, charitable commitments, cricketing fixtures and business. On 21 June 1931, a memorial was erected to the late W.W. Whysall in Mansfield cemetery and was publicly unveiled by Mr A.W. Carr. An extraordinary 15,000 people attended the ceremony that was officially represented by the Lord Mayor and Lady Mayoress of Nottingham, the Mayor of Mansfield and the President of the Nottingham Club, Sir Julien Cahn. This event was heavily covered in the *Nottingham Guardian*, along with several photographs showing Sir Julien seated next to the dignitaries within a sea of bowler hats and trench coats.

The whirlwind of social events continued through the autumn. On 31 October Julien received the Duchess of York at His Majesty's Theatre for a matinee performance of *The Passing of the Third Floor Back* in aid of the Prince of Wales' Builder Fund of Toc H.

The third charity ball for the National Birthday Trust Fund – the British Porcelain Ball – took place on 24 November 1931 upon the re-opening of the new ballroom at Claridge's Hotel. The timing of the occasion was typical for these society events, and very late by modern standards. Guests were invited for 10 p.m. Supper was served at 11.30 p.m. followed by a grand 'Porcelain Buffet' at 12.30 a.m. Carriages were at 3 a.m. Sir Julien had had much involvement in the preparation for this ball. For instance, on 24 September he had presided at a lunch at Claridge's in connection with the ball. Julien managed to persuade many of the leading British porcelain manufacturers, such as Coalport, Crown Derby, Mintons and Wedgwood, to present souvenirs in china to each guest. The firms also lent porcelain to decorate the tables. Lucy Baldwin was Chairman and the Cahns were included in her party at a table decorated by Doulton. However, *The Times* reported that the Cahns also brought their own party, seated at a table decorated with Spode Hunting. Quite how they managed to flit between the two parties is not known!

5

Bodyline & Baronetcy

With their manically busy lives and constant travel, it is easy to forget that the Cahns had three young children. In 1930, Miss Francis Jessica Waite, known by all the Cahns as 'Waity', descended upon Stanford Hall. She became the single most important influence in the lives of Pat, Albert and Richard. Employed as their nanny, she in fact took on the role of pseudo-mother, spending more time and having a greater influence on the children than Lady Cahn. This was very typical of the times and the lifestyle led by the family and was not an indictment on Phyllis Cahn's maternal abilities.

Prior to 1930, the children had had a series of governesses. Waity was horrified by little Richard's legs. He had been dangled by the previous nanny to such a degree that his legs were in danger of becoming bowed. Waity quickly took charge and got Richard strapped to a pair of splints, saving him from becoming bow-legged.

A farmer's daughter from the village of Litchborough near Northampton, Waity had previously worked for another family and arrived at the Cahns in her early twenties with excellent references. Richard adored the occasional trips he took with Waity to stay on the farm with her parents. He was treated like a normal little boy, living on a farm without a servant in sight. Whether it was the lack of grandeur or the fact that it was here that he had his first taste of whisky, stays at the Waites' farm were the highlights of Richard's year.

Waity's rooms at Stanford were opposite the nursery on the other side of the landing. In the process of refurbishing Stanford Hall, a nursery, complete with a sprung floor, was installed on the top floor. There were three substantial cupboards, one for each child, packed full of toys. For ten years, the day nursery was the room in which the children spent most of their time.

Years later, when the children were in their teens, the room was refitted as a library and expensively panelled in wood. On the inside of the door a glass frame was fitted and behind it bookends were glued to the panel. When closed the door swung into place and the imitation bookcase became indistinguishable from the adjacent bookcases. A small wooden plunger served as a door handle. But this was almost imperceptible to the uninitiated, who would find themselves enclosed in a room without a door.

Waity was utterly dedicated to and responsible for the children. She bought their clothes with some occasional input from Lady Cahn. She told Mrs Bentley or Edna what food to prepare for the children. She played with them and taught them to read. Their favourite game was Monopoly; Albert always won and Waity always lost. When they went abroad, Waity travelled with the family. There is a photograph of her alongside the Cahns sitting on a camel in front of pyramids in Egypt. The boys do not have any recollection of her having time off, but one assumes she must have had the occasional respite from her charges. Waity was not responsible for teaching the children, so until the age of 8 the boys went to Miss Hancock's School.

Many of the staff and visiting children were scared of Waity. She was straight talking and didn't stand for any nonsense. Gabriel Jaffé, a contemporary of Albert's and the son of good friends of the Cahns, recalls Waity as being 'strict and grim'. While she may have seemed that way to visiting children, she gave much love and security to the Cahn children and was particularly adored by Albert and Richard. Her relationship with Pat was difficult, but she entered the household when Pat was nine. Pat was of the opinion that Waity disliked her and adored the boys. There was undoubtedly an element of truth to this belief.

The children's rooms were also located on the top floor, adjacent to the nursery and Waity's suite. Pat had her own bedroom and en-suite bathroom. Albert and Richard shared a rather modest bedroom with cane furniture, green curtains and purple eiderdowns. Outside their top window was a Davy automatic fire escape with rope. This wasn't the only anti-fire appliance at Stanford Hall. In fact, there was a complete miniature fire engine housed in the basement fully fitted with a tank and pipes, fortunately never to be used. When they were in their teens, the boys moved downstairs into a large bedroom on the first floor and Pat moved into the elegant Spanish Bedroom.

Back in the 1930s, Waity was perfect teasing fodder for Sir Julien. One rare afternoon, Sir Julien had been playing games with the children in the day nursery. As was commonplace when playing with his children, he had been blatantly cheating. When Waity came in, Albert told her with glee, 'Daddy's been naughty!'

Sensing an opportunity to embarrass Waity, Sir Julien responded with a straight face and typical sardonic wit. 'Don't let me down Albert! You should stick up for your father because he stuck up for you!' Sir Julien thoroughly enjoyed shocking Waity with rude jokes.

The Cahns enjoyed a quieter year in 1932, a year where cricket played a more important part, but still a year when Julien achieved considerable press coverage, due largely to yet another philanthropic donation.

It was an excellent cricketing year for Cahn's side, which was simply too strong for most opponents. The only defeat of the season was inflicted by the visiting South American team. Much to Julien's delight, India suffered a defeat against his team upon their visit to Loughborough Road. Summers, Maxwell, Newman, Seabrook and Morkel all played exceptionally well. Morkel, a South African test player, joined Sir Julien in 1932. A gentle giant at 6ft 3in, he already had a reputation as a first-class all rounder. Some years later, Sir Julien helped him establish his own motor business, Morkel & Carnell, on Derby Road in Nottingham. Audrey Everest, his stepdaughter, tells of how Sir Julien gave Morkel the premises to build his showroom and workshop. The showroom on the second floor was converted into workshops and a lift was installed so cars could be driven into it and taken upstairs. Cahn subsequently put most of his motoring business Morkel's way, purchasing his commercial vans from Morkel & Carnell and having most of his vehicles serviced there.

C.R. Maxwell, also new to the team, was straight out of school. He had performed brilliantly at Brighton College and was one of the best batsmen wicket-keepers of his day.

The team had one overseas match in 1932, in Denmark. Cricket was in its infancy there and the so-called 'test match' in Copenhagen was played on a concrete pitch surrounded by grass at least 4in high, with umpires smoking as they officiated.

The team enjoyed Copenhagen, a buzzing city with plenty of entertainment for the young visitors. Tommy Reddick recalls visiting a late-night funfair, where for a few coins visitors could throw an armful of wooden balls at as many china cups and saucers as they could manage. Unfortunately for the proprietor, he had not reckoned on throwers of the calibre of Robins, Morkel and Crisp. With his china rapidly shattering all around him, the proprietor yelled at the men to clear off.

The highlight of the tour occurred during the unofficial test against All Denmark in Copenhagen. For the first time, and probably the only time, a twelfth man bowled in an international game. Before the match Sir Julien had said it would be a great thrill for his brother-in-law George Wolfe, who was accompanying the side, to play in a test match. He asked Reddick if he would mind standing down and becoming the twelfth man. Unable to refuse, he watched Wolfe walk on to the field in his place.

By the third wicket, a couple of Danes were coping very successfully with Cahn's medium and fast bowlers. Fortunately, Robbie Robins' first six balls completely mystified the opposing team, but then, to everyone's dismay, Robins, probably with an unexpected bout of stomach problems, ran off with no explanation to the pavilion. Although Robins had a fine sense of humour and was the only member of the team who would ever dare to 'pull Sir Julien's leg', this was no joke. No one in the party could bowl leg-spinners except for Reddick, who was seated in the pavilion. Soon enough, George Wolfe appeared at Reddick's side, informing him that he was to report to Sir Julien without delay, and for the time being take over his duties. Sir Julien ordered Reddick to bowl at the top end.

'I can't sir', he replied. 'I'm the twelfth man.'

'Don't worry about that,' Sir Julien replied, 'I very much doubt whether they know the rules anyway!'

Unable to argue with his boss, Reddick followed his orders and bowled. With his sixth delivery he hit the wickets with a googly.

'Alright Tommy,' announced Sir Julien, 'you can buzz off now and send George back again.'

'What about the wicket I have just taken?' Reddick asked.

'Yes, that's tricky,' Cahn answered, 'I'll tell you what to do. Ask the scorers if they would mind putting it down to me.'

No one can recall what was actually entered in the scorebook, but Reddick never forgot the game.

In the summer of 1932 an eloquent letter posted in *The Times* prompted Sir Julien to make his next flamboyant gesture of philanthropy.

Since the 1920s, Professor R.G. Stapledon, based in Wales, had been interested in hill land improvement, believing that the uplands of Britain could provide a major contribution to the nation's food supplies. Working with Abel E. Jones, Professor of Agriculture, he had shown the amazing effects of phosphatic fertilisers on plants grown on upland pastures. In the 1930s, there were new strains of grasses and clovers, and rape was becoming recognised as a valuable crop. Stapledon wanted to show how uplands could be improved on a large scale. Until then, only small studies had been undertaken due to a lack of suitable land and machinery. In 1931, the Plant Breeding Station bought a Caterpillar tractor and on the extensive lands of Captain Bennett-Evans of Llangurig, a farsighted eccentric, Stapledon extended the scope of his studies. The next step was to set up a massive demonstration of all the methods of hill land improvement that the work on Bennett-Evans' land had suggested was possible. However, Stapledon calculated that in order to buy the large area of hill land needed and the necessary machinery, the total capital requirement would be about £20,000 (approximately one million pounds in today's money). When he approached the Treasury for financial backing, he was told that £20,000 was a sum far in excess of what the Government was prepared to pay. Undeterred, Stapledon, together with the Principal of the University College Wales, Stuart Jones, wrote a long letter that appeared in *The Times*, of 11 July 1932.

> Sir – knowing your keen interest in British agriculture, we ask the hospitality of your columns in order to make known what we consider to be an urgent need . . . It is recognised that in our grasslands, we have a very largely undeveloped asset of immense potential importance. It is perhaps not so generally recognised that modern methods of improving grassland can be profitably applied to areas that are today regarded as almost derelict.

They went on to explain how, with the correct strain of grasses and clovers and support by adequate treatment, numerous areas of grassland of negligible value could be radically improved. 'We appeal to all who have the future of British agriculture at heart for financial assistance in order to enable the Plant Breeding Station to conduct the necessary experiments on a larger scale . . . We estimate the sum required to meet these needs at about £20,000.'

The same edition of *The Times* carried an article about Professor Stapledon's work, explaining why the world-renowned agricultural scientist was seeking support for his research.

The very same day, Sir Julien penned a letter to Principal Jones offering an annual sum of £3,000 for seven years, declaring that 'the object for which you are appealing is of an importance which it is scarcely possible to exaggerate'.

Julien was determined that the money be used for the promotion of Stapledon's scheme and not, as some members of the Council had hoped, for the 'general purposes' of the Station. Cardiganshire was full of derelict land and it didn't take long for Stapledon to find a suitable patch. Early in 1933, the Station acquired 2,200 acres of the Hafod Estate near Devil's Bridge, with grazings extending to 1,350ft above sea level and a further 2,700 acres of the Nant Rhys sheepwalk at a height of 1,850ft. Most locals regarded this land as almost worthless due to its elevation and climate. The land was on an estate that had a history of agricultural pioneering, surrounded by romantic and rugged scenery.

The plan was to grass out at least 50 acres of the hill immediately and more each succeeding year so that large areas could be used to conduct experiments. The area was named the Cahn Hill Improvement Scheme and it was to be managed by a representative committee including Lord De La Warr as Chairman and other leading lords and knights, including, of course, Sir Julien Cahn.

Stapledon wanted to show that these unproductive hills could be totally transformed. In an ideal world he wanted to rehabilitate the whole environment, including transport systems, agriculture, forestry and education, but Cahn's gift was specific. He was obliged to limit his activities to large-scale reclamation that would allow by way of spin-off an opportunity for general investigations into the relationship between fertility and vegetation. His ambition was to show that hill land could sustain an acceptable livestock and human population and thus to shame farmers and politicians into admitting the shocking conditions of much of the pasture acreage of lowland and highland Britain. Should the improved hills be suitable for livestock then lowland could be converted to arable production.

The work began on Cahn Hill in March 1933 and progress was rapid. However, it wasn't until 15 May 1933, ten months later, that *The Times* announced that Sir Julien Cahn had responded to the appeal of the Welsh Plant Breeding Station. Perhaps the Cahn publicity machine was rather slower than usual to swing into action. The funds not only enabled Stapledon to acquire the land but also to employ 'a man fully competent in the management and breeding of stock'.

This person was Mr Moses Griffith, previously the Agricultural Organiser for Merionethshire and a well-known breeder of Welsh Black cattle. He became Lands Director.

The Times, of 1 October 1934, carried a descriptive article written by their agricultural correspondent. He stated:

> From the road between Aberystwyth and Devil's Bridge an observant motorist may notice one hilltop standing out strangely green and different from the sombre herbage of West Wales. It is a mark of the work that Professor Stapledon is carrying out under the Cahn hill improvement scheme. Two years ago Sir Julien Cahn and other benefactors undertook to finance for seven years a programme of experimental work to show how far hill grazings could be improved by cultivation and manuring, and by making use of the better strains of herbage plants being bred at Aberystwyth.

The article went on to say:

> The working plan is to produce the maximum amount of winter fodder in the form of grass, rape, turnips, hay, corn and preserved grass; to convert selected portions of the lowland hills into additional farm land; to regrass and improve as much as possible of the rest of the low-land hills and to improve the grazing on selection portions of the mountain sheep walk.

The success of this had already been proved to neighbouring farmers. Lambs were fattened on hardy green turnips. Normally, lambs were sent down to the lowlands for wintering, an expensive process. Stapledon's lambs thrived in the highlands and, as *The Times* correspondent wrote, 'many more fat lambs will be going from the Welsh hills to Manchester'. The scheme was deemed a great success.

During 1932, Julien started to take an active interest in medical developments in matters relating to childbirth. He decided that one of the key objectives of the National Birthday Trust Fund was to promote the use of analgesia for home births. The first phase was the development of a crushable chloroform capsule intended for use during the second stage of labour by a midwife acting alone. The plan was that these were to be presented free of charge to all mothers by the National Birthday Trust Fund accompanied by a card that said 'Motheraid' and the message: 'These are presented free to all mothers by the National Birthday Trust Fund, founded by Mrs Stanley Baldwin, Lady George Cholmondeley and Lady Williams. Chairman: Sir Julien Cahn.'

In 1932, these capsules were used on an experimental basis in various hospitals. Julien wrote on behalf of the Trust to a number of hospitals and local authorities offering to supply them with capsules for three months if they would take part in a large study of their use. He explained that, 'the effect of the small quantity of chloroform contained in the capsules is purely analgesia and does not produce anaesthesia'. Cahn met all expenses relating to this project until October 1933 and this included the employment of a qualified anaesthetist to oversee the trials. For the next ten years, the spearheading of studies such as these was an integral part of Cahn's life.

In the early 1930s, Julien revived his childhood interest in magic. He joined the Magician's Club of London, becoming a full member in 1932 and an honorary Vice-president of the Club in 1933, as well as the chair of the Club's Entertainment Committee.

The Magician's Club had been set up by Will Goldston, who had been the manager of the leading London store for magic – Gamage's Conjuring Department. Goldston had been elected to membership of the Magic Circle in 1905, however, after several months, he stopped receiving any communication from the Circle. It appears that someone forged a letter of resignation purportedly from him. As a result of this fall-out, Goldston called together a secret meeting of some great magicians and in 1911 set up another society called the Magician's Club. Harry Houdini was elected President in 1914 and Goldston Vice-president. At this time, Goldston set up his own business as a magic dealer in premises just off Leicester Square. Goldston took over as President on Houdini's tragic death in 1926, followed three years later by Louis Gautier. Many of the leading magicians of the day joined the Club, although they decided it was to be a club for amateurs too. Although the Magician's Club had been set up as a rival to the Magic Circle, by the 1920s the two organisations co-existed amicably.

When Sir Julien joined the Magician's Club he was in the prestigious company of the leading magicians of the day, including David Devant, Horace Goldin (a Polish-born, world-leading magician credited with inventing the 'sawing a woman in two' illusion, sawing her in half with a buzz saw), Harry Price (a leader in the field of parapsychology), and Servais Le Roy (a Belgian-born magician and genius of illusions).

Professor Edwin A. Dawes, in his *A Rich Cabinet of Magical Curiosities*, describes Cahn as someone 'whose magical abilities apparently approached neither his enthusiasm nor the laudatory appraisal in Goldston's Who's Who in Magic'. Cahn was clearly out of his league. Although it is not documented as such, perhaps Cahn bestowed some of his philanthropy upon Goldston and his Club.

The Club met every Wednesday evening at its headquarters in the National Hotel in Upper Bedford Place, Russell Square, followed by the Palace Hotel on Bloomsbury Street. The 1933 annual dinner was held on Cahn's birthday on Sunday 22 October at the Park Lane Hotel, Piccadilly. Ladies' nights were held bimonthly at the Palace Hotel.

As Edwin Dawes explained, Will Goldston cultivated many personalities via the Magician's Club and was eager to cohort with the rich and famous. These included all the leading magicians of the day, Sir Julien and many other famous personalities such as the singer Sophie Tucker, Sax Rohmer (a prolific writer of mysteries for magazines, books and the stage with an interest in the occult and magic), Viscount Loftus, Hannen Swaffer (famous journalist and spiritualist), Sir E. Denison Ross (Director of the School of Oriental Studies) and the poet Wilhelmina Stitch. How much Cahn had to do with Goldston is unknown, however, it is likely that there was mutual respect. Both were Jewish, Goldston born in Liverpool, Cahn in Cardiff, both were shrewd and extraordinarily able in their chosen fields.

Despite their disparate beliefs in the occult, Will Goldston was greatly admired by Sir Julien and it was thanks to Goldston that, just a few years later, Sir Julien was able to gain rapid recognition in the field of magic.

During the latter months of 1932, Julien was Treasurer for a number of charity balls; the months of November and December were particularly busy. Perhaps the most gratifying event took place on 9 November when, as Treasurer for a special matinee performance of *Bulldog Drummond* held at the Adelphi Theatre in aid of the Actors' Pension Fund, Sir Julien was presented to the King and Queen. Later that month, the Cahns attended a gala performance of the film *The Return of Raffles* in the presence of the Prince of Wales. The Radiant Ball, held at the Dorchester on 29 November, gave particular enjoyment to Julien and was to provide him with inspiration for his own stage performances. The dances were floodlit in different colours – a novel experience for all the guests.

December was hectic indeed. There was a grand concert at the Royal Albert Hall on 8 December. This was of great interest as the New London Philharmonic Orchestra was conducted by Sir Thomas Beecham with an appearance by Cahn's good friend, Malcolm Sargent. On 14 December, Julien attended a dinner at the Dorchester Hotel in support of the Marie Curie Hospital. After Richard's fifth birthday party on 15 December, Phyllis was driven down to London to accompany her husband to the Stage Ball at the Grosvenor House Hotel. The following night the Cahns attended the Silver Rose Ball at the Carlton Hotel in aid of the National Society of Day Nurseries, in the presence of Princess Marie Louise. Just five days later they attended a Christmas matinee performance at His Majesty's Theatre in aid of the Mount Vernon Cancer hospital in the presence of the King and Queen.

To their relief, the start of 1933 was quieter for the Cahns. It was at about this time that Julien commissioned well-known artists of the day to paint pictures of himself and his family. It was quite typical in the 1930s for wealthy socialites to commission leading artists to paint portraits of them, and the Cahns were no exception. Lionel Edwards painted Sir Julien and Lady Cahn when they were out with the Burton Hunt and F.A. Stewart painted them with various other hunts. Both were the foremost equine artists of the 1930s, painting their subjects on location, out in the fields, following the hunts. Sir Oswald Birley, whose portrait of King George V is displayed in the National Portrait Gallery, was commissioned to paint Sir Julien's portrait as he posed in his hunting pink. Frank Salisbury, whose drawing of the Duke of Kent also hangs in the National Portrait Gallery, painted Lady Cahn wearing a beautiful dark-red velvet evening gown.

In between his hunting engagements, Julien spent many weeks at work. There was the occasional social foray and a considerable amount of time spent on the National Birthday Trust activities. At the beginning of the year, he gave money for an extension to the Lucy Baldwin Maternity Hospital that he had funded three years previously. Later that year, Sir Julien was appointed a member of the Council of the Queen's Institute of District Nursing by the Queen, along with Lady Violet Astor, Lady (Rhys) Williams and Dr John Speares. The Trust established a national midwifery headquarters at 57 Lower

Belgrave Street, close to the smart London residences of several of the committee members. The lease, equipment and all furnishings were paid for by Cahn. This became the home of the Midwives' Institute, the Queen's Institute for District Nurses and the National Birthday Trust Fund. Later in the year, the headquarters were officially opened by the Parliamentary Secretary to the Minister of Health, who had hoped to attend himself. Flowers were presented to Lady Cahn.

At the end of March, Julien presented his good friend and doctor Mr Henry Jaffé to the King at a levee held at St James's Palace. In May, the Cahns attended the Famous Film Memories Ball at the Mayfair Hotel in aid of the Princess Beatrice Hospital. A month later they attended an Aelus concert held by candlelight at the Duke of Marlborough's residence, with chamber music conducted by Sir Thomas Beecham.

In itself there is nothing surprising about the numerous social events that the Cahns attended; the number was modest by the standards of the leading socialites. However, the Cahns had only recently landed in society – Julien was *nouveau riche*, wealth attained by commerce and considered just about acceptable due to his hunting and charitable works. But perhaps the biggest hurdle that the Cahns had to overcome was their religion – Judaism – or, as considered by some, their racial heritage.

Today it is easy to forget how rife anti-Semitism was in early twentieth-century Britain, particularly inherent among the upper classes, those very people with whom Sir Julien wished to associate himself. Formal organisations such as the Nordic League were set up to promote anti-Semitism in the 1930s. But there was nothing new about anti-Semitic sentiments, particularly against wealthy Jews and Jews in the British establishment.

During the economic crisis of 1929–31, the radical right made the 'international Jew' scapegoat for the challenging times being experienced by all. International Jewish speculators were blamed for the financial depression that forced Britain to abandon the gold standard. Whenever British national pride was at stake and interests violated, it was attributed to 'the Jew'. Mass unemployment and poverty encouraged people to focus on a nostalgic recollection of a more stable past. Jews, who had contributed so much to the rapid developments in all areas of society, particularly the sciences, arts and mass culture, were frequently blamed for the changes. Changes for the good were dismissed and changes for the worse were focused upon. The following letter, published in September 1930 in the *Daily*

Express and on 26 September 1930 in the *Jewish Chronicle*, epitomises this thought:

> How anyone can prize the downward trend of our national life by the infiltration of a semi-negroid, parasitic scum is beyond comprehension unless you regard the debasement of the country as a result to be desired. All thinking people are aware that the present world depression is a direct result of the Jewish intrigue, as they are also aware that the wave of moral laxity, the debasement of the decencies of life, and the general undermining of the body politic originate from, and are directly attributable to, the same source.

The *Jewish Chronicle* quoted how one paper, in October 1932, stated that, 'At least nine-tenths of the inhabitants of the British Isles think the worse of a man if they are told he is a Jew'.

Discrimination was widely practised. The *Daily Telegraph* carried a job advertisement for a typist stating, 'No Jewesses'. The *British Medical Journal* said, 'No Jews or men of colour'. Jewish teachers found it most difficult to get teaching posts at the better schools. The *Drapers Record* carried an advertisement for the sale of a millinery business with the addendum, 'No Jews entertained'. The Cardiff Credit Traders Association adopted a resolution that the membership of 'folk of alien origin, such as Jews, should not be encouraged'. Reproaches against individual malpractices were levelled at the Jewish community and Jews were indiscriminately considered the principal offenders.

Although the close-knit Jewish community in Nottingham perceived Sir Julien as having abandoned his faith, he did not forsake the community. After the death of his parents, Julien became acutely aware and concerned about the welfare of the elderly within the Jewish community. As his business success grew, so did his desire to do some good for the community to which his parents had been so devoted. In the early 1930s, he gave two houses in Tennyson Street to the Jewish community. These houses were converted into four small flats for the elderly.

In October 1933, Sir Julien bought a convalescent home for children, known as The Chesnuts, Waverley Street, Nottingham. There was accommodation for sick children, children who had been receiving hospital treatment or deserving cases in need of convalescent treatment. Ostensibly it was bought and equipped by Lady Cahn, who was to maintain the institution at her own expense. It was formally opened on 27 October 1933 by the Lord Mayor of Nottingham, in the presence of the Lady Mayoress, Sir Julien and Lady Cahn and Sir Albert and Lady Ball. Julien modestly described the gift as 'one of his wife's little whims', and expressed particular pleasure at the presence of Mr R.H. Swain who had done such wonderful work in connection with the convalescent homes for children at Skegness. Unlike Leicestershire, Nottingham had not had such a home where children could spend a few weeks recuperating. Sir Julien spoke appreciatively of the help given to the scheme by various people, including Sir Albert Ball and Dr. H.N. Jaffé. He said that he would derive much pleasure from visiting the home where he could see the children with 'life's morning brought back and visions of the future'.

The Lord Mayor spoke with emotion. Turning to Lady Cahn he said, 'In years to come children who come to this home will look back upon you as an angel, because you brought a little joy into their drab lives.'

Sir Albert Ball said that for years Sir Julien and Lady Cahn had been trying to be of real service to their day and generation. Sir Julien was one of the most generous-hearted citizens in Nottingham. 'I am proud of his success,' said Sir Albert, 'because he is using it to bring happiness to others.'

Once again it was the time of year for cricket. But poor weather spoiled the start of the 1933 season. The highlight of the first half of the cricketing year was a visit by the West Indies at the end of June; the match ended in a draw. Nevertheless, the team had another overseas tour to look forward to.

The 1933 tour to Canada, North America and Bermuda took place later on in the year than on previous occasions. While this tour may not have been to such exotic locations, the extravagance surrounding the trip was unprecedented. Not only were the Cahn suites on the *Empress of Britain* refitted to meet Julien's requirements, but the send-off was quite spectacular.

On 11 August 1933, Sir Julien gave a luncheon at Claridge's Hotel as a farewell. *The Times* described the event: 'The room was decorated after the form of a cricket ground, with a greensward carpet for the pitch and toastmaster and waiters in whites. The various tables were posted about the room as batsmen, bowlers, slips, mid-on, leg, and so on. The menu was headed "Body-lining (no ducks to be served)".'

Many celebrities were present, including Mr J.H. Thomas, the Lord Mayor of Nottingham, Lord Ebbisham, Mr W.C. Nixon, Agent General for Ontario, Sir George Maclaren Brown (Chairman of the Blue Star Line), H.D.G. Leweson-Gower (who had his own cricket team), A.E.R. Gilligan (famous cricketer and sportsman), G.C. Grant and P.F. Warner (known as 'Plum Warner', Chairman of the MCC). Mr J.H. Thomas proposed the toast of 'Cricket, Canada and the Team', and indicated that he felt that this tour would not provoke any of the recent controversies that had recently worried him as Secretary for the Dominions. He told the team 'not to think little of their opponents' and felt sure that they would do much for the good of the game. The Lord Mayor of Nottingham spoke of Sir Julien's service to the game of cricket.

In Cahn's reply he described the team's previous tours to South America and the visit of a South American team to the UK that followed. He said that he hoped to induce Canadian cricketers to make use of coaching of the highest class so that the game might be developed in Canada to a higher pitch of excellence than it had yet reached.

After a night at Claridge's, the team sailed on the *Empress of Britain* from Southampton on 12 August, arriving in Montreal on 19 August. The *Empress of Britain* represented the height of luxury in cruising. She was designed to be the fastest ship to cross the Atlantic. No expense was spared on the lavish interior, and perhaps the most beautiful public area was the Mayfair Lounge, decorated in walnut with silver designs for the wall panelling. The architecture was inspired by ancient Greece with tall scagliola columns and pilasters. The ceiling comprised a large vault of amber glass with signs of the zodiac around the base. No pictures or records remain of the personal fit-out that White Allom undertook for Cahn's cabins, but undoubtedly they were to the highest of modern standards. As is once again fashionable in cruising today, there was no shortage of activities on board. The modern gymnasium was equipped with a great range of devices, which were put to good use by Sir Julien's team. These included bicycle machines, electric horses and punch balls. The *Empress of Britain* was destined to undertake world cruises, although in the year that Cahn sailed, it did not offer one. The fares for a whole suite in such a world cruise were equivalent to an astonishing £125,000 in today's money.

The team included Blunt, a New Zealand cricketer of the year, and Gibb, both of whom made their debut for the Cahn XI in 1933. The others were Heane, Maxwell, Morkel, Munt, Newman, Peebles, Reddick, Robins, Rhodes, E.P. Solbe, Summers and Swanton. Upon arriving in Canada, the Cahn XI played two matches against Montreal on 19 and 21 August, followed by two against Ottowa on the 23–24 August. There was a slight shock in the initial game when the tourists got into difficulties on a matting wicket and won by a single wicket, but from then on most of the games provided easy wins for the visitors. Matters were not helped by the shock of Reddick requiring an operation for appendicitis after the first game in Ottowa. Julien had already made plans to view hospitals in Canada, to research their maternity facilities, and the Canadian Red Cross had set up a programme of visits to hospitals in Montreal and Ottowa. Luckily for Reddick, therefore, the most senior medical officials, who were accompanying Cahn, ensured that he was offered the very best of treatment.

After Toronto, the team played in Hamilton, London, Chicago and New York, with their final game taking place on Long Island on 8 September before they departed for Bermuda. The Cahn XI didn't rate the cricket in North America, which they considered to be of a low level. More memorable than the mediocre cricket was the team entertainment. Ginty Lush explained that while they were playing in Chicago, 'two rather odd-looking gentlemen arrived in a chauffeur-driven Cadillac to watch. Rather like exaggerated Humphrey Bogarts, they looked dressed to kill – in more ways than one.' At the end of the game they sauntered over to the Cahn players and asked if any of the party would like to 'see something of our fair city's underworld nightlife'. Most of the team took them up on this offer and spent a memorable evening visiting various speakeasies. In January 1920 an amendment had been passed in the USA banning the sale and production of alcohol. Of course, this simply amplified the supply and demand for alcohol and, as it had to be consumed privately, the underground bar was born. Due to its secrecy, the term 'speakeasy' was coined. Prohibition turned the members of organised crime into the czars of their era. Al Capone was the most notorious, organising a network of 700 men, overseeing a bootlegging cartel from Canada to Florida and controlling all 10,000 speakeasies in Chicago.

The team's guides must have been Al Capone's henchmen as they took the players to all of the most infamous speakeasies and introduced them to the key members of the Chicago underworld. While they happily gave information on the people they met during the evening, the guides did not disclose any information about themselves. At the end of the evening, the players were escorted back to their lavish penthouse where a sumptuous meal awaited them. Quite how or why this all came about, the players never found out. Although the prohibition laws were repealed just three months after the team's visit to Chicago in December 1933, various men they were introduced to were 'summarily bumped off' in the intervening few weeks.

While in the USA, the Cahns accepted the invitations of two celebrated hosts. In New York they were invited to stay at the home of Millicent Hearst, the estranged wife of William Randolph Hearst, the massively wealthy newspaper and publishing magnate. At this time, Hearst was living openly with the actress Marion Davies in California while his wife had made an independent life for herself in New York, where she was a keen philanthropist, avid socialite and, most interestingly for Sir Julien, the founder of the Free Milk Fund for the Poor in New York. Julien was charmed and acquired a great deal of invaluable information for the National Birthday Trust Fund. Phyllis Cahn was not so impressed.

'What's the point of having money if you can't get any service?' she asked bluntly.

In Chicago they stayed at the home of the USA's leading magician, John Mulholland. Much to Cahn's disgust, as he had no time for it all, many of the leading UK magicians were heavily involved in parapsychology, either aiming to disprove it or incorporating it into their magical shows. One of Cahn's co-Vice-presidents of the Magician's Club was Harry Price, who spent years undertaking experiments to show how mediums could falsify spirit photographs, trances, the appearance of spirits and messages from the dead. Despite this, he was himself a believer in psychic and occult phenomena but was aware of how less scrupulous individuals deluded the public into believing falsities.

Julien considered everything to do with parapsychology and the occult as utter nonsense, a view shared by his American host, Mulholland. The latter spent many years investigating the paranormal, fortune tellers and clairvoyants and was a total sceptic. In the 1950s, Mulholland was recruited by the CIA to assist them in explaining bizarre occurrences, often accomplished through conjuring or magic. The Cahns spent a fascinating twenty-four hours with Mulholland.

In Bermuda Sir Julien Cahn's team made history by being the first white side to play a club of black men. To mark the occasion a public holiday was declared. The game was played in front of a massive crowd against the Somerset CC. British garrison troops filled one section of the ground, jostling and joking with local Bermudians with whom they had placed bets on the outcome of the match. Spectators covered every inch of the ground, even perching on branches of trees. One tree outside the ground was so heavy with spectators that it collapsed under the strain, with all the occupants fortuitously falling inside the ground!

The Cahn XI played two very good matches against Somerset CC, winning one by three runs due to a magnificent catch on the boundary by Heane and thus dismissing the last man. In the final game against Bermuda, an unbroken ninth wicket stand by Blunt and Maxwell saved the day and meant that, as Sir Julien would have expected, on 16 September the English side sailed for home unbeaten. However, the standard of cricket in Bermuda was first class, especially considering that the tourists' team comprised a test player from New Zealand, two from England and two from South Africa.

Upon returning home Sir Julien was sent a large wreath in the shape of a horseshoe from the Bermudans. It was made of white heather with the nail holes represented by an extraordinary golden-coloured chrysanthemum. No one had ever seen anything like it. Sir Julien ordered his head gardener Freddie Foster to find out the variety of the unusual coloured flower. He took it to the potting shed and gave it to Jo Green, an assistant gardener, to care for. Jo duly sprayed the wreath with water to keep it fresh, but to his horror realised that with every drop of water, the flowers appeared to be developing a chronic form of measles. To everyone's great amusement they discovered that the chrysanthemums had been dipped in a powder that simply faded when it came into contact with water, leaving the pure white colour of the flowers behind.

Despite doing so much for the game of cricket, Cahn was never part of the hierarchy of the MCC, never elected to membership or invited to sit on its committees. Many cricket commentators have considered this unforgivable. However, it is important to remember the era in which Cahn lived, and the status that cricket had in society.

In Jack Williams' book *Cricket and Race* (2001), he explains how cricket in the first half of the twentieth century 'encapsulated the essence of England'. It was a game for the economically privileged and for the white man. Cahn was Jewish and his riches were self-made. Williams noted that it is hard to define the impact of anti-Semitism in cricket, mainly due to the lack of first-class cricketing Jews. There were few, if any, Jews involved in county cricket administration, so Cahn was certainly the highest profile Jew in the game. In that era, Jews were banned from golf clubs and anti-Semitism was rife, particularly among the upper classes.

Of course, there were other reasons why Cahn was unacceptable to the MCC. He made a mockery of the amateur status that was rigorously upheld at the time and was not abolished until 1963. English cricket maintained a division between amateur and professional cricketers. While ways were sometimes found to give the amateurs financial compensation, Cahn was the only major player to take advantage of this loophole during the 1930s. Cricket even had an annual 'gentlemen versus players' game between amateurs and professionals, one of the most important fixtures of the year. Although Cahn's team was officially amateur, in reality it comprised the leading cricketers of the day. Due to the opportunities – financial, travel and lifestyle – that Cahn was able to offer his cricketers, he was able to attract the best players and even pinched potential test-class players at an early age. Maxwell, for instance, was snapped up as soon as he left Brighton College.

On the other hand, when Cahn's XI was at its most successful during the late 1930s, a large percentage of his regular players were recruits from the dominions – three came from South Africa, four from Australia and two from New Zealand. Perhaps the MCC should have been more grateful that Cahn had skimmed off such talent from potential overseas adversaries!

The leading lights in the MCC continued their abhorrence of all Cahn stood for long after his death. In 1954, Charles Lyttleton, 10th Viscount Cobham of Hagley Hall, then President of the MCC, wrote a letter to Harry Altham, Treasurer of the MCC, expressing his concerns about the MCC membership and the need to increase drastically the entrance fees or subscriptions.

> And yet it is so important for us not to put membership beyond the means of the very people we want as members – the young, the 'professional classes' and the Service members. If we apply too stringent an economic sanction, we will find the place full of Sir Julien Cahns.

It was also unfortunate that Cahn's principal dealings with the controlling body of cricket should focus upon the 'bodyline' scandal of 1932–3. As President of Nottinghamshire County Cricket Club and of Leicestershire County Cricket Club he was of necessity vicariously associated with the MCC. After the Bodyline Tour, Sir Julien as President of Nottinghamshire was required by the MCC to act as its intermediary in approaching Harold Larwood.

In brief, bodyline was a cricketing tactic devised by the English cricket team to combat the batting prowess of Australia's Don Bradman for their tour to Australia in 1932. Bodyline bowlers deliberately aimed the ball at the bodies of the batsmen with the aim of creating legside deflections that could be caught by a nearby fielder. The plan was hatched between Douglas Jardine, England's captain, Arthur Carr, Nottinghamshire's captain, and his two fast bowlers, Harold Larwood and Bill Voce. This tactic led to several injuries to Australian players and created very bad relations between the two national teams. Eventually, the controversy spilled over into the diplomatic arena.

As a result, the MCC introduced a new rule giving umpires the power to intervene if they thought a bowler was deliberately aiming at a batsman with the intent to cause injury. To appease the protests still coming from Australia, the MCC also asked Larwood to sign an apology to them for his bowling during the tour to that country, and as President of Nottinghamshire Sir Julien was called upon to relay the message to him. This following quotation is taken from Harold Larwood's book, *The Larwood Story.*

The gentlemen of the MCC did not show their hand until early in the 1934 season and I was certainly not prepared for the devious approach that was made. We were playing a match in Nottingham at the private ground owned by Sir Julien Cahn, who had been president of Nottinghamshire in 1931. He was a wealthy man, a patron of the club, a gentleman, a big businessman who rode in a chauffeured Rolls Royce. During the match I was asked to go and see him. He talked for a few minutes and I knew he was buttering me up for something. Finally he said 'Harold, I'm afraid you'll have to apologise to the MCC'. Harold! Usually I got called plain Larwood. 'Apologise sir? What for?' 'For your bowling, Harold.' 'I have nothing to apologise for sir.' 'Oh, but you must Harold. You must apologise to the MCC for your bowling and you must agree to bowl legitimately in future. If you do you will be picked in the Tests against Australia. But unless I have your word, I'm afraid you will not be considered at all.' I couldn't believe what I had been told and my stomach turned over.

I thought of how I had bowled myself to a standstill in Australia, at the captain's orders, how I had bowled till my side ached, bowled till my toes bled. I thought of how my stomach had revolted against food because of the strain of bowling. I thought of how I had bowled until I was weary, only to have Jardine come across and say, 'Try one more, Harold.' I thought of the cables the MCC had sent me in Australia. There were three of them all signed by Marylebone. The first, addressed to me at the Hotel Australia, Sydney, during the First Test said 'Well bowled Notts.' The second, during the Brisbane Test: 'well bowled, congratulations.' The third one, during the last test 'Bravo'. After a while I said to Sir Julien Cahn, 'I'm an Englishman – I will never apologise.'

Having initially supported Larwood, Cahn had little choice but to follow the orders of the MCC. Larwood commented that as Nottinghamshire President, he would have thought that Cahn would have retained the support he had previously expressed so many times. But Larwood could not begin to understand Cahn's desperate desire to be accepted by the MCC. What he thought in private about the affair we will never know for sure, but we can assume he must have felt badly about Larwood, especially as the MCC failed to fulfil his wishes. Larwood never played for England again.

Nottingham was not the only county to be assisted by Sir Julien. By the mid-1930s Leicestershire County Cricket Club was nearly bankrupt. Cahn arranged for 'Stewie' Dempster, the great New Zealand batsman, to work as his store manager for Jays and Campbells in Leicester so that he could captain the county. In June 1933, he was elected to Leicestershire and became their representative at Lords, serving on the advisory county cricket committee in a post that he held until his death. In 1933, he gave the club £500 followed by £1,000 a year later. Cahn became President of Leicestershire County Cricket Club in 1940 and 1941.

Cahn's championing of cricket went beyond the obvious. Cahn was one of the main supporters of the journal the *Cricketer*. In every edition he advertised his furnishing store Campbells (or sometimes Jays) on the inside of the cover, the most expensive and important slot for advertising. If non-professional or local teams wished to have their matches reported in the *Cricketer*, they had to pay for the privilege. This rule did not apply to the Sir Julien Cahn XI's results. They were reported in return for the substantial sums Cahn paid for advertising.

Although his interest in cricket far surpassed his interest in any other game, Cahn was also a generous supporter of football in the district. The local Nottinghamshire amateur league – the Bulwell and

District – competed for the Sir Julien Cahn Trophy, which had been commissioned in Regent Street, London, in 1922 and given by Cahn to the league. The solid-silver statuette of a player was reputed to be one of the most valuable soccer trophies in the country.

While Sir Julien notched up philanthropic acts, such as donating Newstead Abbey to Nottingham, funding substantial agricultural research and other high-profile gestures worth many tens of thousands, in 1933 another opportunity presented itself that was quite beyond his control. Ironically, it was Maundy Gregory himself who unwittingly presented Cahn with the chance to achieve his baronetcy.

By the late 1920s, Gregory's behaviour had become a political issue. Baldwin was slow to act against the honours fixer. The Government were keen to get rid of Gregory without precipitating a major public disclosure, so they decided to break him financially. They decided to plant a spy in Gregory's camp. Albert (later Sir Albert) Bennett, Conservative MP for Nottingham Central and assistant party Treasurer, was instructed to obtain a list of clients whom Gregory intended to put forward for honours so that the Conservative Central Office could veto these names in advance and thus ensure that none of them got on any honours list. Gregory's position depended upon his ability to deliver the goods for which his clients had paid him. Unfortunately, at this stage Baldwin was defeated in the general election in May 1929 and a Labour Government was formed with support from the Liberal Party. Bennett received his own baronetcy in the Dissolution Honours of June 1929 at the same time as Julien Cahn received his knighthood for 'philanthropic and public services', and it may have been as a result of these chores.

Unfortunately for Gregory, he was unwilling to curtail his extravagances even after the source of their funding, honours brokerage, began to dry up. In 1930, the executors of the estate of a Sir George Watson tried to reclaim money that Watson had given Gregory for honours, honours that had not been forthcoming. While they settled out of court, after the first instalment Gregory was broke.

In increasing desperation, Gregory managed to sell papal honours. He also befriended a lady and persuaded her to change her will in his favour. Dying just a year later, the death was considered sufficiently suspicious to result in a police inquiry and exhumation. In desperation, Gregory tried to tout honours again and was eventually exposed by

Lieutenant-Commander Leake. Maundy Gregory was the only person charged under the terms of the 1925 Honours (Prevention of Abuses) Act, facing subsequent imprisonment and exile.

'Honours List Summons Issued!' – in 1933 the *Daily Sketch* announced that a charge was to be brought by the Director of Public Prosecutions against a man called Maundy Gregory. In the preceding twelve years several men who had acquired titles had been subject to comment in Parliament or the Law Courts. These all related to surprising and embarrassing revelations about the manner in which they had obtained their honours. Gregory's charge was that he had attempted to obtain a sum of money from a retired Naval officer by offering to secure for him a knighthood or baronetcy, according to the sum he might be willing to pay. The Honours (Prevention of Abuses) Act 1925 made it an offence for anyone to promise or try to secure an honour in respect of payment or other consideration.

Although Gregory was successfully prosecuted, it was very much in the Government's interest that the details of the case remain hushed up. They were desperate to ensure that the general public did not learn of the extent of honours touting. As a result they decided to offer Gregory a deal. Although he would have to serve a short term of imprisonment, they would secure his financial future if he went permanently to live in France. This eventually happened. He was met at the prison gates, whisked away to France, given accommodation in Paris and a quarterly pension, all in exchange for never disclosing his identity or referring to his past. Gregory remained in Paris until his death in 1941.

Tom Cullen, in his book *Maundy Gregory Purveyor of Honours*, suggests that Maundy was not paid by the Conservative Party but rather that the Conservative Central Office acted as an honest broker in bringing together a group of noble lords and knights who had been Gregory's clients in the past and who were prepared to underwrite his future in return for silence. It appears that the payment was made by none other than Sir Julien Cahn.

Neville Chamberlain, Chancellor of the Exchequer from 1931 until succeeding Stanley Baldwin as Prime Minister in 1937, partook of the Cahns' hospitality when he stayed with them from 16–17 October 1933. This stay at Stanford Hall would have been to discuss Sir Julien's donation of funds to the Conservative Party in order to hush up the Maundy Gregory affair. If it is indeed true that Chamberlain harboured anti-Semitic feelings, his political charm would have ensured that these would have been kept well under wraps in his associations with Sir Julien, who was so conveniently assisting both the Conservative and Labour parties to get out of a potentially seriously embarrassing political scandal.

Some months after Gregory had left Wormwood Scrubs, Stanley Baldwin approached Prime Minister MacDonald and asked that Sir Julien Cahn should be made a baronet in return for paying Gregory £30,000.

The following is an extract from Ramsay Macdonald's private diary for 13 December 1933:

Baldwin came into the Cabinet room in the morning, sat down and straight away asked what I had against Julien Cahn. I said he was one of those Honour hunters whom I detested, that his friends and agents had beset me for a long time for a baronetcy for him, that he was not a commendable person, that he had put money into 'Everyman' stating it was in my interests – in short just the man whom I should not dream of honouring. I had let it be known that do what he might no recommendation for an honour to him would be put up by me. Baldwin replied that I must yield and when I asked why he said that Maundy Gregory's papers and Maundy Gregory's presence here would stir up such a filthy sewer as would poison public life; that many innocent persons had become indirectly involved; that all parties were involved (I corrected him at once and said, not ours. He smiled and said that unfortunately friends of mine were. I replied that if they were I knew nothing about it. Then I remembered that Clynes & Henderson were mentioned at an earlier stage) that people like Churchill, Chamberlain, Birkenhead were involved; that Gregory had been used by Lloyd George & Bonar Law; that the subscription lists for the rebuilding of St George's Chapel Windsor were involved and several other things. Gregory, as indeed I know, was a blackguard who netted innocent people who did nothing that was irregular or bad, but whose associations with those who had enshrouded them in a cloud. The dunghill had to be cleared away without delay and £30,000 were required to do it. So I had to give the Honour. I pointed out that if I did so the many people who knew of Cahn's baits to me would say at once that he had made one tempting enough and I had taken it and that in order to do what he wanted I should have to accept odium and be quite unable to explain it away. I asked him to consider the matter for a day and see me again.

The next day Baldwin relented and it was agreed that the question of Cahn's honour should be postponed until the next list, in May.

MacDonald resisted for six months but his diary on 19 May 1934 noted: 'Mr B . . . involves me in scandal by forcing me to give an honour because a man has paid £30,000 to get Tory headquarters, and some Tories living and dead out of a mess.'

A month later, Sir Julien Cahn was given his baronetcy in the King's Birthday Honours List of June 1934, ostensibly for 'services to agriculture'.

6

One Big Family

Sir Julien Cahn received his baronetcy in the King's Birthday Honours List on 4 June 1934. His official title became Sir Julien Cahn Bt. of Stanford-upon-Soar in the county of Nottingham. He was immensely proud of his honour and immediately created his own coat of arms. The society book, Debrett's *Peerage and Baronetage*, describes the Cahn coat of arms as, 'Gules, a cross raguly ermine between in the second and third quarters a fleur-de-lis or crest. In front of a fox's head erased two branches of willow in saltire proper.' In layman's terms the crest includes willow to represent Julien's love of cricket and a fox's head to represent hunting. The motto is '*Possunt quia posse videntur*', which translates as 'They are able who believe they can'. How neatly this summed up Sir Julien's success – he believed that he could achieve his baronetcy and indeed he did.

A few weeks after the receipt of his baronetcy, Julien was asked to become Vice-president of the Royal Society of Arts. Although it has always been known by its shortened name, its full title is the Royal Society of Arts, Manufactures and Commerce – and thus it becomes clear why Sir Julien was asked to become involved. It was a radical body that sought to challenge the status quo, seeking to 'embolden enterprise, enlarge science, refine art, improve our manufactures and extend our commerce', as well as alleviate poverty and secure full employment. Its core values mirrored those of Cahn's. Such an association enabled Julien to meet on a regular basis with other leaders of the manufacturing and design industries, in particular notable businessmen such as Samuel Courtauld, owner of Courtaulds, and Sir Henry Leggett, Managing Director of the British East Africa Corporation.

Such connections were vital for the continued growth of Jays and Campbells. In 1934, the business was so successful, employing more and more people, that Julien decided to build a new headquarters, the finest, most prestigious business headquarters in Nottingham, if not the whole of the Midlands. The new offices were at Talbot House, Talbot Street, not far from their existing headquarters on Upper Parliament Street. The immaculate offices were completed in 1935. In the reception of Talbot House were seated two beautiful girls, dressed in black and white, responsible for operating the telephone and manning reception.

The block was completed with a flat at the top of the building and an integrated barber's salon. Julien's private bathrooms were fitted out with the finest art-deco marble. There was a modern lift and telephone exchange. As if that was not enough personal accommodation, Julien disposed of his flat at East Circus Street and acquired a house at the corner of Clarendon Street. He installed a housekeeper and it was here that he had lunch every day, and on the rare occasion he needed to stay in Nottingham, he would spend the night at the house.

Most nights, however, were spent at home, at Stanford Hall. Every morning at 8 a.m. prompt, Sir Julien and Lady Cahn would convene in the bottom half of the dining room for breakfast. The top half of the room was used for dinner. Breakfast, which typically included kedgeree, a fish dish and an egg dish, was laid out in silver dishes to which the family helped themselves. The large panelled dining room had mouldings painted in green and white, complemented by curtains made from crimson and buff-coloured velvet. There were three Persian carpets scattered on the floor, covering the polished wood block. There were two large tables placed in a T configuration with eighteen finely carved Georgian dining chairs each covered in crimson silk velvet.

During the weekdays, the children would take their breakfast with Waity in the school room at the top of the house. Manners were to be strictly adhered to and the children had to finish every last morsel on their plates. Albert loathed porridge. 'You will stay at the table until you have finished!' announced Waity firmly as she left the room. Checking to make sure no one was looking, Albert crept to the radiator and tipped the porridge down the back of it. When Waity returned Albert had a cherubic smile on his face and an empty bowl. As far as he knows the porridge was never found – so perhaps it is still there today, a solidified lump wedged behind an ancient radiator!

The weekends were special, for it was only on Saturdays and Sundays that the children could eat breakfast with their parents in the dining room. Sir Julien would read the newspaper and had his post placed on his desk in his library to be dealt with after breakfast. The rest of the family received their post at the breakfast table. Like most youngsters, the children rarely received any mail. However, one Saturday there was a letter addressed to Miss Patience Cahn. 'It's a bill!' she announced in dismay. Pat looked closer. 'It's a bill for Car Opody. I haven't bought any Car Opody. What cheek to send me a bill for something I've never shopped for! I haven't even got a car!' 'Give it to me!' demanded her father. When he read the letter he roared with laughter. 'Chiropody, Pat!' he explained. 'What you have done to your feet.'

After breakfast, Julien would read his post in his library, carefully studying the words through his monocle. Then Cahn's young sons, Albert and Richard, would carry their father's briefcase from the library to the front door of Stanford Hall. 'Be careful! It's too heavy for them Julien – they'll get a rupture!' Phyllis would exclaim every morning. But the boys enjoyed their little duty, it was one of the rare occasions they had anything to do with their father.

Albert, aged 9, and Richard, aged 7, had to walk a long way with their father's heavy brown crocodile-skin briefcase. They didn't notice the stunning ornaments of Chinese origin. They tore past the William and Mary grandfather clock embedded in a black and gilt lacquer case in 'Chinese taste'. They ignored the 2ft-high Chinese elephants embossed with red and gold dragons and aptly defined in the inventory as 'grotesque', and the Chinese sacred ram incense burners that sat alongside Tibetan bronze elephants on top of an antique Chinese black and gold lacquer cabinet with red and gilt decorations. The antique Chinese draught screen carved with figures, dragons and birds might as well have not been there. But the boys always slowed down when they walked past the pair of bronze statuettes. Each over 2ft tall, they were of Sir Julien and Lady Cahn in hunting costume, on marble pedestals, and looked slightly out of place among the oriental *objects d'art* but, nevertheless, slightly frightened the boys with their uncanny resemblance to their parents.

Hidden between all of the highly valuable artefacts were a few surprises – items that most certainly were not sourced by the very proper White Allom. These included an innocuous French bronze model of a monkey on a couch and an intricate marquetry inlaid box that upon closer inspection would reveal themselves to be erotic collectibles. Any naïve young maid diligently undertaking her dusting duties would have had the shock of her life if she lifted the lid to clean inside. Perhaps these objects added to the reputation of debauchery that some tried to tarnish Sir Julien with, a reputation for which there appears to be little factual substantiation. What these antiques did show is that Sir Julien was no prude and thoroughly enjoyed teasing and even on occasion shocking friends and family.

The baronial hall was decorated in a mock Tudor style with vast, highly polished flagstones upon which lay original Persian carpets. Stone archways embraced the front door. The windows were framed with heavy crimson velvet curtains. The panelled ceiling was, in fact, carved out of plaster made to look like authentic wood. To complete the Tudor look the hall was furnished with large antique oak refectory tables, a 6ft antique oak cupboard dated 1679, antique carved oak coffers and troughs. Jacobean oak chairs with seats and backs in leather and armchairs painted with shields were strategically placed for decoration rather than use.

As the children arrived with the briefcase, a footman would open the door and Albert or Richard would hand their father's case to the chauffeur who would be waiting on the front steps. Normally, this was Robson, the head chauffeur. Cars were a vital part of Cahn's life. Of course they were a necessity for Sir Julien's daily trips to the office in Nottingham, and tours across England and Europe, but perhaps of equal importance was all they represented – Cahn's success and social standing. Sir Julien only wanted the best. He had a stunning chocolate and cream Rolls Royce fully equipped with a cocktail cabinet; a robin's egg blue Rolls Royce classic Phantom bought new in July 1932 for £2,500, restored over the years and sold most recently at auction in 2004; a black Rolls Royce especially kitted out for hunting and shooting, equipped with a shoot brake with seats running down the side with a gun rack in the centre; a Wolsey, which was used to collect the shopping and take the children on school runs; a van that was used for collecting milk; and a bus, used predominantly for transporting the cricket team.

Over the years, Julien had many different cars, particularly Rolls Royces. It was said that after Sir Julien achieved his baronetcy he had a Rolls especially commissioned, with a body that was taller than usual to allow him to sit in the car with his top hat on. A fine story, but unsubstantiated in fact. However, it is fact that in the 1930s when one purchased a Rolls Royce the engine would be bought from Rolls Royce but the chassis was made separately, designed to the new owner's unique specifications. One day, shortly after he had received his baronetcy, Sir Julien walked into Mulliners, the Rolls Royce garage in Berkeley Square, London. He was approached by a young salesman.

'Who can I get to help you, Sir Julien? Captain Smith or Major Brown?'

The reply was withering.

'With the order I'm about to place you'd better find me the General!'

Such an acerbic response was typical – Sir Julien vehemently disapproved of people who used lowly titles.

Julien had had a peripheral involvement with the Army for many years. He had been appointed an honorary colonel in the Lincoln Territorial Army, and once a year dressed up in his full regalia to take part in the manoeuvres on Cherry Hill. Besides this he never participated in active duties.

To drive and maintain his collection of cars he had to have a chauffeur. But Sir Julien did not employ just one chauffeur – at any one time he employed three.

The head chauffeur was Thomas Robson. He was Sir Julien's preferred driver and it was Robson who was trusted to take Sir Julien on all his long-distance drives, including many trips abroad. Postcards sent by Robson from Grand Hotel du Cap d'Antibes explain that he drove Sir Julien to the south of France and on to Italy twice in 1938, once in February and again in November of that year. In the earlier years, such foreign trips were even more frequent. It was a fabulous experience for the chauffeur from Nottingham to stay in such luxurious, world-renowned hotels. At Dover it was possible to drive one's car onto a train that was ferried across the Channel making drives to the Continent easy and practical. Cahn travelled to Europe extensively this way, visiting all of the major cities such as Vienna and Paris for work and pleasure. Letters from his principal shop manager, William Yarnall, date back to trips the two men took together to Vienna in 1920.

It was during one of the many trips to France that Sir Julien acquired his most precious and beloved collection of forty Napoleonic soldier models. These statuettes were of French regiments between 1800 and 1840 and were displayed in a large 9ft oak bow-fronted display cabinet, fitted with internal electric lights and with a silver plate back mirror, in the lobby of the Badminton Hall. The toy soldiers were made by French prisoners of war, who used their own clothes to create the uniforms for the models. Along with his collection of cricket balls and bats, the soldiers were his prized possessions. Like so much else, they disappeared after his death. Robson drove with extra care when returning these special artefacts to Stanford Hall.

Robson took huge pride in the maintenance and care of his vehicles. His daughter, Audrey Concannon, has a letter of commendation that Robson received from the Rolls Royce Owners Club. It reads:

> We understand our inspecting engineer had an opportunity of making an examination of Sir Julien Cahn's car with you recently. In his report to us he emphasised the care and attention that has been given to it. Therefore we congratulate you and inform you that we are sending you a Certificate of merit and a RR Badge no 2976 to be a permanent record of our appreciation.

It was explained to Robson that badges were only given to drivers who had earned it, in recognition of keeping the cars in their care in excellent order. He also received a reward of £5.

Jerry Perkins was the second chauffeur taking over from John Swift. The second chauffeur did many of the school runs. Billy Redmayne was the third chauffeur. He sadly died while on holiday in 1934 and was replaced by Walter Tacey. The chauffeurs were responsible for filling up the cars with petrol from the underground tank adjacent to the garage. This was no quick task for the fuel had to be pumped up by hand. And this had to be done with great regularity as the cars only managed 8 or 9 miles to the gallon.

At the East Leake, Nottingham entrance to Stanford Hall, Sir Julien fitted electric gates – a complete novelty for the 1930s. The gates were operated by two plates, upon which the car had to stand in order for the gates to open. Unfortunately, they soon became the bane of the chauffeurs' lives and a horror for visiting drivers. Unless the car was driven absolutely straight onto the plates the gates wouldn't open. Woe betide those visitors who had a light-weight car! If the car was too light, the gates would not swing far enough to latch back and to the horror of the occupants, the gates would swing forwards again and hit the car. Fortunately for Sir Julien, this was not an era of litigation but, unsurprisingly, the gates were rarely used.

On a typical weekday morning, it would be Robson standing on the steps, the door of the Rolls Royce open to receive Sir Julien. They would drive in companionable silence the 10 miles to Nottingham.

Each morning, whatever the weather, 16-year-old Roy Dexter would be waiting patiently on the doorstep of the offices for Sir Julien's Rolls Royce to come into sight. Dressed in a brown uniform, especially made by a livery tailor in Clumber Street, the jacket had forty-nine brass buttons arranged in two rows of sixteen and one row of seventeen buttons. Roy had to get up early in order to polish them every single day. Upon sighting Sir Julien's car, he would rush forwards and open the boot, removing Cahn's crocodile-skin briefcase, while Robson opened the door for Sir Julien to get out of the car.

Sir Julien would walk through the reception every day, in a slow, quiet manner looking straight ahead, with his perfectly polished brogues sinking deeply into the 4in-thick red carpet. He would never engage in conversation with any of the staff unless there was a specific matter to be dealt with. Roy would open the lift and together they would ascend in silence up to the top floor of the office block. There, Sir Julien would enter his large office, where his co-director and trusted business partner and financial advisor, Robert Doncaster, would be waiting for him. The two men sat opposite each other at a large desk. In the next-door room was a large boardroom that housed a horseshoe-shaped table with a glass top arranged in three pieces that, as Roy Dexter recalls, were impossible to put together.

After Julien was deposited in his office, Roy would sit outside the office in darkness, next to a telephone on the top floor waiting for a call from reception. Pretty Miss Clark was in charge of the telephone exchange, and young Roy's heart leaped every time the telephone rang. If Sir Julien had a guest, Roy would have to descend in the lift, collect the visitor, bring them up to the top floor and introduce them to his boss. He recalls that certain 'horsey-looking' ladies visited regularly, some of whom supplemented his 5s a week wage quite considerably with half a crown at a time. On Saturday afternoons, Roy would be back in the office, cleaning the deep-pile carpet, which he likened to a bog, with a hard wire brush. After three or four years, Roy was sacked due to a particularly arrogant young man calling the lift himself, striding straight past the terrified Roy, and walking into Sir Julien's office unwelcomed and unannounced.

Sir Julien had a number of personal secretaries. Miss A.M. Lane was personal secretary to Cahn and Sir Robert Doncaster from 1930 to 1948. Gwen Drury was another personal secretary from 1929 for a few years. Together, the two ladies were known as the Drury Lane partnership. Julien was extremely kind to those staff who were loyal to him. In the early 1930s, he helped Miss Drury buy an Austin 7. Those were the days prior to driving tests and her driving skills were somewhat limited. Part of the arrangement was that during the day one of Cahn's chauffeurs would turn the car around so that it was pointing in the right direction for her journey home.

Miss Lane was a serious young lady who preferred to concentrate on her work in the office. Cricket was the bane of her working life. How annoyed she became when whole days were wasted accompanying Sir Julien to his cricket grounds at Stanford Hall or Loughborough Road, where she was to remain on standby should Sir Julien wish to dictate a letter between innings.

Mina Whitelocks, an employee of Cahn's Nottingham Furnishing Company, rather enjoyed watching her employer play cricket. She recalled how there was a band playing classical marches and other popular tunes during the game at Loughborough Road. Whenever the band stopped playing, much to Mina's quiet amusement, Sir Julien joined the crowd in clapping the performers. He even stopped to clap when he was fielding, completely ignoring the ball as it passed his way!

In 1934, after he was made a baronet, Cahn's social activities increased considerably, so he employed a social secretary – Miss M.V. Wren, known by the family as Jenny Wren. Cahn became extremely close to Jenny and, although it was never proven, it was believed by many that Julien had a relationship with her.

Over the years there was much speculation as to whether Sir Julien had affairs. Rumours spread among the staff of shenanigans at Stanford Hall; Charlie Firth, the former estate carpenter, suggested stories of bedroom hopping in his memoires. Staff at Talbot House would comment upon the beautiful ladies that would visit Sir Julien. However, there is no evidence to confirm any of this, and it can not be known for sure whether or not Cahn was unfaithful. There is no doubt that he was a ladies' man. He enjoyed the company of women and spent much time with ladies of society through his charitable undertakings. He also spent much time away from home, away from his wife, and these simple facts would have made excellent fodder for the gossip-mongers.

Joy Tacey, daughter of the third chauffeur, remembers how as a little girl she would secretly peer out of her window and watch guests cavorting around the swimming pool at the midnight parties, mainly organised by and for the cricketers. On one occasion she recalls seeing a lady wrapped only in a bath towel walking around the pool being filmed by a man. To the young girl's amazement, the lady dropped her towel but the man carried on filming. What happened next, Joy never knew as her mother pulled her away from the window. As Sir Julien was one of the few, if only people, at Stanford Hall who had a cine camera and knew how to work it, Joy was probably correct in surmising that the man was Sir Julien himself.

Jenny Wren was an insipid-looking female in her early thirties. As Cahn's personal secretary she was his confidante, working with him every day. Self-confident, and at times brazen, members of staff at Stanford Hall recall an incident that for many would have caused deep embarrassment. Not for Jenny Wren. One afternoon she was climbing into the Rolls Royce with Sir Julien and as she stepped forwards the elastic on her large, bloomer-style knickers gave way. She simply stepped out of them, took them off and carried on getting in the car.

One day Jenny Wren arrived at Loughborough Road with Cahn's mail for his signature.

'You're late!' he muttered darkly.

'Yes, I'm very sorry Sir Julien!' Jenny replied. 'But the bus was so crowded, I couldn't get on it. I had to walk.'

'That's ridiculous!' he declared. 'I shall get you a car!'

And so he did. When Jenny roared up the drive in her immaculate top-of-the-range sports car – an SS Jaguar – eyebrows were raised.

A few of the senior staff had their own offices, Miss Cherry and Jo Mahoney, one of Sir Julien's solicitors, included. Nancy Cherry was in charge of all twenty girls who worked in administration. Perceived as a bit of a battleaxe, she ruled her teams with a rod of iron. Mina Whitelocks was in charge of ordering stationery for all of the shops. She recalls how Miss Cherry would silently pad into the main office and stand at the back waiting to pounce upon any girl who made the grave mistake of returning late from lunch. Mina never experienced the Cherry whip, but she knew that girls who were late were severely reprimanded.

The administration girls sat in a large open-plan office. They were responsible for writing out, by hand, all of the sales information gathered from each store around the country. Hire-purchase ledgers were of foolscap size, well bound with each page interleaved with a thin sheet of plain paper faintly lined. The plain paper enabled notes to be made relating to each account. Notes of interviews, arrears letters and other critical information were painstakingly entered so as to maintain a concise record of each deal made. Every branch had its own ledger, a copy of which was kept at Talbot House. Each evening, Roy Dexter had to wheel the ledgers on a trolley and place them in the strong room, behind fireproof doors.

Nancy Cherry was a member of the Nottingham Mechanics Institute and regularly lunched there at a table shared with Dr Spencer, Mr Addelsey and Eric Pensen. One day she came in brighter and breezier than usual, and when asked why she was extra happy she explained that Sir Julien had sent for her that morning and said that he understood she was going on holiday at the weekend.

'Where are you going?' he asked.

'With my sister on a Mediterranean cruise, Sir Julien!' she replied.

'That will be very nice, and may I ask what it will cost?'

She told him the price per person, upon which he promptly wrote her a cheque to cover their combined outlay.

Such behaviour was typical. For a man who rarely spoke to his staff, it seemed inconceivable that he should know so much about them. They could never understand how their gauche and distant employer was always aware of their personal problems. Whether he perceived that Mina Whitelocks was upset, or whether Miss Cherry had told him, Mina never knew. However, one day he approached her and said that he had noticed that she was worried about something. Mina explained that her mother was very sick with gall-bladder problems. Sir Julien immediately organised for Mina's mother to be cared for and operated on by a Mr Webber, a leading consultant at the Peel Street Hospital in Nottingham. Sadly, Mina's mother did not recover, but Mina never forgot Sir Julien's kindness. This story was repeated time and time again among all Sir Julien's staff, at work and at home.

On another occasion, Mina recalls falling on wet leaves and badly spraining her ankle. It was so swollen that she was unable to walk on it and so couldn't get to work. When Sir Julien found out, he ordered Robson his chauffeur to pick Mina up from her home in the Rolls Royce and return her in the evenings until her foot was better. Mina recalls Robson arriving in his peaked hat and all the neighbours peering out of the windows at the Rolls Royce that had pulled up outside her house. Robson even had to carry her to the car. In those days, there was no such thing as statutory sick pay, so staff were most reluctant to be off work.

The two major social events of 1934 were the Young Britons Ball and the Winter Rose Ball. 1934 was the first of many years in which the

Cahns opened their gardens at Stanford Hall to the public in aid of the Queen's Institute of District Nursing. Normally, a cricket match was organised, so that visitors could watch the match as well as enjoy the beautiful surroundings. It was rare that Sir Julien charged people to gain access to his premises, but on this occasion guests paid a nominal fee, all of which and more (contributed by the Cahns) was given to the charity. In return, the guests were treated to sumptuous teas, served from striped marquees. Mrs Bentley made fabulous petit fours in the Cahn cricket colours of pink, pale blue and black. Bespoke culinary centrepieces were created for every occasion.

The guests were free to wander around the extensive grounds and gardens of Stanford Hall. The immediate grounds were about 40 acres while the estate itself, including all the farms, extended to around 3,000 acres. To maintain the beautiful grounds a considerable retinue of staff was required. There were groundsmen, gardeners, a gamekeeper and a water bailiff.

At the front of the house was a bed planted with roses, including the pale-apricot-coloured rose named after her ladyship – the Lady Cahn. Heliotropes were set in beds of calceolaria and begonias flowered in large borders. Neatly boxed yews surrounded perfectly manicured lawns. Adjoining the hall was an architectural gem known as the Italian Piazza, which was erected under the supervision of Italian consultants. The floor was created in small blue and orange mosaic work and in the centre was a fountain that tapped into a natural spring. The fountain 'played' through the combination of pumps and artificial light. This was another area in which Sir Julien could indulge his fascination for lighting effects. In the early 1930s, a minor earth tremor caused the concrete above the natural spring to crack and the spring flooded the basement corridors, taking three days to pump out.

There was a fabulous vegetable garden and a compound full of thousands of strawberries. The latter was the frequent sneaky haunt of many of the children of the staff. The vegetable garden supplied the needs of all the family, guests and staff – comparable in size to a medium-sized market-garden business today. The king of this gardening empire was red-headed Freddie John Foster, head gardener. His considerable knowledge and gardening skills produced not only stunning looking gardens, but award-winning crops of fresh produce and delicious fruit and vegetables enjoyed by all who lived at Stanford Hall. For several years, Foster entered vegetables into the Royal

Horticultural Show in London on behalf of Sir Julien and he always came away with a trophy or rosette. Foster's charming daughter Millie, known as Miss Foster, worked at the local school as assistant teacher alongside Miss Entwhistle, a masculine-looking woman who terrified all the local children.

Foster was assisted at various times in the gardens by Wallace Coutts, known as Jacky, Sandy Thomson, Harry Chambers, Albert Wormall and David Morris. Morris stayed on after Sir Julien's death, worked for the Co-op and took over the running of the gardens. Jo Green was the youngest of the gardening staff. He lived, along with five others, in the Bothy (a room where the unmarried male servants lived above the gardening preparation area). As the youngest of the group, Jo was responsible for getting up first in the mornings, unlocking the doors, stoking the fires and cooking breakfast for the other men. Although the gardening staff did not consider themselves hard done by, they did not receive the same level of care as the house staff. They had to make their own breakfasts and were catered for by Mrs Tuck, wife of Arthur Tuck, groundsman, rather than Mrs Bentley, the head chef. Along with many of the younger staff, such as Jo Howitt, who was the 'odd-job' man in the house and principal washer-upper in the pantry, Jo Green was recruited to assist Sir Julien with the magic shows. He helped with many of the scene shifts and was privy to most of the extraordinary magical secrets.

The gardening facilities were numerous. There were potting sheds, mushroom sheds, fruit houses, carnation houses, a melon house, orchid houses and a palm house, which was Foster's favourite. There were rows of heated greenhouses, growing grapes, peaches, nectarines, raspberries, strawberries, cape gooseberries – a particular speciality –and every other conceivable fruit and vegetable. There were five gardeners allocated to work just under the glass and many more men worked outside in the grounds. As they had the best equipment and the latest growing techniques, fruits were often grown out of season. Although commonplace today, this was extremely unusual during the 1930s. Strawberries were forced to be eaten in March and sweet, yellow tomatoes frequently went missing. These were Richard's particular favourites and he devoured as many as he could, much to Foster's eternal annoyance. Every morning, Mrs Bentley would stop at Freddie Foster's house to discuss the menu for the day, so that he could provide the necessary fruit and vegetables.

All of the flowers used to decorate the hall were grown for the purpose. Lady Cahn was an accomplished flower arranger and took pleasure in selecting colour schemes and displays for her interior decoration, directing Waity as to which flowers should be positioned where. Phyllis particularly enjoyed wandering through the gardens and glasshouses selecting the flowers, but her pet hate was the geraniums. Each year, they grew over 600 geraniums for planting out at West Bridgford cricket ground.

The head groundsman was a Mr Leefield. He changed his name from Leipfried to Leefield at the beginning of the First World War. As far as Sir Julien was concerned, Leefield had the most important job – ultimate responsibility for the maintenance of the cricket grounds at Stanford Hall. As far as Lady Cahn was concerned, Foster had the most important job as he was the provider of the magnificent flowers, fruit and vegetables. Unfortunately, Foster didn't approve of Leefield, wary of his German extraction. Leefield was assisted by other groundsmen. Arthur Widdowson was responsible for the initial laying of the principal cricket pitch at Stanford Hall in 1928, and together Leefield and Widdowson maintained the main cricket pitch to test standard. Even the secondary pitch, which was used by the staff and village for practising, along with the state-of-the-art bowling machine, was spotless. Arthur Tuck was in charge of the lawns, the bowling green – which was at the front of the house and kept to the most immaculate standard – and 'a pitch and putt' golf course. He was also responsible for the proper nine-hole golf course. They were joined by Harry Leatherland, 'red-faced Harry', who was sometimes estate carpenter, other times groundsman, sometimes carter and always responsible for delivering fresh vegetables grown on site to the houses and flats of staff members.

The Winter Rose Ball in aid of the restoration of Emmanuel Church and the winter relief fund for Camberwell was chaired by Princess Marie Louise. Julien Cahn was a Vice-chairman in conjunction with the Earl of Atholl, Lady Dalrymple-Champney, Admiral of the Fleet Earl Beatty and Mrs Warren Pearl. While the cause would have held little interest for Sir Julien, the company into which he was thrust most certainly did. To impress his co-chair people, Sir Julien offered to pay for the band.

At the same time, he was a Vice-chairman for the Young Britons Ball. He arranged for Walford Hyden and his Café Collette Orchestra, as well as Jack Harris and his orchestra, to play for the ball, with the American Elizabeth Welsh singing.

In December 1934, Sir Julien fell ill with a severe bout of influenza. Quite simply he had been doing too much: attending too many balls, committee meetings, managing the hunt and his business. Much to his regret he was forced to withdraw from some of his charitable commitments.

His illness was exacerbated by the bodyline cricketing scandal that had just come to a head. In January 1935, along with the whole of the committee, Sir Julien resigned as President of Nottinghamshire Cricket Club, addressing his resignation letter to Captain H.A. Brown, Secretary of the Nottinghamshire County Cricket Club, and forwarding a copy of the letter to the press. The long-standing bowling dispute involving Nottinghamshire Cricket Club, the Australians and the MCC was finally resolved in March 1935. At the Nottinghamshire CC annual meeting, the members agreed that they would, in line with the MCC's request, condemn the 'direct-attack' bowling. The members also rescinded the no-confidence vote on the committee that had been passed in January. They also re-elected Sir Julien as President. All was peaceful once again.

At the end of that month, Sir Julien resigned from the Burton Hunt and accepted the Mastership of the Woodland Pytchley. This was no surprise. Members of the Burton had been complaining since 1932 that Cahn hunted the areas where he could be sure of sport at the expense of less popular coverts. This meant that the hounds were not properly encouraged through the woodland areas. If the hounds took a long time to scent out the smell of the fox, it became boring for the riders who had to stand at the side of the woodland, waiting and doing nothing. It is easy to imagine Cahn running out of patience, insisting that the company get on with the thrill of the ride.

Discontent bubbled slowly with accusations being made that the Master was unavailable to hear complaints, was out of touch with those in the countryside and was losing members' support. However, his offer to resign was rejected and for the next three years these bubbles of discontent reared up to the surface and then were suitably dissolved, until another one arose. In 1935, the Chairman of the Hunt Committee called for a resolution stating that they (the Committee) were completely satisfied with Wright (the Huntsman) but that his horsemanship would show to better advantage if he were more suitably provided with horses. This criticism was directed at Sir Julien who supplied the horses. The Committee refused to accept this resolution, which was, in their opinion, not their affair. The Chairman therefore resigned, followed swiftly by Sir Julien as Master. Sir Julien disliked petty politics and squabbles with a vengeance, and he would have immediately cut them off from his philanthropy. His forced resignation caused a great deal of controversy. Cahn's generosity was missed by many of the local farmers. The Burton Hunt was now divided and upset.

The Times of 24 January 1935 reported that at an extraordinary general meeting of the Burton Hunt a vote of censure was passed on those who sent an anonymous telegram to Sir Julien Cahn which resulted in his resignation. A vote of thanks to Sir Julien was carried unanimously, and the opinion was voiced that 'it would be very hard indeed to find a Master to hunt the Burton country as successfully as he has done for the past nine seasons'.

Perhaps at this point, Sir Julien submitted his name to the Quorn, expressing his interest in taking on their Mastership. The Quorn is where hunting began and it remained the most prestigious of all the hunts. Its founding father, Hugo Meynell, was the first gentleman to exploit Leicestershire's natural advantages as a foxhunting country, and in the late eighteenth century this earned him a reputation in fashionable London and throughout all the great country houses in the land.

It was widely known, certainly among his family, that Sir Julien fervently aspired to assume Mastership of the Quorn. But this was to be denied him. He even bought land in his quest to be accepted – a covert near Wymesfold and another one named 'the curate' – coverts that had once belonged to the Quorn, which he now hoped to return to them.

The only real opportunity to assume Mastership had presented itself in 1928 and then in 1930 when the Masters changed. At that time, Sir Julien had his knighthood but had not yet been awarded the baronetcy. Why would they have wanted Sir Julien, a Jewish shopkeeper, as their Master? It surely was inconceivable that the most English of all English institutions could have accepted him. Sir Julien must have realised that. Instead, in 1930, Sir Harold Nutting became Master and continued in this role until 1939, when, with the arrival of the war, most gave up hunting altogether. Sir Harold had partly earned his fortune from bottling Guinness. A senior Army man, Lieutenant-Colonel Sir Harold Nutting, was a perfectionist and dedicated to the hunt, and he successfully ensured its financial well-being.

Instead, Sir Julien agreed to become Master of the Woodland Pytchley Hunt. With its large grass fields and thick, thorn hedges with a ditch on one side, it was considered one of the toughest of the Leicestershire territories to hunt. The Pytchley was a first-league hunt. In the 1920s and '30s, Melton Mowbray became one of the most fashionable places to stay for the winter season. Edward, Prince of Wales, who was to be Edward VII briefly before abdicating, adored hunting in Leicestershire particularly with the Quorn, Cottesmore and Belvoir hunts, but the Duke of York, who became King George VI, rode in the Pytchley country for several seasons. Sir Julien was Master of important territory.

It soon became apparent that only a handful of relationships had broken down at the Burton Hunt, between a few vociferous and influential members. The staff were so loyal to Sir Julien that a number of them followed him to the Woodland Pytchley. These include the 'whippers-in' (the men who help the huntsman look after the hounds in the kennels and keep all the hounds together when out hunting), Fred Phillpotts and Cecil Gooch. They were joined by the Hunt Secretary, Captain Charles Deane. During his first season as newly appointed Master, a large number of member supporters from the Burton Hunt travelled with their horses in a special train, laid on by Sir Julien, for a day's hunting with the Woodland Pytchley. Either there were genuinely no hard feelings towards their previous Master or, on a more cynical note, perhaps they were pleased to be able to partake once again of Sir Julien's considerable generosity.

These were busy years for Sir Julien, years when he had numerous social and charitable commitments, weekly trips to London and regular lengthy trips abroad. He didn't remain long as Master of the Pytchley. However, he did take on another commitment, a commitment that was to fulfil yet another of his dreams.

All of his life Sir Julien had had a fascination with magic. In the early 1930s, he became involved in the Magician's Club and attended performances of the leading magicians of the era. However, he had not the time or the opportunity to actively indulge his interest in magic until he was well into his fifties.

In the 1920s, Julien would visit Professor Edwards' Magic Emporium in Stoughton Street, Leicester. It was here that, in 1925, a young man called Eddie Ward linked up with Edwards and various other magicians in order to start a magic society that they called the Leicester Magic

Circle. Shortly afterwards, Wilf Hubbard opened his magic shop in Leicester opposite the station and this revived interest in magic locally. It was frequented by Chris Van Bern, a famous magician who changed water into wine, made flowers appear in his buttonhole and was the first magician to use a gramophone in his repertoire, talking to a record that spoke back to him. No doubt he provided some of the inspiration for Cahn's famous gramophone opera trick. Van Bern also changed oversized playing cards into a crying baby, a telephone into a bouquet of flowers and developed many other startling effects.

In 1935, the Leicester Magic Circle moved premises to the White Hart Hotel, an old coaching inn. The members realised that if the society was to move forwards and grow it needed to be run on a proper business footing. They approached Sir Julien to become President. His interest in magic was widely known, for he was already a member of the prestigious Magician's Club in London. Other members of the Committee included famous illusionists such as Chris Van Bern and D. Deveen (who subsequently wrote a book entitled *Cigarette Magic*), W. Cyril Gibbons (whose stage name was Cyraldo) and Eddie Ward. Julien accepted the position with glee and spent more and more time watching, reading and learning about magic from the masters.

September 1935 was an important time for the Cahn family – it was the first occasion that all of the Cahn children had been sent away to boarding school.

Patience, known as Pat, was Sir Julien's adored eldest daughter, the apple of her father's eye. Initially, she was educated at the PNEU School on Waverley Street, an independent preparatory school in Nottingham where she made some of her closest friends. At the age of 12 she was sent to board at Moira House, in Eastbourne. Although it was far away, it was convenient in so far as Albert and Richard were also sent to a small prep school in Eastbourne, St Cyprian's. On occasion, the boys were allowed to visit their elder sister at school. Albert was particularly privileged to be invited to join all the girls for tea. The food was superior to that at St Cyprian's and Albert couldn't believe his eyes when he was offered cakes. 'Can I have another one please?' he asked the stern-looking, pig-tailed girl sitting next to him. 'Pat Cahn's brother wants another cake!' she whispered to the girl sitting next to her, who in turn relayed the same message all the way down the long row of seated girls until the message arrived at the girl in charge of the remaining cakes. As the cakes were passed back up the long table, the message was repeated, much to Pat's great embarrassment.

Pat was a willful girl and enjoyed flouting the rules of society, particularly flirting with the boys. Perhaps after pushing one too many boundaries, she was removed from Moira House and brought home to be educated by a French tutor called Marcelle. Later she went to the Monkey Club, a finishing school in London where she became very friendly with the ward of Vic Oliver, the famous comedian and violinist. Oliver, an Austrian Jew whose real name was Jo Plotz, was married to Sarah, Winston Churchill's daughter. Vic Oliver became a frequent visitor to Stanford Hall, performing in the theatre as well as enjoying his host's productions.

Albert and Richard were both sent to boarding school at the age of 8. Sir Julien chose St Cyprian's for his sons after playing a memorable game of cricket against a side that included Bill Tomlinson, the school's headmaster. Tomlinson impressed Sir Julien, extolling the virtues of his school, explaining that his charges were more or less guaranteed to get into the leading public (private) boys' schools at the age of 13. With such famous alumni as George Orwell, various Indian princes and attended by the sons of most of the leading industrialists of the day, Sir Julien needed little persuading. Indeed, among Richard Cahn's fifty contemporaries there was Alan Clarke MP, the son of H. Sichel Sohne, the German creator of Blue Nun wine, the son of Lord Halifax, the son of a bishop and many other notable names, none of whom the Cahn boys stayed in touch with.

In September 1935, the boys were dispatched to school via a train from Leicester accompanied by their governess, Waity, and their large school trunks. Crossing London, they caught the 'school train' from Waterloo where, unlike the pictures conjured up in the Harry Potter books and films, fifty little boys sat in their school uniforms gazing miserably out of the train windows. At least little Richard had his brother Albert to look after him. Albert had had no one. Sir Julien and Lady Cahn never visited their sons at school. In fact, the only people who took an interest in the Cahn boys during term time were Ernest and Ada Atkinson, friends of the Cahns who lived in Alfriston, and Great Aunt Sheba, the aunt who had facilitated Sir Julien's triumphant win on the Derby in 1929.

The highlight of the week was the Sunday visit to Aunt Sheba who lived in the Grand Hotel, Eastbourne. Aunt Sheba, who was in fact Phyllis Cahn's aunt and the member of the Wolfe family whom Sir

Julien held in the highest esteem, was a red-haired lady who, upon her husband's premature death, retired to a suite in the Grand Hotel. With no children of her own, she took a keen interest in the Cahn boys. Albert had already left St Cyprian's but Richard was allowed to take a friend with him as they walked the half a mile or so to the hotel every Sunday. The boys would eat as much as humanly possible, storing up for the interminable week ahead.

It was the Atkinsons, however, that gave Richard the highlight of his Eastbourne years. At a cost of 10s, they paid for him to go for a ride in a light aeroplane high above the white cliffs of Dover and along the Sussex coast line. This gift experience was kept from Sir Julien for quite some time as he most certainly would not have approved! After a particularly scary flight in Russia, a country Julien had visited as part of his medical research in 1932, he distrusted aeroplanes and swore never to fly in one again.

While Richard shone at mathematics, Albert's talents lay in horse riding. No country estate was complete without its stables and horses. Horses were a vital part of the Cahns' life, essential for hunting and a passion for Albert Cahn. Charlie Rodgers was the head groom, living in a house with his wife attached to the garages and stables. He taught Albert to ride and was largely responsible for assisting him to become a proficient show jumper.

Albert was an exceptionally talented horse rider, which in the eyes of his father slightly made up for both the boys lacking in terms of cricketing skills. By the age of 8 Albert had competed at Olympia and was winning show jumping and dressage classes in every show and gymkhana he entered. In 1932, Albert won a staggering nine silver cups at the Kingston Show, organised by Lord and Lady Belper at their home Kingston Hall, Kegworth. Sadly for Albert, his father didn't show any interest and he never watched his eldest son win at the shows. The only support Albert had was from Waity, who never failed to cheer on her young charge. Nevertheless, Albert was expected to perform on horseback at Stanford Hall whenever his parents had guests staying for the weekend. On Sunday mornings a full set of show jumps was erected on the field below the gardens and Albert was expected to demonstrate his prowess on the back of his beautiful iron-grey horse called Silver. Silver had been bought from a famous horse dealer called Fred Todd – 'the finest horse that ever looked through a bridle!' When Albert eventually outgrew Silver, Todd agreed to take the horse back and put him into retirement. Some years later, Albert discovered that he

1. Julien and Phyllis Cahn's wedding, 11 July 1916.

2. Phyllis Cahn.

3. Julien Cahn in his early thirties.

4. Papplewick Grange.

5. Housemaids at Papplewick Grange.

6. Staff outside Papplewick Grange.

7. The Cahns with their hunting entourage.

8. Picture of Julien Cahn as Master of the Burton Hunt as appeared in the *Whitehall Gazette*, February 1927.

9. Sir Julien Cahn's XI *c.* 1931.

10. Claridge's ballroom, 11 August 1933.

11. Nottingham Furnishing Company truck.

12. Nottingham Furnishing Company on Parliament Street, Nottingham, 1931.

13. Sir Julien Cahn XI, photo from the opening match of the 1938 season against Nottingham University at Loughborough Road. Back row: R.E.C. Butterworth, C.R.N. Maxwell, J.A. Walsh, J.B. Hall standing behind V.E. Jackson with J.G. Lush & J.R. Gunn (umpire) far right; front row: D.E.P. Morkel, F.C.W. Newman, Sir Julien Cahn, R.C. Blunt, G.F. Summers.

14. Richard, Phyllis and Albert Cahn, *c.* 1934.

15. Sir Julien Cahn dressed up to receive his baronetcy.

16. Portrait taken by Brassano.

17. Julien and Phyllis Cahn with their staff on their first day at Stanford Hall, 1928.

18. Stanford Hall, Loughborough.

19. Cahn's bedroom.

20. The baronial entrance hall.

21. The drawing room.

22. The dining room.

23. Julien Cahn's library.

24. The Italian gardens.

25. The badminton hall.

26. Stanford Hall's swimming pool.

27. The theatre.

28. The Stanford Hall theatre stage.

29. Bob Mason with a sea lion.

30. Richard, Pat and Albert, 1937.

31. The Duke of Westminster, Lord and Lady Belper, Sir Julien and Lady Cahn and other dignitaries at Kingston Hall.

32. Cahn's Rolls Royce.

had in fact sold Silver on and the horse continued in his winning vein for many more years.

As Albert grew older, he would frequently join his parents hunting. Pat and Richard never developed the same skill for riding. In fact, Richard recalls that one of the few times he rode a horse he managed to clamber onto the horse's back and found himself seated backwards, facing the horse's rump! On another occasion, he quickly lost control of the horse and found himself trotting down the road to Rempstone, whereupon the horse decided to enter the open door of Rempstone church. When they were introduced to hunting both Albert and Richard were subjected to the barbaric tradition of 'blooding'. When someone, normally a child, witnesses their first kill (when the hounds kill the fox) the fresh blood of the fox is smeared on the child's face. Richard, who was squeamish at the best of times, was quite disgusted by this ritual and it put him off hunting forever more.

At the age of 12, both boys were sent to public school. Albert was sent to Harrow, apparently because it was smaller than Eton and thus it was considered that he had a better chance of getting into the first cricket XI. Unfortunately for Sir Julien, while both his sons inherited his ineptitude for the game, neither of them inherited his passion for cricket. In 1938, Patsy Hendren, one of the most famous batsmen to play for Middlesex and England, was appointed cricket coach at Harrow, resulting in Harrow's first win against Eton for thirty-one years. Albert, then fourteen years old, was already well established at the school. George Wolfe, Sir Julien's brother-in-law, was friendly with Hendren, and approached him about Albert.

'If Albert Cahn gets into the first XI at Harrow I'm sure that you will receive a fabulous present!' he whispered in Hendren's ear, none too subtly.

'If you gave me £1,000, I still couldn't get him in!' replied Hendren acerbically.

Unfortunately, the pressure on Albert to play cricket only reinforced his dislike for the game. It is ironic that despite all of their first-class coaching, neither Albert nor Richard had any greater skill at the game than their father. Although Richard was to become interested in cricket as an adult, eagerly taking advantage of his MCC membership, the true love of the game was only passed on to Sir Julien's eldest grandson and namesake. Julien, eldest son of Albert and born long after Sir Julien's death, has contributed much to the cricket training of the UK's under-privileged youth.

Meanwhile, in 1937, Richard was still at St Cyprian's when at 5 a.m. the school burned down. Fortunately, no one was hurt but it signalled the beginning of the demise of the school. Richard doesn't recall any member of the Cahn family rushing down to check if their little boy was alright! Instead, he remembers a sense of adventure as the boys were hurriedly sent to Whisper's School in Midhurst, which was at that time fortuitously empty. By 1939 and the onset of the war, St Cyprian's was to close its doors, never to re-open. The memories of this school were not particularly happy ones for either boy, although little Richard enjoyed peaceful moments spent on his school allotment, a precursor of his future vocation in horticulture.

Richard was expected to join Albert at Harrow in 1939. However, at the beginning of the war, a bomb was dropped on the Harrow playing fields, and so Sir Julien quickly sought another school for his youngest son. Uppingham was considered a safer venue and certainly nearer to home, and thus Richard was dispatched there for a miserable four years. The harsh regimes of public school, along with the pervasive anti-Semitism, made Richard's school years desperate. Fortunately, he was an able scholar and spent his time immersed in his books, unusually for the time studying both classics and science.

Despite living in such lavish surroundings, Sir Julien tried hard to instill in his children a sense of value and an understanding of money. His ambition, often expressed but never realised, was for both his sons to train in accountancy prior to joining the family business. During their childhoods, the boys were given minimal pocket money for which they had to prepare ongoing profit and loss accounts. These were then presented to their father on a weekly basis before he issued them with their next installment of pocket money. Phyllis Cahn thought her husband quite mean in the way that he controlled the children's pocket money and would frequently hand over coins to her children, surreptitiously and on strict instructions not to tell.

Richard was a very slight boy and his mother was concerned that he was all skin and bones. To Albert's dismay, Phyllis offered Richard 2s for every pound of weight he put on. Despite eating as much as he could, he didn't put on much weight and earned very little extra money.

While they were never really short of money, the Cahn children were not flush with cash to spend as they wished. When he was

15, Richard sold his impressive stamp collection in order to finance a motorbike. Under the terms of a trust set up by Cahn in 1928, the children would not come into any money until Richard, the youngest, reached the age of 21. Initially, this trust was to divide the income of his companies equally among his three children. However, these conditions were later changed, so that under the terms of his will the funds were divided, four sevenths to Albert, the eldest and heir, two sevenths to Richard and one seventh to Pat. Clearly, Sir Julien did not believe in female equality. In fact, this was probably done in light of the fact that Sir Julien's hereditary baronetcy would pass to Albert, who would need additional funds to execute it. Even so, considering the huge wealth that Sir Julien had enjoyed during his lifetime, the children did not inherit great sums. Most of the money had been dissipated on his death or given up in death duties, income and higher rate taxes that equated to 98p in the pound.

Despite all of their wealth and materialistic luxuries, the Cahn children were shown very little attention by their parents. This was typical for the era. The children used to put on their own shows in the nursery to which the staff were invited to attend; these shows were never viewed by their parents. The pillowcases (stockings were too small) stuffed full of toys for the children at Christmas were selected by Waity.

Occasionally, on a quiet evening, Sir Julien would ascend to the day nursery on the top floor to play Ludo or card games with the children. He started off teaching them 5 Card Nap and moved on to Whist and then Solo Bridge. However, he refused to play Monopoly because the board stated 'pay super tax' rather than 'pay surtax' – super tax being an American term and thus an incorrect description. Cahn, in a peculiarly pedantic manner, refused to endorse a game that could teach his children a false fact. Instead, the children played Monopoly with Waity, who always lost.

Shortly after Richard went to boarding school, Waity was given her own flat in Nottingham and started work for Sir Julien at the Nottingham Furnishing Company. Working in administration, she became a firm friend of Nancy Cherry who was in charge of all the 'girls' at Sir Julien's business headquarters.

In 1935, Sir Julien sponsored three German Jewish girls, refugees and possibly distant relatives, to come to England under his care. Hilda, Helga and Ruth were put up in a house purchased especially by Sir Julien in Sherwood. Waity was moved into the house to care for them. The three girls received an excellent education under the guidance of Sir Julien and they eventually all moved to the USA. But Waity remained an integral member of the Cahns' retinue.

Music was an essential part of Julien's life. During the weeks in which he made his slow recovery from influenza in 1934 he spent many hours listening to opera on his newly acquired gramophone. Julien particularly enjoyed the human voice and although he organised all the modern bands of the day to play for his various charitable events, it was opera that he favoured listening to. In an evening, beautiful voices could be heard singing Verdi and Mozart, arias floating through the corridors. Inside the morning room, Sir Julien would be following the scores, conducting an imaginary orchestra viewed by a make-believe audience. Family and servants were strictly prohibited from entering the room while the music was playing. The operas were played on his auto-change gramophone, a unique record player that could hold up to twelve records picked up from one stack and deposited upon another for automatic playing. Sir Julien owned every single opera that was available on record, a total of 124. This would prove to be extremely useful for his infamous 'opera' trick, which he was to perform in the late 1930s. Records in those days were made from shellac, a material made from the excretion of a beetle, a cotton compound, powdered slate and a wax lubricant. They were extremely brittle and with the slightest movement were easily broken. Richard called the autotrope record player the 'cruncher' as it tended to crunch up the records.

Wherever possible, Sir Julien tried to get involved in live music. He had attended the Nottingham Harmonic Society's performances since childhood, a choir and orchestra founded for the musical education of the people of Nottingham.

During the first fifty years of existence, it attracted some of the leading conductors of the day. Charles Hallé visited regularly, Sir Arthur Sullivan conducted a performance of his oratorio *The Martyr of Antioch* and in the same season Dr Hans Richter conducted a concert of music by Dvorak.

By the turn of the century, the Society had become so well known and proficient that Henry Wood, later Sir Henry Wood, founder of the Promenade Concerts, used to travel up from London by train once a week to rehearse the choir and orchestra. The works they performed included the Handel oratorios, the large choral works by Beethoven,

Haydn, Mendelssohn, Mozart etc. but also relatively modern works for the time: Wagner operas (in concert form), Parry and Gade.

The competence of the Society continued to attract the best conductors and choral trainers during the 1930s, in particular Roy Henderson and Sir Hamilton Harty. By this time, the Nottingham Harmonic Society was firmly established as one of the leading provincial choruses in Britain.

While their musical skills were unquestionable, the management of the Society proved another matter and during those inter-war years, finances became severely strained. By 1934, it was apparent that the regular engagements of professional orchestras would be too costly for the Society. The members tried desperately to raise funds through various fundraising initiatives. The obvious solution was to reduce the number of concerts, so only two were planned for the 1934–5 season. During this time, Sir Julien was promoting concerts as a means of raising money for the National Birthday Trust Fund. Arthur Foulds, the son of Charles Foulds for whom Sir Julien had worked at the start of his career, discussed the Society's financial hardship with Sir Julien, who in turn came up with a solution. He explained that the Society would be likely to suffer from competition with his charity concerts, and so he offered to merge the two, and to take on financial responsibility for the cost of two choral concerts in each season. In addition, he agreed to contribute 25 guineas per concert towards the working expenses.

When President Alderman Manning died in April 1934, the obvious successor was Sir Julien. G.C.A. Austin, in *The History of the Nottingham Harmonic Society* written in 1955, describes the association with Sir Julien as resulting in 'a dazzling array of celebrity names' appearing on the concert list. Of course, it also secured the Society's financial stability.

Sir Julien organised leading international artists to perform at the Albert Hall in Nottingham – artists such as Yehudi Menuhin, Horowitz, Gigli and Conchita Supervia. When the Harmonic Society sung Delius' *Sea Drift* accompanied by the London Philharmonic Orchestra, they were conducted by Sir Julien's good friend, Sir Malcolm Sargent. On 17 January 1935, there was a fabulous concert performed by Horowitz and Conchita Supervia. Then on 27 March 1935, the Society sung *The Apostles* in memory of Sir Edward Elgar, who had just died, accompanied by six leading soloists and the London Symphony Orchestra. With Sir Julien at the helm, only the best would do.

On 12 December 1935, Heifetz performed, conducted by Roy Henderson. During the 1935–6 season, the stars were Tauber, Heifetz and Corto. The London Symphony Orchestra accompanied two other works in the season, Elgar's *Music Makers*, conducted by Harty with Enid Cruikshank starring, and Vaughan Williams' *Sea Symphony*, conducted by Sir Malcolm Sargent. Interestingly, there was no Messiah concert that year, perhaps due to Sir Julien's distaste for such religious music.

Julien tried to pass on his passion for music to his children but with little success. Albert was taught the oboe, Pat the flute and Richard the organ. Julien himself was a poor viola player. The unlikely ambition was for the four of them to form a quartet. Shortly before being shipped off to boarding school, 8-year-old Richard hatched a plan. The *pièce de résistance* in the entrance hall was a 6ft-wide, three-tiered carved antique oak arms rack that contained seven ornate ceremonial swords and spears. Clearly meant for decoration rather than use, this point was missed by the normally meek-mannered Richard who decided to test the efficacy of the weapons. Richard had taken a dislike to his organ teacher, Mr Barton Hart, who, undeterred by Richard's lack of musical talent and spurred on by the considerable fees he was earning for teaching the recalcitrant young boy, nagged and chastised Richard week after week. Richard had had enough. He marched into the entrance hall, checked no one was looking and grabbed the smallest of the ceremonial spears. Crouching behind an oak coffer, he lay patiently in wait. Sure enough, the doorbell rang, a footman opened the entrance door and in strode the unsuspecting music teacher. Then Richard charged. Spear pointing directly at the man, little Richard leapt forward and gave chase. The terrified organ teacher ran straight out of the front door never to be seen again. And so ended Richard's organ lessons. Although Richard was told off for this escapade, his father thought the whole incident hilarious and the tale was recounted with much mirth for many decades.

In addition to music, Julien had a great passion for literature. He was extraordinarily well read and with his photographic memory could quote from numerous volumes. Despite this, he never encouraged his children to read and their nursery was almost void of books. Caroline Weinberg was a leading figure in the Nottingham Jewish community. She founded the Jewish Girls' Club, which taught music, eurhythmics, cookery and tennis to young girls. She organised many concerts and dances and was much admired by the Cahns. In the 1930s, she formed a literary society with the help of Sir Julien and Lady Cahn, to which eminent speakers were invited, including Sir Norman Birkett (leading QC), Blanche Dugdale (niece of Lord Balfour) and the leading Romanian Jewish scholar Moses Gaster.

While there were no overseas tours in 1934 or 1935, the Sir Julien Cahn XI team scored such huge totals that E.E. Snow considered them to have been a sufficiently strong side to have probably finished in the top half of the county championship. As an example, Morkel and Summers both exceeded totals of 2,000 runs.

R.J. Crisp was the only newcomer to play for the side in 1936. He was a very fast bowler, possibly the fastest in the world and a big hitter who played in four test matches for South Africa against Australia in 1935 and in five tests against England.

Between his two grounds, Cahn welcomed all of the major touring teams that visited England, with the single exception of the Australians, as well as county and club teams in profusion, typically attracting crowds of 5–6,000. All of the Sunday games played by the team took place at Stanford Hall. Every team was treated to lavish hospitality and the joys of country-house cricket. Luncheon feasts were served in striped marquees in the grounds. Post-game activities included formal evening dinners often followed by swimming parties or squash competitions. It has been said that cricket cost Sir Julien in the region of £20,000 per year. That is equivalent to just under £1 million today.

By the summer of 1936, Cahn had accumulated probably the finest team of cricket players in the world. He was able to attract and retain the very best cricketers. He paid them well and gave them a fascinating life. This inspired extraordinary loyalty. While his players may have joked privately about their captain's lack of cricketing prowess, they held him in the very highest esteem and were utterly respectful to him in every other way. Of course, not everybody was lured to join the Cahn line-up. Tommy Wass, Nottingham's greatest wicket-taker, expressed his disapproval of Cahn's hire-purchase business and said, 'I'm not working for a fellow who sells you a lot of furniture and takes it back six months later.'

Wass's sentiments were the exception. Most of the young, talented cricketers of the 1930s would have leaped at the chance to be employed by such a bountiful benefactor.

Harry Blankley of Crossman Street, Sherwood, wrote a charming letter to a local Nottingham newspaper. He explained how he had played for the Civil Service team who played against Cahn's team in the summer of 1920. He was a left-arm bowler and had already taken a few wickets when Cahn came in. Cahn was playing his stroke well after Blankley made a mess of his stumps. After the game, Blankley got talking to one of Cahn's players. He was told, 'you won't be asked to take a job in any of his shops after bowling him first ball!'

All the same, Blankley went on to say what a generous man Julien Cahn was and how everyone in the city was delighted when he received his knighthood. He also commented that he often wondered what would have happened if he had not 'boobed' by bowling Cahn out first ball that afternoon.

So as to maintain their amateur status, Cahn employed many of his cricketers in his shops. In reality, they worked in Cahn's vast furniture business during the winter and when they were not on tour. Tommy Reddick was one of the very few with an agreement and ended up managing twelve furniture shops in the south of England. He started his career studying methods of furniture manufacture at one of Cahn's associate upholstery factories. Within three months he was moved to a large Jays store in Manchester for the winter. The following are examples of the roles the cricketers played in the Cahn empire. Tich Richmond became manager of Smart & Brown on Parliament Street when his contract with Nottinghamshire County Cricket Club ended. John Scotton and Henry Pattinson were also shop managers. F.W. Newman was a shop supervisor and later a director of the firm. Roger Blunt spent time in the advertising department, Dennis Morkel was set up by Cahn in his own motor business, John Hall was funded by Cahn to run his own rope and twine business in the centre of Worksop, Ray Munt was supported in running a wine and spirits firm and George Heane became a farmer, working one of Cahn's farms.

Tommy Reddick was one of Julien's key players. Many of the stories he told were pulled together in an article written by Gerald Pawle for *Wisden Cricket Monthly* in September 1982. Although he travelled the world, Reddick claimed that there were no experiences quite as remarkable and bizarre as his demanding apprenticeship with the Cahn circus, a phrase much banded around.

Young and inexperienced, Reddick recalls that Sir Julien seemed a hard and unreasonable task master. At the start of his employment he played very little, and so secretly went to Worcestershire for a trial. Furious, Cahn decided, nevertheless, to give him a few chances, but demanded that Reddick attend every match.

> When I did get a game, I found I did not have to compete only with the opposition, often of test class – I had to compete with my own side. Twice I was blatantly run out by players anxious to remove any challenge from a newcomer. It was a cut-throat business with no holds barred.

The players knew that if they played well their jobs were safe. Reddick stated that 'you have no ideas of the strain we played under'. He described a particular match played against Warwickshire in a roaring gale:

> A ginger-haired bowler was swinging the ball fantastically. I was soon out and in came Maxwell, one of the most brilliant batsman wicket-keepers I have ever seen.
>
> 'Don't worry Sir Julien,' he said as he left the pavilion, 'just leave it to me!'
>
> He was out immediately and we barely struggled past the hundred. Cahn sent for his right-hand man, Lofty Newman.
>
> 'Maxwell and Tommy Reddick will never play in my side again', he ordered.
>
> Enraged by this unexpected defeat, he then departed to Monte Carlo. As it happened he made some money and when he came back I went to Newman to find out the form. Newman said he didn't know, told me just to lie low, don't do or say anything. During the next match I kept out of sight while Sir Julien tossed. Then Lofty produced a blank team sheet. When they got to number four I thought my fate was sealed, but Newman suggested me at number five and Cecil Maxwell at six. Not a murmur. This was typical of the situation we had to contend with regularly.

Legend has it that Denys Morkel, assisted by his lifelong friend and teammate John Hall, committed what must have been one of the most audacious of acts. Unusually for him, Morkel was going through a lean period, not playing up to his normal standards. He was becoming increasingly concerned that Sir Julien would not re-engage him for the following season. At the end of each season, Cahn would look through the score book and decide who was to stay and who was to go. Morkel's scores were not looking good. So, together with Hall, he hatched a plan. It is not known exactly where the team was when the treachery was carried out, but it must have been by the seaside. At 2 a.m. when all were fast asleep in their luxury hotel rooms, Morkel and Hall crept out and went back to the cricket ground. They broke into the pavilion and grabbed the Cahn XI score book. They then ran down to the shorefront and hurled the book into the sea. Needless to say, they feigned amazement at the disappearance of the score book the next day. But it did the job, for Cahn had no record of Morkel's recent scores and re-engaged him for the following year.

Although it must have been stressful for the young players, it was also an exciting and lavish life, packed full of wonders, fun and luxuries that these men would never have experienced otherwise. For most, it was worth the pressure of having to play well.

A less pleasant tale that elucidates both the pressure Cahn's cricketers were put under and the strings that Sir Julien was able to pull, was recounted by Joseph Shrewsbury, who himself had little positive to say about Sir Julien. He recalled playing in a match against the Cahn XI at Stanford Hall. He played for the Nottingham Post Office, whose home ground for fifty years had been Trent Bridge, making them the second oldest side to play there after the county side. Cahn's team included Newman, Blunt, Dempster, Maxwell, Morkel, Woodhead and Simms. The Post Office team decided they had nothing to lose and having won the toss elected to bat. They eventually declared 166 for 6 – a score that didn't go down well with Sir Julien. When Cahn's team batted, the score was 6 for 2 in the space of four overs, and then, amazingly 44 for 6. That was the end of their success for the day. Dempster and Simms dug in and managed to survive to 111 for 6 at close of play. Shrewsbury recalls seeing the anxious look on Sir Julien's face during those last few overs; defeat by a comparatively unknown club side was unthinkable. The Post Office saw it as a moral victory and they had an ebullient journey home.

As was their custom, the Post Office team sent the usual reports to the sports editors of the two Nottingham morning papers and the two evening papers. They were surprised to find no mention of the match in any of the papers on the following Monday. Enquiring as to the reason for the omission, they were politely informed that Sir Julien's secretary had phoned on the Saturday evening and asked that no reports of the match should be published. Shrewsbury recounts that they never got a satisfactory explanation, although the results of the game and the comparative scores were reason enough. Some weeks later, in conversation with a journalist for the *Journal* and *Evening News*, Shrewsbury was told that it must be remembered that Cahn had tremendous influence in business circles, including the local press. None of the papers would risk losing the large advertising revenue in connection with his furniture stores. Some may say that little has changed over the last century.

While Julien expected commitment and high standards from his players, he also subjected himself and his children to the same harsh practice regimes. At his secondary ground at Stanford Hall there was a net where Sir Julien had his practice sessions with Chesham, his engineer, and the bowling machine. Cahn was one of the first cricketers before the Second World War to have a bowling machine, imported from Australia. Richard and Albert recall the device vividly, mainly because as young boys they were terrified of it! The bowling machine was effectively a giant catapult that hurled the ball into the air with amazing accuracy. It was a wooden contraption on wheels with an arm. The ball was put loosely into a jaw, at the end of which lay a small piece of leather and a drawing pin which was inserted into the ball either to the left or right of the seam. This imparted the spin to deliver a leg break or an off-break. To operate it the strap was pulled one way for spin, the other way for googlies. The speed and trajectory were regulated by the distance the catapult was drawn back – and the user had to be quite strong to operate it. The bowling machine was kept at Stanford Hall for the use of the Cahn family, and was used as little as possible by the two Cahn boys.

Interestingly and somewhat surprisingly, although both Albert and Richard received the very best coaching at Trent Bridge from Fairfax, neither of them was ever taught how to bowl. Their coaching was limited to batting only – they were not even taught the rudiments of bowling. No one, his sons and the coach included, would have questioned Sir Julien's instructions. One must assume that this was due to Sir Julien's disappointment that neither of his sons was left-handed. In those days, every team would boast a left-handed slow spin bowler, so left-handed bowlers were very much in demand. Although Albert bowled quite successfully underarm for his prep school's first eleven, unsurprisingly he made no inroads into cricketing success at Harrow.

Despite the many stories about his poor playing, Sir Julien did have a couple of personal notable cricket successes – in particular against one of the world's greatest left-handers, Frank Woolley. In any match that Woolley played in, Cahn would always go on to bowl when Frank came in to bat – and invariably he trapped him.

'Here comes my rabbit,' Cahn said as Woolley was approaching the wicket.

Then Cahn served up an innocuous delivery. Ginty Lush recalls watching Cahn play against Woolley at Stoke-on-Trent and Loughborough and both times Cahn gained Woolley's wicket.

On one occasion in an over before lunch, Cahn bowled Duleepsinhji, probably India's greatest batsman, with a very high-pitched full toss. Halfway through the ball's flight, Duleepsinhji seemed to lose interest and sat on the end of his bat handle awaiting a return from outer space. The look of consternation on his face when the ball landed flush on top of two trembling bails was a picture indeed.

These personal cricket successes were commemorated in the form of Julien's most prized objects – six cricket balls, mounted on silver and ebony stands. The balls commemorated matches in which Sir Julien had taken a wicket. The details of the match, including dates, were engraved onto the silver stands. Along with the huge books on magic with ornate locks, their keys dangling from a chain fastened to the cover, written by Will Goldston, they took pride of place on Sir Julien's mantelpiece in his library.

During the mid-1930s, Sir Julien was invited to join a number of extremely prestigious organisations, bodies that would bring him even greater respectability and influence at the very heart of national and international affairs. In 1934 he joined the council of 'The bribery and secret commissions prevention league'. More importantly, in 1936 he was appointed a Founder Member of Chatham House, at the same time as Viscount Astor and Sir Henry Price. His appointment followed a now familiar routine. He was considered an interesting, influential man of commerce and social standing, but he swayed the decision by making a substantial donation of well over £1,000.

The Institute of International Affairs, now known as the think tank Chatham House, was set up in 1919 to encourage and facilitate the scientific study of international questions and to provide and maintain information on international affairs. In particular, it researched international politics. Stephen King-Hall, in his publication entitled 'Chatham House: A brief account of the Origins, Purposes and Methods of the Royal Institute of International Affairs', published in 1937, states that the purpose of Chatham House was 'to collect, examine and distribute information on imperial and foreign, political, economic and social problems'. The Institute owes its development to generous benefactors who came forward at critical stages of its development. Cahn gave his considerable sum in 1936. Although there were 2,400 members, there was only a handful of Founding Members.

In 1936 Sir Julien offered a cup to the Leicester Magic Circle that was to be given to the member who presented the most original effect. It was to be known as the Sir Julien Cahn Cup and is still presented annually. That first year, the cup was won by Cyraldo (Cyril Gibbons), who went on to acquire many of Cahn's magical effects after his death. Jack Chesham, Sir Julien's trusty magical sidekick and estate engineer, was also a member of the Leicester Magic Circle and he was one of three judges charged with selecting the winner for the Sir Julien Cahn Cup in 1938.

On 20 May, the Leicester Magic Circle met between 10 p.m. and 2 a.m. to have a rendezvous with the famous Horace Goldin, billed as the Royal Magician, who was performing nearby. It is notable that many events during these years took place in the early hours of the morning. Either our forebears had much more resilience and required less sleep, or they were able to take regular afternoon siestas. Later on in the summer, the Circle was visited by the Great Levante, who was performing at the Opera House in Leicester.

On Saturday 22 October 1936, the Leicester Magic Circle gave its first public show at the Little Theatre, Dover Street. The Grand Night of Magic received phenomenal newspaper coverage. At the second annual dinner on Thursday 16 November, Lady Cahn presented Cyraldo with the Sir Julien Cahn Cup. In its first year, the Leicester Magic Circle made over 500 appearances in different venues. With its extraordinarily high standard of magic, the Leicester Magic Circle was already established as one of the leading magic societies in the United Kingdom, as indeed it remains today.

At the end of the evening of the second annual dinner, Sir Julien announced that he would be taking his cricket team on a tour to the Far East in February 1937 and that he had been invited to attend the Singapore Magic Circle annual dinner.

On 30 December 1936, Sir Julien invited all of the Circle members to Stanford Hall. For the first time, Sir Julien presented a one-hour magic show, where he performed alongside Rupert Hazel, Mario de Pietro and others.

Earlier in the year, Sir Julien had bestowed a little of his philanthropy upon the local community in Stanford-upon-Soar. For the coronation of King George VI and Queen Elizabeth, all the children in the village were given a china cup and saucer as a souvenir. It was paid for by the Cahns and had a picture of the King and Queen and Princess Elizabeth on it. Each cost 2s 1d. It has been said that Cahn contributed little to the local community. Although he had no interest in the local church, he did raise funds to assist in the repairs of the roof and he also organised and paid for the choir boys of Stanford to go on an outing every year, which in latter years saw them collected in the cricket bus and given a ride on *My Sweet Princess*, Lady Cahn's boat.

7

Upstairs & Downstairs

It's Christmas day in the workhouse, the time of all good cheer,
The in-mates hearts were full of gladness and their tummies full of
  beer.
Out spake one bold old pauper, his face as gold as brass
You can keep your Christmas puddings and throw them on the
  grass.

Despite the fact that he himself had invented this, Julien considered the verse absolutely hilarious. When his sons started laughing, at what, they never quite knew, he almost split his sides with mirth.

'You have an excellent memory Albert! Now repeat it with the correct finale.'

'No you will not!' Phyllis quickly interjected. 'Please Julien, don't teach the boys such naughty rhymes.'

Phyllis had a wry grin on her face as she recalled some of the other wicked ditties and songs that her husband had invented, many composed at the expense of friends or staff, and was relieved that he was not spurting forth the particularly crude one about the wife of their cricketer Harry Munt.

Sir Julien loved words – particularly long and unusual ones. After the first completed edition of *The Oxford English Dictionary* was published in 1928, he spent many pleasurable hours reading the tome and, assisted by his photographic memory, he learned new words. Richard recalls asking Waity why Daddy didn't speak English. When his father reprimanded him for telling 'a terminal logical inexactitude', it is hardly surprising that the little boy had no idea that he was being told off for telling a lie! Similarly, 'Stop that concatenation of strident cacophony!' did not result in a reduction of noise. Julien realised that others viewed his use of the English language as pretentious. He did not care. It was a combination of the simple joy he gained from language and his fascination with the British establishment that resulted in a desire for correctness in every aspect of life, whether that be dress code or manners. He was equally pedantic about pronunciation. 'Golf' was pronounced in its proper manner as 'gof' and 'laundry' as 'lowndry'.

Among friends and family, Cahn was known for his wry sense of humour. One December he sent Christmas cards adorned with a photo of the Chief Rabbi to all of his Jewish friends.

In January 1937, Julien decided to float his company. He formed the company Jays and Campbells Holdings Ltd to acquire the entire capital of his various companies, George Hopkinson Ltd, Gosford Furnishing Company, Jays Furnishing Stores and J. Symons & Co. Together these businesses owned 150 furniture stores located in every major town around the country. The holding company, of which Sir Julien was Chairman, had a capital of £3.5 million, one-half in Five-and-a-half cumulative preference shares and the other half in Ordinary shares. The following week a public offer was made of the Preference shares ensuring that Cahn kept the equity. *The Times* stated, 'On a three-years average, the profits of the operating companies cover the Preference dividends more than three times'.

It also explained that the company had been established over fifty years ago and had been gradually built up until it achieved a turnover of £2 million in 1937, the majority of the funds coming from hire purchase. The three directors (Sir Julien, Sir Robert Doncaster and Joseph Freedman – the latter a cousin of Sir Julien) agreed to sign five-year agreements to maintain continuity in management. Julien owned the vast majority of the shares, whereas Robert Doncaster was very much a minority shareholder. This is the first time that Cahn's financial affairs were put into the public domain, and few were surprised to realise that he headed up a business empire worth over £100 million pounds in today's money.

At the beginning of February, the Cahns found themselves in the company of the Queen once again. Queen Mary attended the premiere of *The Great Barrier* at the Gaumont Cinema in Haymarket and among her party were the Cahns, the Baldwins, the Marchioness of Anglesey and the other committee members of the National Birthday Trust Fund. During 1937, Julien was on the committee, normally in the position of Treasurer, of numerous other fundraising events, ranging from film premieres for the Widow and Orphan Fund of the National Union of Journalists to the 'Anti-Dud Ball', the Primrose League Ball and the Ivory Cross Fund. On several occasions, Sir Julien was the speaker at a dinner. One example was a fork luncheon held at Claridge's in November in aid of the Royal Society for the Blind, where Cahn spoke alongside the Earl of Athlone. As President of the Bavarian Christmas Tree Ball (how ironic that the Cahns were sponsoring this), Phyllis and Julien were entertained by Lady Diana Cooper, the social celebrity and actress. In January 1938, the Cahns were invited to attend a private viewing held by the Mars Group of an exhibition to meet Corbusier. This is just a snapshot of their social commitments and simply covers the events they attended in London. In addition to these, they attended hunt balls across the country, private parties and social events in the Nottinghamshire area. They also entertained on a large scale at Stanford Hall.

The visitors' book from Stanford Hall records that there were guests staying most months throughout the 1930s. While many of the signatures are indecipherable, some are clear – the names of Chamberlain, Baldwin, Horowitz, Rothschild and Sargent are all easily distinguishable. The fabulous rooms located on the ground floor were designed especially for entertaining. All were filled with valuable antiques, most sourced from great houses, castles and abbeys by White Allom, and paid for by Sir Julien. All of the carpets and soft furnishings were bespoke, mostly made in France, and with the exception of a few curtains, much of the material was woven especially for the job. The Légion d'Honneur bestowed the award of Officier on Sir Julien. This is a prestigious decoration given by the French to distinguished foreigners; individuals whom the French believe have made a significant contribution to their country or are well disposed towards the French and have held eminent positions. Such awards are made to this day and frequently no specific reason is given. We can speculate that Sir Julien's honour was given due to the vast sums of money he spent in France and the considerable trade he carried out with the French.

Guests would have been entertained in the drawing room, morning room, lounge or very occasionally the boudoir. All were finely decorated rooms of substantial proportions.

The morning room was painted green, complemented with long silk green curtains. A comfortable room that opened up into the gardens, it was decorated with Chinese lamps, oriental cabinets and red lacquer Chinese wall panels. Although the boudoir, with its blue, silver and rose silk curtains, Chippendale settee and Hepplewhite chairs, was certainly the more refined and exquisitely beautiful room, it was the morning room that was most commonly used for entertaining.

The lounge was a large traditional room with grey soft furnishings, chesterfield settees, mahogany and rosewood tables, card tables, writing tables and numerous chairs. Four decorative leather mural panels in walnut frames were fixed to the walls depicting oriental hunting scenes. This room was used the most by the family and housed a Nake table billiard game with all its accessories and a Balby Product Champion novelty pin table.

The smartest parties and balls were held in the drawing room. This beautiful room even had silvered cornices that were highlighted by the long blue and silver silk brocade curtains. The floor was polished blocked parquet. At one end stood the boudoir grand Steinway piano in rosewood. As none of the family played the piano to any standard, Sir Julien purchased an electrical piano player attachment so that the piano could play itself! The furniture in this room was quite magnificent. There were sixteen Louis XVI armchairs, console tables, carved settees and many Chinese artefacts dating back to the mid-eighteenth century, including a pair of Canton enamel lanterns that came from the Summer Palace in Peking, brilliantly decorated in *famille rose* enamels on an Imperial yellow background.

After dinner, the men would normally retire to the billiards room. The full-sized table, which was valued at the equivalent of £11,000 in today's currency, stood in the centre of the room. Two settees and ten chairs lined the room for onlookers. This was clearly a man's room. There was a roulette table, board and counters and a variety of smoking accessories, including an ebonised pipe rack with sixteen long stem meerschaum and other pipes, various cigarette and cigar boxes, including a cigar box in the shape of a motor car with rubber-tyred wheels. Sir Julien smoked only the finest Punch Havana cigars, lighting a large, fine-quality specimen every night after dinner. However, after a couple of puffs he threw them away. Whenever Phyllis's father, Grandpa Abe, came to stay, he would sneak into his son-in-law's study, relight the cigars and finish them off. Being so aware of social etiquette, Julien was highly critical of anyone who didn't light his cigar properly. The cigar had to be held in hand and not puffed until it was completely lit.

A large carved oak staircase rose from the ground floor to the first floor where, in the central section of the house, the main bedroom suites were located.

There were an extraordinary twenty-seven bathrooms in Stanford Hall, and many more lavatories! Unusually for grand houses of that era, almost all the bedrooms were en suite. Valued guests were put up in one of the fabulous suites on the first floor. The King Charles, the Italian and the Spanish suites each comprised a vast bedroom, dressing room and bathroom interconnected.

The King Charles bedroom was a walnut carved and panelled room highlighted with silver. The walls were panelled with a grey silk moiré enriched with crimson and grey Genoa velvet (Genoa heavy velvet was cut against a glossy satin background; a particularly expensive process resulting in the finest of fabrics). The same fabric was used for the long crimson and grey velvet curtains. A dark crimson fitted carpet lined the floor.

The chimney-piece was constructed from red marble with a white hearth. Iron fleur-de-lis linings and a panelled iron back added to the period feel. Forming the centrepiece of the room were two 3ft-wide walnut bedsteads, finely carved with silvered sides with head panels covered in velvet and moiré. All of the Stanford Hall guest rooms had box hair stuffed mattresses. The beds in the King Charles suite were piled high with pink silk bound blankets, down pillows, antique oriental bedspreads embroidered with flowers and a rich gold appliqué with fringed border, as well as crimson silk eiderdown quilts. Silk fringes, canopies and tassels completed the look. The furniture included a Queen Anne walnut cabinet, bureaux, tables, chest of drawers and chairs. The contents of this suite alone were valued at the equivalent of £38,000 in today's money.

All of the bedroom suites were accessorised to make guests feel as at home as possible. The Spanish bedroom was fitted out with a cycle polo game, squash racquets and balls, leather blotto, ink bottles, pen holders and stationery case for guests needing to write letters, match stands and ash trays (for many guests smoked during that era), trinket boxes and vases. While most rooms had working fireplaces, and in the winter these were kept burning for guests, each room was also fitted with electric fires. In addition, all of the major bedrooms had a metal bell push with flex and plug with at least two buttons – 'maid' and 'valet'. When staff were required, the guest would simply push the appropriate button and their allocated member of staff would come running. It is not surprising that many guests stayed for weeks at a time, sometimes remaining at Stanford Hall even when their hosts had departed abroad. Such comfort could not easily be found elsewhere.

While it was pure luxury and indulgence for the guests of the Cahns, life was not so easy for the staff. The most important member of the Stanford Hall household was the butler. Butlers were like managing directors of an enterprise. They were in highly trustworthy positions, but, as in any organisation, some took advantage of this. During their marriage, the Cahns employed six butlers – Campbell, Dutton, Bridgman, Jones, Godson and Pack, with Dennis Bridgman being the longest serving.

Dennis Bridgman was butler from 1932 until 1940. A popular and respected man, he lived with his wife and son in a flat in the main house. Bridgman came to Stanford Hall with an excellent pedigree, having previously been footman to the Duke of Wellington and worked for the Duke of Grafton. Bridgman was known colloquially as 'Pop', and he certainly was a father figure for most of the servants. The Cahn family and their guests referred to him and all the other staff by their surnames – in his case simply 'Bridgman'.

The Cahns had numerous house parties, with plenty of guests staying at the same time, sometimes for several nights. On such occasions, Bridgman's family would not see him for days on end. He would be up well before dawn, snatch a few hours sleep after all the guests had gone to bed and resume this gruelling routine until the guests departed.

As was the norm for all country estates, during the season guests were often invited to join Cahn's shooting parties. Mr Crisp was the gamekeeper and was employed to breed pheasants and partridges. Each member of the family had their own gun, or guns in the case of Sir Julien and Lady Cahn, who each had their own pair of Holland & Holland guns. Typically, the ladies had 20-bore guns and the men 12-bore guns. The children had guns with small bores.

Crisp had to oversee all the preparations prior to a shoot. He ensured that the guns were cleaned and properly prepared. They were stored in the gun room next to the main hall, although in time this room was to be shared with the monkeys! In those days, the gun cabinets were never locked, but no one would have dared to touch them.

Over the months and years, the woods were especially prepared, making them an ideal habitat for the birds to live and breed in. Crisp successfully bred hundreds of birds. On the day of a shoot, Crisp organised local farmers as beaters. These men would go into the woods to disturb the pheasants. The birds then flew out of the woods, unwittingly setting themselves up to be shot. After they had been shot, the pheasants were hung in Crisp's semicircular thatched outhouse. When they were ready, Crisp would pluck the birds and deliver them to Mrs Bentley for cooking.

The Cahns always had dogs, and certain dogs would assist in the shoot, collecting the dead birds. One of Sir Julien's first dogs was a Dalmatian by the name of Spot. He was buried in a grave in an area of copse known as the 'Dog Kennel Wood'. The small headstone notes that he was killed in that field in a shooting accident. Another Dalmatian was Henry, who died of old age but was remembered by a china replica that lived on the dining-room table and was also called 'Henry' by all the family. Alice, Lady Cahn's maid, had a small Pekingese dog named Ping, which was in fact Lady Cahn's but ostensibly became Alice's pet. The dog was later to be immortalised in a painting by Sir Oswald Burleigh at the feet of the Cahn children.

Out of season, family and guests could still enjoy shooting from the clay pigeon shooting tower. In fact, this tower was more frequently used by staff who would climb up it and lie on top to sunbathe.

Crisp was an amiable man who patiently taught the Cahn boys how to shoot. Richard recalls trying to shoot pigeons and rabbits. When the Cahns wanted to go further afield to shoot they would be taken in the black Rolls Royce that had been especially kitted out in red leather with a gun holder in the centre. Crisp loved the outdoor life and he adored his job.

The life of the housemaids at Stanford Hall was not as onerous as in many country houses of the day. While they had to undertake mundane tasks for the Cahns and their guests, the servants did not have to do much to look after themselves. Their meals were cooked for them and their laundry whisked away and returned washed and ironed. All the same, by today's standards work was all-consuming. The staff had just one day off each month.

Housemaids and footmen were expected to get up at 6.30 a.m. and congregate in the kitchens for a cup of tea. The kitchen staff rose a little earlier. The housemaids all wore cotton, blue-and-white striped dresses with gathered skirts, a stitched belt and white apron. Perched on their heads were quaint white starched caps. Stockings and sensible low-heeled black shoes completed the outfit. They were responsible for general cleaning around the house. Scrubbing steps and floors were all part of the daily routine.

At about 10 a.m. all the servants, including chauffeurs, grooms, groundsmen, maids and footmen, convened in the servants' hall for tea, coffee and bread and butter. Particularly favoured was Mrs Bentley's dripping spread on the bread. A couple of hours later the staff returned for lunch. They ate lunch before the family and guests as they were required to serve at table.

After lunch, normally served at about 2 p.m., the housemaids were free. Some of them would nip into town for a spot of shopping, perhaps visiting Morgan the cobblers in Loughborough, others relaxed in their rooms or roamed the extensive grounds. Then, just before 5 p.m., they changed into their afternoon uniform and returned again to the servants' hall. For many this was the best meal of the day, for the table was set with bread, jam and cakes. After their high tea, they still had a few more duties to perform, depending upon how many people were in residence at Stanford Hall.

The floor in the great hall was the constant bane of the housemaids' lives. Every afternoon when Sir Julien returned home from the office, the chauffeur would hoot to announce their imminent arrival. The footman on duty would rush to the front door to open it and take great enjoyment sliding across the great smooth, shining stone slabs in the hall, invariably leaving behind black gashes where his shoe polish had rubbed off. Immediately, the housemaids would have to rush behind the footman, frantically re-scrubbing the floor to get rid of the marks before Sir Julien entered the house. Despite the daily *rapprochements* from the housemaids, the footmen were not prepared to forego their little skate to the front door.

Most of the housemaids' evening duties had to be done while guests were at dinner. Beds were turned down, hot-water bottles were placed in beds, bathrooms were tidied, towels straightened and curtains pulled. Being the most junior maid, Una Walton also cleaned the other maids' and footmen's bedrooms. In her first week of employment she turned down the footmen's beds in the evening, assuming that everyone's beds should be treated in the same manner. This caused great mirth and amusement among the footmen when they arrived back to their rooms and found they had been subject to the same luxurious treatment as the family.

As the second most senior housemaid, Mabel was responsible for cleaning the most exquisite bathroom in Stanford Hall. Indeed,

Antique Collector magazine believed it to be the finest bathroom of the period to survive in Britain.

> The Adam Bathroom was appropriately furnished and a jib door in one corner leads into a room, reconstructed as an octagon with a glazed roof. The corners contain entrance, shower, lavatory with window over the park and a bidet with a window. The bath is the main feature of the room. Set in a recess lined entirely with Norwegian Rose marble the bath is of white marble sunk into the floor. Above is a central niche lined with white marble, the bronze figure of a boy upon a conch shell illuminated from behind; the effect of light and the water gushing from the shell to pound down on the marble floor is unforgettable, as the bather steps down the white marble steps into the rising water. To either side of the top steps is a low marble wall with shallow soap dishes carved into the top. The ultra-refinement of craftsmanship is to be found here in the minute brass plug holes at the base of each depression. A child could swim a couple of strokes in the bath without reaching the great brass levers set in the wall which operate the mechanism of the draining grille and water mix and flow.

Mabel would pretend that she was bathing in the bathroom. On occasion, she would stand on the low platform that was in fact a weighing machine and watch the elegant pointer on the wall move until it accurately showed her weight. She would stand dreamily gazing into the full-length mirror fitted in one recess, and reluctantly chivvy herself along to clean the shower in another.

The footmen had the most fun when the Cahns were entertaining as they were expected to help out at dinners. John Albert Langsdale and Bill Cover were two cheeky lads who both became footmen in their teens. What fun they had at formal dinners! Footmen were required to stand behind guests' chairs, serve food as necessary and generally fade into the background. As Langsdale and Cover entered the dining room they would rapidly scan the faces of the guests and race each other to stand behind the chair of the prettiest woman in the room. The loser would inevitably have to suffer the knowing smirk of the winner throughout dinner.

As in most substantial households, there were several footmen who reported directly to the butler. Ernest Fletcher was a senior footman employed at Stanford Hall for over ten years. He had previously worked for Dr and Mrs Jaffé, the Cahns' good friends. Although grand by most standards, their house was a fraction of the size of Stanford Hall, so realising that he would have more varied and challenging work at Stanford Hall, they offered Ernest's services to the Cahns. A tall man with a gentle kindly manner, he was particularly liked by the young Cahn boys. Eric Fletcher, Ernest's younger brother, visited Stanford Hall on many weekends. He recalls some of the varied duties that Ernest had to fulfil. These included cleaning the silver, much of which was stored in a massive walk-in safe. Rouge powder was made into a paste and applied to the silver using a finger. Although this was an effective way of cleaning it, it was hard work and time-consuming. Ernest's favourite items were Sir Julien's unique collection of cricket balls each mounted on a silver salver and the solid silver coach with eight horses that stood proudly on the sideboard in the dining hall. The under-footmen were tasked with cleaning the everyday silver – the silver plates used for the Cahns' everyday dining.

In the early 1930s, the telephone exchange was put in – one of the first telephone systems to be installed in a domestic residence. The exchange was in the pantry and was manned at all times by Ernest or one of the other footmen. Every important room in the house had its own extension. If a member of the family wanted something, they would ring the pantry or request an outside line – East Leak 233 or 234.

Lady Cahn loved her animals and when one of her dogs was sick, she asked Fletcher to administer its medicine. The only way he could get the dog to stand still and open its mouth was to hold it firmly between his legs. Lady Cahn was horrified when she learned that Fletcher had acquired ringworm as a result.

A warm-hearted lady, Phyllis cared deeply for all of her staff. Whenever she learned that they had personal problems she went out of her way to try to help. Eric Fletcher remembers the furore after Ernest fell off his motorbike. Similar to many young men, Ernest rode a motorbike and inevitably had an accident on his way home, somewhere near Trent Bridge. Although he was not too badly injured, Lady Cahn insisted that her chauffeur collected Ernest from his parents' home and returned him there on his day off. Imagine the wonder of the neighbours as the shiny cream and brown Rolls Royce pulled up majestically in front of the Fletchers' modest mid-terrace home. The chauffeur walked around to the back of the car, opened the door and out hopped Ernest, attired in full footman's livery in dark blue, tails and silver buttons encrusted with the Cahn crest. The local children flocked all around, staring agog at the splendid car and Ernest's garb.

When the Second World War started, Ernest joined up and fought in the Far East where he had a traumatic time being held as a prisoner of war in Singapore. Upon release he joined the services of Lord Wakehurst, who took him to Australia. He spent the rest of his life there, marrying a lady who also worked for Lord Wakehurst, and living in comfort in Tasmania until his death.

Arthur Harrup was another senior footman and was to become the longest-serving employee of the Cahn family. Along with all of his normal duties, he had the special task of dealing with Simpkin and James, the Loughborough-based grocers and purveyor of fine wines, spirits and liqueurs. Stanford Hall had an extensive cellar, a cool dark room with curved ceilings, proportioned exactly as a proper working cellar should be. Although Sir Julien drank very little alcohol, the cellar was stocked full of the best wines and liqueurs. A fine organiser, Arthur would liaise with Mrs Bentley, the cook, and the butler to ensure that the correct wines were ordered and available for every function.

The rooms were cleaned on a rota, each room receiving a thorough clean on a different day of the week. Everyday grates were cleaned and laid in each room. The maids used white lining paper covered with black lead polish that was put at the front of each grate. Once bedrooms were vacated by family and guests, beds were made, clothes tidied away and bathrooms cleaned. On occasion, the staff would wonder who their master and mistress really were, for Sir Julien and Lady Cahn would go away, leaving their visitors to stay on at Stanford Hall for days at a time. Certain guests would leave plenty of mess. The worst offenders tended to be the visiting cricketers who enjoyed partying well into the night. They stayed in the new wing that was built over the theatre. Even if no one was staying there, the maids had to pull the curtains in all the bedrooms at night and open them up again in the morning.

Some girls had specific tasks. Elsie Bennett was responsible for cleaning out the monkeys' room – a particularly unpleasant and smelly task. Alice, Lady Cahn's personal maid, loved animals, so she cared for the performing canary, Garbo, and the budgerigar, Sunshine, and kept their cages in her room. Both Joan and Elsie, who were housemaids, helped out in the nursery and occasionally, when Miss Waite was absent, they helped put the children to bed.

Most staff arrived at Stanford Hall through connections. Some, such as Ernest Fletcher, were recommended to the Cahns by other families; others were friends or relatives of existing staff. At just sixteen, Una Walton was the youngest of all the housemaids and the younger sister of Elsie, Ida and Freda Walton, all of whom worked for the Cahns. The family came from Durham, an area of the country where there were few prospects for young girls. Elsie, the eldest, responded to an advertisement for staff and joined the Cahn family when they were living at Papplewick Grange. It wasn't long before Ida joined her, followed shortly by Freda, who worked in the kitchens as a maid under Mrs Bentley and Edna. In 1936, Elsie Walton left Stanford Hall. She was missed.

'I wonder if Elsie's younger sister has left school yet?' Rhoda, the head housemaid, asked Mabel, her second in command.

As it happened, Una, aged 16, had just left school and her mother thought it an excellent idea to pack off her youngest to join her sisters several hundred miles away. While she was desperately homesick initially, Una quickly became a key member of the household. A petite girl, she was snapped up by Sir Julien as a stage assistant for his magic performances. Being so small, she was ideal to wriggle through the various tubes and boxes that played such a major role in his illusions. Earning £2 per week, she considered herself to be well paid.

Keeping jobs in the family was commonplace. Another example was Alice (Lady Cahn's personal maid) and her sister Lucy Stowe, who was a more junior housemaid. Perhaps not surprisingly, those families grew. There were an extraordinarily high number of marriages that occurred between various members of the Stanford Hall staff, particularly among the young maids and footmen. Edna, the cook, married Jack Percival, a gardener; Kimberly Jones, a butler, married Alice Stowe, Lady Cahn's maid; Mabel, the second most senior housemaid, married Sandy Thomson, the second-in-command gardener.

Where positions could not be filled through friends or relatives, vacancies were advertised. Sir Julien's businesses spent enormous sums on advertising in newspapers all across the country. None of the papers wished to risk losing Sir Julien's considerable advertising revenue, and there were several occasions when the papers held back from writing derogatory editorial for fear of upsetting the holder of the purse strings. So when Sir Julien's secretaries placed job advertisements, needless to say they obtained prime position within the papers. They did not limit their searches to the local Loughborough and Nottingham papers, but often put adverts in national papers. As all the positions were live-in, it mattered little where the staff came from. Typical of the advertisements seeking domestic staff was one placed by the Cahns in *The Times* early in 1941: 'Parlourmaid required to work with butler in country house. Good wages to experienced woman.'

If a member of staff wished to leave their current employment, it was not uncommon for their employer to assist them. For instance, the following advert was placed to assist Albert Wormall find a new position: 'F.J. Foster, gardener to Sir Julien Cahn, can thoroughly recommend A.J. Wormall as Head Working Gardener. Fully competent in all branches. Aged 34.' In fact, Wormall did not leave, and he and his new wife, Freda Walton (previously a kitchen maid), eventually moved down to Sussex with Lady Cahn after the death of Sir Julien.

The spring of 1937 were quiet months for the staff at Stanford Hall as Sir Julien was fully engrossed in business matters at home, and then the Cahns took a three-month tour abroad and so had little time for entertaining. When the Cahns went abroad on long trips, sometimes for up to four months at a time, this gave the house staff plenty of time for spring-cleaning. The staff particularly enjoyed these months as they could use all the facilities of the house whenever they wished and their working days were short. Una Walton remembers being responsible for the valuable rugs that lay on the floor in the great hall. On warm, dry days she and one of the other maids would have to carry the heavy rugs onto the lawn, pulling them back and forth across the grass to freshen them up. They were then left on the lawns for a couple of hours to air. When Rhoda looked outside one morning and noticed the rugs still lying on the lawn she was livid. Una was severely told off but fortunately for her it hadn't rained that night, so no damage had been done to the rugs, and she received a reprimand rather than being sacked.

On 30 April 1937 Jays & Campbells had their first publicly recorded Annual General Meeting held by Sir Robert Doncaster, as Julien Cahn was in Singapore. He reported that the business had opened twenty new stores in the past year and that the turnover and profitability of the business looked set to increase substantially. Even stronger growth occurred in the following year.

In the spring of 1937, Sir Julien took his cricket team on a nine-match tour of Ceylon and Malaya. The side arrived in Colombo on

4 March and consisted of Cahn, Dempster, Crisp, Peebles, Morkel, Maxwell, Butterworth, Lyon, Rhodes, Reddick, Hall, Goodway, Summers and two New South Wales bowlers who joined the team in Ceylon – Mudge and Walsh. Mudge finished second in the batting averages with 570 runs at an average of 48.83 and Jack was second in the bowling with 45 wickets at 14.22 apiece. The two Australians then went back for the rest of the England season to be joined by Lush the following season. During the 1937 trip, E.G. Wolfe, Cahn's brother-in-law, acted as manager. The team travelled from Colombo to Singapore then on to Kuala Lumpur, Ipoh and Penang.

For many of the players this trip was perhaps the most enjoyable, despite the countries still being under the control of the Raj. They entered a world that was alien to most of them, exotic and enchanting. The only downside was the intense heat and humidity.

John Hall had become well respected by Sir Julien and took on the role of Cahn's bookmaker whenever Sir Julien fancied his chances on the horses. Cahn never put on more than 1s – a modest and restrained sum for such a wealthy man. Although he feigned indifference as to whether he won or lost, he would telephone Hall from wherever he was in the world to find out the result of the race. As John Hall, or JB as he was affectionately known, discovered when he had to place the call himself from Ceylon, the cost of the telephone call was invariably substantially more than the bet itself.

Of the five games played in Ceylon, the most important was that against All Ceylon, which was won by 6 wickets. On the first day of the opening match they discovered that Irish stew was on the luncheon menu. The team were so taken aback that such a hearty, hot meal was proposed, they decided to reject all solids until the evening meal. Breaking all local health rules, they stripped off during the lunch break and lay prone like a row of corpses on trestle tables with electric fans going full blast above them. Charlie, the Tamil dressing-room attendant, then strolled down the line like a hospital matron, ladling into their gaping mouths a mixture of iced minerals, fruit and gin which he politely served from a dirty-looking bucket.

At a farewell lunch given by the Ceylon Cricket Association, Sir Julien was presented with an ebony elephant with a silver howdah and silver trappings; Lady Cahn received a silver cup with fine Kandyan engravings. The players all received silver ashtrays. As part of the ceremony, copious quantities of tea were brewed for the visitors and each member of the party was presented with tea in Kalutara baskets, the traditional baskets woven out of stiff palm leaves from this south-western Sri Lankan town.

The Cahn XI was the first English side ever to visit Malaya. While they were there, a three-day game was played against All Malaya, but was drawn due to rain. There were three country matches in which the local sides proved vastly inferior to the tourists, who were well on top in every game, winning one by an innings. A photograph shows the team in casual whites and open-collared shirts with short sleeves, with the exception of Cahn who was wearing a white suit, the Cahn-coloured tie and two-tone leather shoes.

During their stay, Cahn and his cricketers were guests at a dinner hosted by the Malaya Magic Circle, at Circle House, Amber Road, Singapore. It was quite a new magical society, having been formed in November 1935 with fifteen members. Now, only 16 months later, it boasted some 110 members, a phenomenal growth, and its aim was to create branches throughout Malaya and to work for charitable causes, including the education of poor children.

The President of the Malayan Club, Mr. M.D.P. Gilroy, in toasting the guests, said:

> This function marks a truly great occasion in the history of the Malayan Magic Circle, as we have with us tonight that distinguished amateur magician, Sir Julien Cahn. On behalf of the committee and members it gives me the greatest pleasure to extend a very hearty welcome to Sir Julien and Lady Cahn and their party. Apart from being Vice-President of The Magicians' Club, London, Sir Julien as chairman of their Entertainment Committee is an asset which is the envy of all magicians' clubs.

Mr Gilroy went on to say, 'We wish him and his team success during their stay in Malaya, but at the same time I hope his side will go easy with the "hat tricks" and that Malaya will produce the odd ducks and eggs from their "bag of tricks".'

In response, Sir Julien remarked that he thought he was a better magician than he was a cricketer. He agreed with the views expressing the fellowship of cricket but he opined that there was a greater fellowship among magicians. Travelling in the USA and many parts of the world, he found from his visits that among the fellowship of magicians was the ever-striving desire to work for charitable causes.

'I do not know whether I've heard of any Magic Circle which is more successful and prosperous than yours and I do hope that you will exist for many years to come and go from strength to strength,' concluded Sir Julien, who was accorded Honorary Fellowship of the Malayan Magic Circle.

Cahn is not recorded as having performed at the dinner but there was really no need, for after the meal, the company was treated to an excellent show of oriental magic by Mr Tan Hock Chuan.

In Colombo the opposing side included a fine Singalese player called de Saram who at Oxford had been a tennis and cricket blue. Stewie Dempster made a dive at short leg to snap up one of the very few chances offered by de Saram. At the crucial moment, de Saram's cumbersome pith helmet fell over his eyes causing a complete blackout, and that was that. De Saram went on to become Ceylon's captain, but in 1962 he was a key figure in the right-wing, military-aided attempt to unseat the democratically elected Government of S.W.R.D. Bandarnaike. The coup failed, and de Saram was incarcerated for a long time in Colombo jail.

The team stayed at the Gall Face Hotel, a beautiful, superbly run hotel that is still of world-class standard today. The manager of the hotel recommended the Englishmen visit the fine tailors of Colombo. Consequently, some members of Cahn's side visited a shop one morning to be fitted out with short white tropical dinner jackets. The tailor delivered the garments beautifully cut and finished to their rooms at the hotel by 4 o'clock the same afternoon. Surprisingly, no account was tendered right up until the night before they sailed for Singapore.

Reddick recalled that, 'The ship left early and as we crept from our rooms at an unearthly 5am each debtor disappointingly found his way barred by a body lying prone across his bedroom doorway with something ominously sharp sticking out of his belt. Needless to say, we paid up, chop, chop!'

In Singapore the team was showed around the Singapore Naval Base. The guide was a pompous young Navy officer. At the conclusion of the tour, he asked if they had any questions. Reddick said he was surprised that in spite of the fact that so much of the machinery of the base was below ground, the vital mechanism that controlled the entrance of the dry dock was above ground, a tempting target for any Japanese bomber. He looked at him and drawled, 'You don't really imagine those monkeys will get as far as this?'

Upon his return to England, Julien had to take some time to fulfill his duties as President of Nottinghamshire County Cricket Club. He prepared a book that was published in 1938, entitled *A Hundred Years of Trent Bridge*. This was distributed to all 4,000 members – each with a compliment slip inserted saying that the book was given personally by Sir Julien Cahn. Many of these books are still floating around today and unfortunately are not the collector's items that their fervent owners hoped they would be.

In 1938, Cahn supplied a loudspeaker set for the cricket ground. He also offered to pay the cost of coaching for three years. While this had great benefits for the Club, the offer was not quite as it seemed for it was also of considerable benefit to Cahn himself. George Heane and Stuart Rhodes played for Sir Julien's team. He paid for them to play for Nottingham and suggested they be joint captains in 1935. Although these men were officially amateurs, they were part of Sir Julien's big 'scheme'. He officially employed his finest cricketers within his furniture shops but they were released from their shop duties whenever cricket called, which was very frequently indeed. Similar to many of Cahn's team, Rhodes went on to manage a number of shops, including a large store in Southampton.

In March 1938, the Willowbrook coachworks supplied a new twenty-seater coach with a Leyland Cub chassis and petrol engine for the use of Sir Julien's cricket team. This fine vehicle with its registration plate of EAL 7 was painted in the Cahn cricketing colours of pink, pale blue and black and ran for him until the beginning of the Second World War. Unfortunately for Walter Tacey, Cahn's third chauffeur, the coach became his downfall.

Sir Julien's team lost only 19 out of 621 cricket matches played. Tacey was responsible for driving the cricket coach on the first occasion in three years that the Cahn XI had lost a match. Perhaps subconsciously picking up on the bad mood of the players, Sir Julien's in particular, Tacey was inadvertently careless as he drove the coach back through the narrow gates into Stanford Hall. To his horror, he managed to scratch the side of the new bus. Venting his fury, it is said that Sir Julien fired Tacey for his carelessness. Whatever happened, Tacey left Sir Julien's employment and started a taxi business in Loughborough. Lady Cahn, who was upset by the whole episode and obviously had a soft spot for the Tacey family, visited Walter Tacey twice at his taxi stand to try to persuade him to return to Stanford Hall. Her cajoling offers of re-employment were politely turned down.

During those three months in the Far East, Julien had missed his classical music. He did not enjoy what he perceived to be the discordant oriental melodies and could not wait to return to his operas. While he was practising his viola or pretending to conduct the operas emanating at full blast from his gramophone, a number of his employees were also indulging their musical talents. Although he would never have admitted it, Julien was sorry that the impenetrable class barriers forbade the pleasure of making music together with his staff. Herbert Firth, the estate joiner, made instruments – ukuleles, banjos, violins and drums – as a hobby. Herbert Reginald Firth, along with his wife Mabel and three sons Charlie, Jack and Cyril, had moved to Stanford Hall in 1929 from Lincolnshire. Firth had been recommended to Sir Julien by the land agent Guy German. Bert Firth was a very skilled craftsman, carpenter and joiner and was put to work on a diverse range of projects from day-to-day maintenance in the house to props for Sir Julien's magic. Some of his unusual work included two semicircular seats that stood at the front of the hall, gates for the south lodge and a large cage that housed the monkeys in the gun room. As a young teenager, Charlie Firth was employed to work in the gardens under Freddie Foster.

Julien would smile wryly at the noise the footmen and other staff would make from their eclectic collection of instruments as they wandered over to Firth's house at Gould's Barn, armed with food, beer and whisky to make music and fun from six in the evening until the early hours of the following morning. Their music-making was really rather good, so they decided to form a band called Stanlea, an abbreviation of Stanford and East Leake. They played quite regularly in pubs in East Leake. Bridgman and Robson reported back to Sir Julien on their musical progress, but to his regret, he was never able to listen to them himself.

8

Grand Illusions

During 1936–7, Sir Julien's desire to be connected with the crème of the world's musicians reached its pinnacle. He was able to facilitate this through his presidency of the Nottingham Harmonic Society. Cahn organised and paid for the Vienna Symphony Orchestra under Dr Felix Weingartner, with Albert Sammons as solo violinist, to come to Nottingham and perform on 26 October 1936 as a birthday treat to himself.

In May 1937 Sir Julien announced that his arrangement with the Society would cease, but that he would continue to give financial help. He did this for one more season. It was around this time that his health started to give him concern, and this propelled Sir Julien to cease many of his peripheral commitments. Austin writes in his history of the society that while Sir Julien's scheme saved the financial situation at the time and provided orchestras, conductors and artistes that the Society would never have otherwise encountered, the members perhaps had it rather too easy under Sir Julien's financial stewardship. At the same time, Arthur Foulds resigned his position as secretary after sixteen years and the position of chorus master also became vacant, so the society was filled with new blood. Indeed, the Lord Mayor was asked to take over the presidency from Sir Julien and in fact, the position was held by Lord Mayors for many years after. Although Sir Julien was no longer actively involved, when he sponsored the tour of the great pianist Moiseiwitsch several years later in 1943, he organised for him to play in Nottingham.

In February 1937, Julien arranged, with the help of Foulds, for the world-famous Russian bass, Feodor Chaliapin, to tour around all the major cities in England, starting at Covent Garden in London. Cahn paid all of Chaliapin's expenses. The proceeds of the concerts were to be given to the National Council of Social Service in distressed areas.

Once again, the appeal was being supported by Julien's good friend Lucy Baldwin. This tour was, with hindsight, particularly special as Chaliapin died a year later of leukaemia aged just 65.

Hunting was an activity that Julien had no desire to give up. In 1937 Sir Harold & Lady Zia Wernher, Cdr Alexander and Capt J.D. Hignett resigned as Joint Masters of the Fernie Hunt. Sir Julien was elected as the new Master although, according to George Thompson who wrote *History of the Fernie Hunt 1856–1987*, a couple of people had reservations. He was right in surmising that Cahn was not really a 'countryman'. It was Lady Cahn who enjoyed hunting and was a fearless rider. Her husband partook of the sport but did so to promote his social standing.

Fernie country lies to the south of the East Midlands, bordered in the north by the A47 Leicester to Peterborough road, with Market Harborough sitting in the middle of the territory. It was much more convenient for Sir Julien. Nevertheless, due to his numerous other commitments he was often late to meets and had to appoint Col Breitmeyer as Field Master. During the previous years as Master of the Burton and to a lesser extent with the Woodland Pytchley, Cahn had been able to hunt as he pleased, answerable to no one. Things were not quite so easy-going at the Fernie. Cahn was a controversial appointment, although it has been noted that those with a sense of humour appreciated his eccentricities.

Ulrica Murray Smith was of the opinion that, 'The meet was the only part of a day's hunting which he really enjoyed. He would only stay out for an hour or so and then retire into the back of his Rolls Royce, where he would find a three-course lunch ready for him.'

Once again, Capt Deane followed Cahn as he had from the Burton Hunt to the Woodland Pytchley and now onto the Fernie. Looking after Cahn's duties in the country, Capt Deane was also employed as Hunt Secretary for a year or so, until the conflict of interest was considered such that he was replaced. The 1937/38 season was not considered a successful one. This was due to a shortage of foxes and a criticism of Peaker, the Huntsman of the past ten years. Peaker had been seriously ill and had been forced to take his eye off the ball. In addition there was some disgruntlement among farmers about a lack of liaison. It clearly didn't help matters that Sir Julien lived out of the Fernie country and Capt Deane had other duties.

One day John Swift, second chauffeur, was driving Sir Julien home in the Rolls Royce after a day of strenuous hunting.

'Halt the car Swift! I need to micturate.'

'One moment Sir!' replied Swift, desperately hoping there would be somewhere appropriate to pull over on the straight road ahead of him. Robson had briefed him on Sir Julien's vocabulary. Fortunately 'micturate' was one of the easier words to remember as it actually sounded like 'urinate'.

'Oh, no hurry!' muttered Cahn as he pulled off one of his hunting boots. Swift glanced in his mirror and to his bemusement saw his master 'micturating', or in the vernacular 'peeing', into his boot. The expression on Swift's face must have been priceless.

'Don't worry – the boot is waterproof!' announced Cahn with a glint in his eye. 'It won't stain the car.'

'What about the boot, Sir Julien?'

As he uttered the words, images of the boot room at Stanford Hall came to mind – row upon row of boots and shoes for every purpose. Swift instantly realised exactly what would happen to the boot.

'I don't intend to hold a boot full of urine all the way home.' Swift stopped the car and rushed around to open Sir Julien's door.

'Here you go! Dispose of it!' ordered Sir Julien as he carefully handed the warm and heavy boot to his chauffeur. 'No – don't pour it out, just propel the boot over the hedge!'

With a brief nod and a smile, Swift did as he was ordered and they continued on their way home.

The boot room in the basement of Stanford Hall contained all of the boots and outdoor shoes owned by the family. It was the domain of the footmen.

'I've never seen so many boots in one room!' exclaimed Bill Cover, a junior footman, whose job it was to keep them all clean and sparkling.

Perhaps unhappy with the shoe-cleaning prowess of his staff, Sir Julien organised a shoe-cleaning competition. Little did he realise that his son Richard, having spent so much time in the pantry, particularly under the watchful eye of footman Ernest Fletcher, had acquired outstanding shoe-polishing skills himself. The staff lined up in the brushing room, next door to the boot hall and the drying room (that housed a 'Spik' glove-cleaning machine with accessories) and set to their polishing. At the end of the line stood the shortest contestant, young Richard. He rubbed and rubbed the two-tone brogues until they sparkled. The contestants then left the room while Sir Julien undertook his judging. Without any hesitation he selected the two-tone brogues at the end of the line. With great hilarity the winner was brought in front of Sir Julien. The competition certainly had the desired effect. No servant wanted to be out-shone by a little boy and the standard of polishing increased dramatically thereafter.

Both Julien and Phyllis loved animals, and their home was full of dogs and horses as well as several rather more exotic species. Throughout her life Phyllis gained a huge amount of pleasure from choosing presents for friends and family. On her regular trips to London she spent long hours browsing the shops on Bond Street. While she had little trouble choosing trinkets and clothing for her friends, and adorable toys for her children, the annual task of selecting a suitable birthday present for her millionaire husband, the man who had everything money could buy, taxed her ingenuity. During the mid-1930s she hit on a successful recipe – animals! Phyllis bought Julien two small monkeys, Humbolt Woolies of South American extraction, the only breed considered to be absolutely safe with humans. Julien was thrilled with the new pets. He called them Winnie and Neville, named after Churchill and Chamberlain. The monkeys lived in an enormous cage, the size of a room, in the gun room, eating fruit. They provided much entertainment, peeling bananas for the Cahn children who visited them whenever they had friends over.

Sunday tea was always a big weekly event at Stanford Hall. Tea was taken in the lounge and Winnie and Neville were allowed out. Their regular trick was to climb up the curtains, making it extremely difficult to recover them. There was one member of the household who was never allowed to take tea with the monkeys in the lounge, and that was Waity. Whenever Neville saw Miss Waite the governess, he urinated! It was a regular cause of embarrassment and mirth. On another occasion the monkeys caused great havoc when a celebrated news cameraman had his reels uncoiled from their cans.

In 1937, Phyllis was faced with the same birthday dilemma once again. This time she startled Chesham, the estate engineer, by announcing conspiratorially that she wished to present Sir Julien with sea lions. Mr Chesham, having recovered from the initial shock, went off to London where he managed to purchase two male sea lions from London Zoo at a cost of £60 each. Being somewhat difficult to get hold of, Phyllis had to wait a further nine months for the arrival of the two females. When the October morn dawned and Sir Julien saw the creatures frolicking in the Stanford Hall swimming pool, he was overjoyed. He was even more thrilled to learn that another two sea lions would be arriving the following year.

Aqua and Charlie were almost fully developed males from California. But the swimming pool was far from an ideal home for them, as the water quickly became slimy. Sir Julien summoned Robert (known as Bob) Mason, a tall, thoughtful man who ended up with one of the most unusual jobs on the estate. In 1937 he was employed as the Water Bailiff in charge of the trout fishing at Stanford Hall. In his extensive programme of developing the estate, Sir Julien had drained and cleaned up the lake area. Originally it had been extended from a somewhat small area of water by diverting a stream. Coarse fish were removed and the lake re-stocked with trout bred on the estate. Bob Mason was engaged on this task, so it seemed natural for Cahn to move him from the fishery to the sea lion pond.

'I want you to oversee the building of a special pool for the sea lions,' Cahn announced. 'I've employed a keeper from London Zoo to assist you. In the meantime I've organised for you to go down to London Zoo for a week's worth of sea lion training. They will be your charges from now on!'

Bob Mason was stunned. He knew nothing about sea lions, but was delighted to be given the opportunity to learn. Soon he discovered that he had an extraordinary hitherto undiscovered talent for sea lion training!

Every day fresh fish was delivered from Grimsby for the sea lions. During winter they were fed three times a day, on whiting and herring. During the summer, they only required two meals – however, these meals were normally timed so that any guests could attend 'the feeding of the sea lions' – a high point of their visit to Stanford Hall.

It took nine months for the purpose-built pool to be constructed, during which time the sea lions were the only swimmers in the swimming pool. During the construction, Albert and Richard played pranks on the builders. One day, playing with the rail trucks that were used for moving the materials up and down the slope to the pool, the boys released the wagon from the top of the slope, and as it shot down the rails towards the builders they realised the danger. Albert shouted just in time for the workmen to jump clear. Albert was in great trouble with his father for this – a memory that has stayed with him his entire life.

Freda and Ivy, the two female sea lions, arrived in the summer of 1938 and moved straight into their new home where the males were waiting for them. The sea lion pond was created at the foot of a gentle slope known as The Dell. It was approximately 35 yards long by 25 yards wide, 7ft deep in the middle, tapering to 2ft deep at the sides. At the wider end, nearest to the lake, there was a stone structure that the sea lions used as their sleeping quarters. Close to the water's edge, a see-saw diving board was constructed made with special sprung ends, which allowed the sea lions to jump off the diving board without damaging their spines. Time and time again, the creatures would pull themselves up the shallow steps, climb onto the diving board and hurl themselves into the water. The sea lions' home cost Cahn about £3,000.

Sadly, a short time after they moved into their new home, Charlie died, apparently as a result of having eaten large amounts of stones. However, the remaining three sea lions thrived, relishing the time and attention given to them by Bob Mason, their new but very effective trainer. 'Until ten months ago, Mr Robert Mason had not even seen one of these amusing creatures,' declared the reporter from the *Loughborough Echo* in the 19 August 1938 edition. 'Today, he is justly proud of the feats performed by his charges.'

Bob successfully trained the animals to perform a series of routines, including imitating the famous Guinness poster advert, where a sea lion balanced a bottle on his nose. They swam up and down and balanced coloured sticks and balls offered by the guests. Aqua, who was the most intelligent of the three, obeyed Bob Mason's invitation to take the ball up the steps to the roof of the sea lion house, lie down when instructed, 'shake hands' and clap his 'hands' (flippers) when bidden. He would even kiss the cheek of the trainer on request.

During the few years that the sea lions lived at Stanford Hall they gave numerous people great pleasure and entertainment and were always incorporated into the fundraising events that the Cahns organised.

As an adult, Julien Cahn displayed little interest in or involvement with the faith and practice that had been a ruling passion in his father's life. He never went to synagogue and did not keep a kosher home. All the same, he would never knowingly eat seafood or pork and on the whole his diet comprised mainly of vegetables and fish. The Cahns had many Jewish friends and they were sensitive to their requirements. Dr and Mrs Jaffé, close Nottingham friends who kept a kosher kitchen, were very regular visitors to Stanford Hall. Lady Cahn always ensured that their food was prepared, as far as possible, to kosher standards.

It was Phyllis Cahn who insisted that their children have some Jewish upbringing. Both boys were circumcised eight days after being born, as is standard Jewish custom, and upon attaining the age of 13, they both had Bar Mitzvahs. By this time, 1937 in the case of Albert and 1940 in the case of Richard, Sir Julien was so anti-religion that he did not even attend his sons' Bar Mitzvahs. This must have raised many an eyebrow among the Jewish community, as the Bar Mitzvah is considered a rite of passage, one of the most important occasions in a Jewish boy's life, typically attended by all friends and family and an excuse for a big party afterwards.

By all accounts Richard's Bar Mitzvah was a light-hearted event. The event was held at the Serabskis' house in Derby – long-standing friends of the Cahns. Serabski had taught Richard his prayers, songs and psalms. Having learned and recited realms of incomprehensible Hebrew verses, he was then expected to make a speech to the congregation at the reception afterwards. The audience welcomed Richard with raucous clapping and waited in avid anticipation for his speech, having been impressed by the young boy's cantoresque singing. Richard stood in front of them but although the Hebrew words had flowed easily the English words failed to arrive.

'Stop making me laugh!' he roared at his elder brother Albert, who was sitting in the front row pulling faces. And then, to the bemusement of all present, Richard promptly sat down, forgoing the well-prepared speech. And thus was his launch into manhood!

The Cahns were particularly friendly with two prominent Jewish families – the Jaffés and the Snappers. W. Max Snapper was president of the congregation. He was delighted when, in 1935, Sir Julien announced that he wished to establish a club for Jewish youth. After purchasing a large Victorian property on Waverley Mount, Sir Julien organised and paid for it to be refurbished and fitted with an assembly hall, dance floor, kitchen, games room, badminton and tennis courts, as well as rooms for meetings and religious classes. When the Waverley Mount Community Centre was opened in November 1939, and donated in its entirety to the congregation, it enhanced the community's social life considerably.

Unfortunately, the community centre never proved financially viable, and while Sir Julien made good the annual deficits during his lifetime, it was unsustainable after his death. In 1940 it was requisitioned by the Army and after the war the house was sold for £15,000 and this money was used to set up youth facilities and provide religious education next to the Shakespeare Street synagogue.

Julien had not rejected his religion lightly. He was a voracious reader. He digested newspapers, journals and books covering national and international news, politics and history. It is said that he studied every single religion and rejected them all. But just because he didn't practice a religion, this did not change others' perception of him.

As a rationalist thinker, Sir Julien only believed in things that could be explained logically. As such he dismissed much of religion. He did not believe in the supernatural and many of the so-called 'psychics' that sat at the fringe of the magic world. But he loved tricking others. He was fascinated by the way the human mind worked, how people could be deceived into seeing only the things that the performer wanted them to see. If something seemed impossible or unbelievable, Sir Julien would analyse and investigate until he came up with the logical and rational solution.

An advertisement placed in *The Times* of 3 September 1936 clearly elucidates the racial hatred that Sir Julien, as a prominent albeit non-practising Jew, had to face on a daily basis. Written by Graham Seton Hutchison, for and on behalf of the National Workers Party, the advertisement, headed 'Sir Charles Hyde and the Birmingham Mail – an Apology' was written in the form of a letter. Seton Hutchison wrote that in the pamphlet *Truth* he had made the statement that the *Birmingham Mail* was controlled by Sir Julien Cahn, under the heading 'Our Jewish Masters'. He went on to say that there was no foundation for this statement, that the *Birmingham Mail* had always been privately owned by Sir Charles Hyde and he unreservedly apologised to him for the statement. Of course, there was never any apology made to Sir Julien Cahn for the offence he must have felt.

The publication *Truth* had started off as a Governmental magazine, which under the editorship of Henry Newnham had developed strong anti-Semitic tendencies. *Truth* was secretly controlled by Sir Joseph Ball of the Conservative Research Department, a department that had been developed by Neville Chamberlain. It was believed that as Chamberlain found events turning against him he increasingly used *Truth* to discredit his opponents, such as Churchill. *Truth* alleged that the British press was Jew-controlled and it attacked Jewish financiers with foreign names and English aliases.

The rabid anti-Semitism in England that the Cahns were so aware of only strengthened Julien's decision to undertake what was to be his most ambitious building project of the decade.

For some years Cahn had been working on his magic skills. Although he was a superb orator and could conjuror up much of the necessary showman's gloss, it was evident to himself and to his audience that his skills did not lie in sleight of hand. He enjoyed the big illusions, the grandiose spectacles. While plenty of thought and preparation went into the construction of the tricks and effects, they did not require great technical skill on the part of the magician. Large stage illusions were perfect. Cahn had the money, access to the best magical brains in Europe, his own innovative thinking and numerous staff to help.

What he did not have was a dedicated space in which to perform and entertain audiences. For some time he had been using the beautiful badminton court as a makeshift theatre. Unfortunately the family played badminton every Sunday afternoon, his wife played the game at other times and it was hardly an ideal venue. In 1936, after yet another clash between himself and Phyllis for the use of the court, he had a flash of inspiration.

'I'll build myself a theatre!' he announced. And what a theatre it was to become.

The architect selected to design and oversee the build was Cecil Aubrey Massey, the leading cinema and theatre architect of the day. He had trained in Bertie Crewe's office working on the large theatres and music halls that Crewe designed before the First World War, and in the early 1930s had worked for Sydney Bernstein designing the Granada Cinemas in Tooting and Woolwich, two highly acclaimed cinemas. Each of these theatres had a fully equipped stage, organ, orchestra pit and complete suites of dressing rooms, similar to that which was to be built at Stanford Hall. However, even Massey with his extraordinary pedigree must have been somewhat taken aback by Sir Julien's brief. For not only did Cahn want a theatre of grandiose proportions, he also wanted a bomb-proof air-raid shelter.

Cahn was a deep and prophetic thinker, although he rarely shared his thoughts. During those glorious inter-war years, while many were so adamant that war was over forever, Cahn was sure that it would be rearing its ugly head again, very soon. Understandably sensitive to the ardent rise of anti-Semitism both in the UK and across Europe, he foresaw the threat that Germany posed and the coming of the Second World War. By the mid-1930s Cahn was increasingly worried about the prospect of war and of aerial attack, and decided to take action. It made financial and logistical sense to combine the two schemes by building an air-raid shelter under the theatre. Cahn had the money to look after himself and those closest to him and he intended to take every possible step to ensure their future safety. Frequently prophetic, a few years later, once the war had started, Cahn pronounced to his sons, Albert and Richard, that the third world war would be fought against the Muslims.

Gossip was rife as always, and some suggested that Cahn received a substantial grant to build the shelter and that he, 'rather craftily, used this construction to provide a cheap foundation for his theatre'. This belief was never substantiated and it was subsequently discovered that, under the legislation of the Civil Defence Act of 1939, the maximum sum available, even if Cahn had been eligible, would have been £812. Hardly a noticeable sum for a project that was to cost him over £70,000.

While Massey designed the basic building, the theatre, the air-raid shelter and the suites of rooms above the theatre, he left the interior to a Mr Joe Redding, Managing Director of White Allom Ltd. White Allom Ltd had already gained Sir Julien's approval. They had been the interior designers for the massive refurbishment of Stanford Hall when the Cahns took residence some ten years earlier. Joe Redding was often employed by Massey as his chief designer, so he was the obvious choice for both Massey and Cahn.

The architect and designers certainly had to work hard for their fees. Sir Julien demanded detailed sketches, with a full perspective of all work prior to approving it. While he had no problem envisaging and planning his magical illusions, he could not understand blueprints or elevations for buildings.

Although White Allom Ltd oversaw all of the internal design, they sub-contracted the air-raid shelter to British Air Raid Shelters Ltd, a firm that went bankrupt during the completion of the main shell of the building. 'Get hold of E. Hammond & Sons!' ordered Sir Julien. They were the trusty firm of builders from nearby Loughborough whom he regularly used for building projects, some of their finest work being the completion of the swimming pool and its surrounds. When Sir Julien spoke, Hammonds listened and sure enough they were prepared to work night and day to get the job finished. At times there were over 150 men working on the build.

Unfortunately the change of contractors mid-project did cause one or two rather major hiccups. Perhaps the worst was the discovery that subsequent to the laying of over 20ft of concrete and rubble to reinforce the ceiling of the air-raid shelter, the water pipes had been forgotten. Therefore large holes had to be drilled through the concrete in order to insert the water pipes to take the water and heating to the shelter below.

When finished, it was said that the air-raid shelter could be sealed against a gas attack for two days. The doors were like those on a submarine; they shut and locked with a large turn wheel in the centre to seal them. Included in the basement was the air-conditioning plant and emergency generator. Joy Tacey, the young daughter of one of Sir Julien's chauffeurs, remembers a practice escape from the air-raid shelter through the escape tunnel at the rear of the building. The tunnel emerged into a field near the lake. The staff crawled through the tunnel one by one, until Edna, the second cook, got stuck. A large lady, she started giggling uncontrollably, collapsed in a heap causing a substantial bottleneck of staff unable to escape.

The theatre was built at the eastern end of the main hall. Sir Julien and his special guests would enter the theatre from the hall through his sumptuous private foyer. Bedecked with seven 10ft-tall French windows and walls finely decorated with small paintings of horses, the foyer led to a curved terrace around a semicircular pool illuminated from beneath. Walking straight ahead through the double doors, they would arrive at the centre rear of the auditorium with a view straight to the stage.

The public entrance, accessed via double doors to the right of the main façade, led into a small foyer with a box office on the right-hand side. It is unlikely that the box office would have had much use in Sir Julien's era as the vast majority of performances were free for guests. On the few occasions that guests were charged the funds were always donated to charity.

There were two stairways rising up from the foyer. The right-hand staircase entered the single floor auditorium at the rear while the left staircase entered at the front stalls level. A stage entrance was tucked away at one end.

Above the auditorium a domestic floor was built to house the bedrooms where visiting cricket teams were accommodated in pre-war days and where injured soldiers stayed during the Second World War. Situated beneath the stage were six dressing rooms and a bathroom and a large green room accessed via staircases leading to both sides of the stage.

No expense was spared in building the theatre. It was lavishly extravagant and utterly modern; a fully equipped professional theatre of quite considerable proportions. It is believed that the theatre cost £73,000 – equivalent to about £3 million today. Subsequently the theatre has been referred to as 'The Glyndebourne of the Midlands'.

The auditorium seated an audience of 352 and it was frequently filled up. The rake (or slant on which the rows of chairs were built) was excellent, so every seat afforded a good view of the stage. The seats themselves were extremely comfortable – tip-up chairs covered in rust-coloured velvet. For live performances, Sir Julien and his guests would sit at the front and for cinema shows at the rear. The front and back rows had wider seats and greater leg room especially designed for the slight Sir Julien. When Julien visited other theatres he always purchased two seats for himself – one for him to sit in, the other as a repository for his coat and hat.

The stage, lighting and projection equipment were provided by specialist firms. The projection suite comprised a projection room, mercury rectifier room and rewind room, and was reached by a ladder from ground level, leading to its own private staircase. The equipment, including the twin manually-fed carbon arc projectors, was up to the best 1930s standards and everything met the requirements of the 1923 Cinematograph Act. The film projection apparatus was the very latest equipment from Gaumont British Duosonic. There was a cyclorama and, above the stage, contraptions incorporating counter-weight flying gear.

Even the ventilation system was the most modern then available. Sir Julien, who felt the cold, wanted to ensure that he and his guests could relax in a perfect ambient temperature. Warm air could be sucked in and withdrawn through the floor of the theatre. It was said that all the air in the auditorium could be changed in the space of nine minutes.

Considerable attention was paid to the lighting. Sir Julien was fascinated by lighting effects and they were to become the mainstay of many of his performances. The auditorium was lit by 960 lamps, each lamp concealed in the vertical and horizontal covings of the walls and ceilings, the lights arched up the walls and across the ceiling, mostly pointing towards the stage. These were complemented by two large ornamental plaster vases.

The stage was bathed in light by 28,000 watts of spotlights. The bulbs were operated by electromagnets from a finger-controlled switchboard by which almost any colour scheme could be devised. The reporter from the *Loughborough Echo* was particularly impressed.

He wrote: 'The depth of colouring is all controlled and it is possible for the lighting to seep through so slowly that changes in the colouring are almost imperceptible.'

The Blackburn Starling stage lighting control board was state of the art. The lighting operator was located so that he could see the effects from the audience's point of view. Although the London Palladium was to get a similar system a few years later, in 1938 Stanford Hall was the only British theatre that had a remote board.

All of the best cinemas built in the 1930s had Wurlitzer organs that rose from a well. The organs were played in the film intervals. An ordinary organ was not good enough for Sir Julien's magnificent theatre, so he scoured Europe for the very best model. During one of his many trips to Paris, he bought a remarkable Wurlitzer organ that had been built by Wurlitzer's Tonawanda factory for the New Theatre Madeleine in Paris in 1926. Julien paid £20,000 for the organ and dispatched it to Stanford Hall on 25 May 1937. It was then modified, enlarged with a fifth rack, and installed so that when the theatre was complete in 1938, the organ rose up, thanks to a hydraulic lift, from a well in the centre of the orchestra pit, reaching stage height when in use.

This Wurlitzer organ was the only one of its kind in Europe; it possessed an automatic programmer made by Wurlitzer in the USA that from a punched music roll in a special unit played the organ 'by itself'. This hidden device, concealed behind the grille, featured prominently albeit clandestinely in Cahn's magic shows, enabling him to present the organ that played by itself. It also had features whereby the playing could be speeded up or slowed down, synchronising the music to the magic tricks with fabulous effect. It could play an extraordinary array of different sounds, from every conceivable instrument and percussion to mechanical sounds such as the toot of a train and even the human voice.

Fifteen players could be accommodated in the orchestra pit, but part of the floor was removable so that an orchestra of up to seventy-five musicians could be seated.

There was great pressure put on the workmen to finish the theatre in time for Sir Julien's birthday in October 1937. In order to complete it on time, men worked day and night, floodlights enabling work to carry on after dark. The *Loughborough Echo* reported that 'Lights reflected in the sky and there is considerable activity.'

The interior of the theatre was quite stunning. A rose pink carpet complemented the light pink of the frescoed walls. The frescos represented 'pagan mythology in a modern baroque style'. The lower parts of the walls were panelled in mahogany veneer topped with a wide band of ebony. The entrance doors were also mahogany veneered. But the real work of art lay in the frescos.

Beatrice MacDermott was the artist chosen to carry out the decorative work in the theatre. The private theatre at Stanford Hall was an important commission for such an up-and-coming mural artist. She had painted the Midland Hotel at Morcombe and went on to paint the cruise liner, RMS *Caronia*. She was known for her stunning screen designs. MacDermott was one of the founder members of the newly formed Society of Painter Decorators that aimed to make decorative art, including murals, more accessible to the masses.

The theatre took her many weeks to complete, during which time she lived in one of the tenant farmer's houses on the estate. The Cahn children, the Bentley girls and the children of the other servants would watch her in awe as she lay on her back at the top of a scaffold, paintbrush in hand, bringing scenes to life on walls and ceilings, painting Da Vinci style.

MacDermott painted the walls, ceiling panels and the sliding screen. Her work was considered to be imaginative, produced 'in a delicate, formalized style'. She painted a sliding screen, 12ft by 22ft, which was used instead of drop curtains in front of the stage. This was quite unique for the 1930s as it was operated by the touch of a button. The design depicted Orpheus and the Bacchante but included some personal touches such as a representation of Cahn's pet sea lions. With the introduction of fire curtains and health and safety regulations the sliding stage screen was removed in the latter half of the twentieth century and is assumed lost. It must have been the largest screen ever painted. The front of the safety curtain which is still in existence depicts Stanford Hall in the year 1740.

The interior was enhanced even further by 'a variety of delicate tapestries which formed the curtains, silks of many hues being changed to almost any colour by the clever spotlighting, while a variety of amazing patterns could be thrown on those curtains by the Brenograph'. A Brenograph was a magic lantern that could project special announcements, scenic effects and patterns onto the theatre curtains by using multiple lenses and moving slides with intricate fades and dissolves. It was the only one of its kind in the country.

Announcing the improvements to the house and grounds, the *Loughborough Echo* of 19 August 1938 said: 'The theatre, erected at a cost of many thousands of pounds, is one of the most remarkable in this country. Its lighting, furnishing, and general appointments are delightful in every respect. The fittings are modern in the extreme.'

The opening public show was on Wednesday 28 December 1938 and was a Variety Show in aid of Loughborough Hospital. Once again a reporter from the *Echo* was there. His prominent headline read: 'Sir Julien Cahn – Magician and Illusionist – Remarkable Show in Private Theatre!'

A full dress rehearsal had taken place on 17 December to which Will Goldston had been the principal guest. Goldston, the founder of the Magician's Club, visited Stanford Hall at least twice, in February 1934 and in December 1938. Sir Julien presented his show to applause from Goldston who subsequently wrote in the visitors' book, 'A delightful show', no doubt impressed by the fact that Sir Julien had told him that the illusions had been devised by him and made in his workshops – perhaps not always a strictly true comment, as many of the original concepts for the illusions were borrowed from other magicians, adapted by Sir Julien and then constructed in his workshops.

Sir Julien was mentioned from time to time in the magical press. *The Magazine of Magic* and *Goldstons Magical Quarterly* congratulated him when he was created a baronet in 1934. It was noted that he became a member of the British Ring of the International Brotherhood of Magicians, the world's largest group of magicians, attending the annual banquet in 1937.

Sir Julien's picture featured on the front of the *Magician Monthly* of October 1937, under the heading 'Magicians You Read About'. The article within stated:

We are proud to publish the photography of Sir Julien Cahn who is well known to all magicians. His interest in magic is not merely a 'book' interest but he is a practical amateur artiste and he owns the most unique collection of stage illusions in this country. His home is equipped with a theatre which seats 300 people and magical performances are often given by Sir Julien to his friends.

At a magical spectacular held on 28 December 1938, Chesham told the *Echo* reporter that the programme would last over two hours. Guest artistes included Ena Baga, the organist who played Gershwins' *Rhapsody in Blue* on the Wurlitzer showing off the many effects in her programme; the Grace Core Ballet; Phil Meny and his Hungarian Orchestra, and Sutherland Felce, a well-known compère for commercial radio programmes. Sir Julien introduced several new illusions, including a Houdini-like trick where a girl escaped from a 'genuine steel safe'. One of the most amusing was the Slimming Machine, into which a rotund young lady entered to emerge greatly slimmed down just a few moments later.

Another illusion that was most popular with the audience involved an old-fashioned farmyard pump that produced jugs of fine, foaming ale on command. According to the *Loughborough Echo* the pump was encouraged to put in a little overtime, so that the local police superintendent was rewarded with a glass of excellent ale. The then Mayor of Loughborough, Councillor G.H. Dean, was invited to help with this trick. Disappearing young ladies were included in the programme, two vanishing from a large box suspended in mid-air. A girl was produced from a very large top hat, empty seconds earlier; another popped out of a tea chest.

The reporter from the *Loughborough Echo* described the performance on 28 December as follows:

Sir Julien Cahn's beautiful modern theatre in the grounds of Stanford Hall was seen by many Loughborough and district people for the first time on Wed evening when Sir Julien presented a variety of entertainment on behalf of Loughborough Hospital. Nearly four hundred invitations were issued and the large audience saw a show that could hardly be bettered in a first-class London theatre with the many facilities and props at their command. The performance was preceded by a remarkable lighting effect. The theatre was plunged into darkness and soon the bare outline of a tree was seen. Then various other lights were introduced and the sombre scene slowly changed into a glorious garden, with life-like trees, flowers and birds. The singing of the song, 'Trees', by a soprano voice, added to the effectiveness of the item. Another attractive part of the programme was the recital on the theatre organ by Miss Ena Baga, the only lady Wurlitzer player to broadcast. With the console she came into the view of the audience by means of an invisible moving platform, and she gave a programme which included numerous effects, with drums, castanets, xylophone and triangle. Her playing of the late George Gershwin's Rhapsody in

Blue was most effective. Others who assisted in the programme were Mauricette, a delightful Austrian soprano with a remarkable talent for whistling, the Grace Core Ballet in graceful ballet and speciality dancing, Mr Sutherland Felce a well known compère for commercial radio whose musical yarn of the king with the terrible temper was the best thing he did, and Phil Meny and his Hungarian Orchestra, with an excellent xylophonist. The audience was very enthusiastic throughout. Among those present were Lady Cahn, Sir Edward Packe and Lord Crawshaw, all of whom brought house parties, Mr Lawrence Kimball MP and Mrs Kimball, and the Mayor and Mayoress of Loughborough. Programmes were sold by five nurses from the General Hospital. The proceeds at the moment amount to £130 but further sums have still to come in.

The proceeds of the event were given to the Loughborough Hospital Carnival Committee.

Within a short time, Sir Julien had filled his theatre with almost every known magical device so as to amuse and mystify his audiences. His cast and stage hands were recruited from the parlour maids, footmen, gardeners, secretaries and other household and office staff. The smallest most attractive girls were selected as helpers. One young and very able assistant was a secretary of Sir Julien's. She wore glasses that unsatisfactorily reflected the lights when she was on stage. Not wanting to lose her, Julien organised for her to be fitted with one of the very first set of contact lenses.

The audiences were visiting friends, cricketing teams, tenants of the estates with their families and local clubs, societies and groups that he entertained for charity. Undoubtedly many of these audiences had little choice but to agree to be entertained. There were a number of charity performances and open days at Stanford Hall where guests were charged to view the shows and the money donated to charities. Visitors paid an extra sixpence for the theatre show of 'lighting effects and the sunlight scene'.

Sir Julien had a particular fascination with large stage illusions and during the 1930s he assembled a substantial collection of props, many of which were specially constructed for him. For a short time he engaged P.T. Selbit as a magic consultant. Selbit, whose real name was Tibbles (Selbit – spelled backwards), was a prolific inventor of magical effects and widely respected. His most famous trick was 'Sawing Through a Woman', which was first presented in London in 1921. He placed a pretty girl in a long box and would then saw the box, and her, in half with a double-handed timber saw. Afterwards the girl would jump up from the box unharmed. Another of his famous illusions was the 'Spirit Painting' in which a picture mysteriously appeared on a previously blank canvas.

By cultivating this association, Sir Julien was able to acquire most of Selbit's illusions, including 'The Maids of the Mist'. Selbit sold many of these illusions to Sir Julien at vastly inflated prices. This lucrative arrangement came to an abrupt end when Cahn's estate engineer, Jack Chesham, became privy to a conversation which occurred between Selbit and another magician:

'Oh, hello Selbit – what are you doing these days?' asked the magician. Selbit replied 'I'm doing Sir Julien Cahn!' Chesham duly reported the conversation back to Sir Julien and the cosy arrangement that Selbit had hitherto enjoyed was terminated immediately.

Among other of Selbit's illusions that he sold to Cahn was 'The Idol of Blood' – a thrilling mystery where the Idol destroyed a living girl while surrounded by the audience. 'Growing a Girl' was an illusion in which he placed a girl in a cabinet. She was stretched then 'dissected' and put back together again, emerging from the cabinet as a fully grown woman.

One of Cahn's favourite illusions, using the principles of the famous Pepper's Ghost trick, and created through the use of mirrors, glass and clever lighting effects, was 'The Statue'. Wearing his dinner jacket, Julien would walk through the audience carrying a large marble statue, showing it to members of the audience as he passed. He would carefully place the statue on a pedestal on the stage. Having admired it from all angles he would then sit down on a chair and to the bemusement of the audience seemingly fall asleep. As he 'slept', the features and hands of the statue were seen to slowly change from white marble to pink, the vital hue of life. The statue would then descend from the pedestal and move down to where Sir Julien was sleeping. Bending down, it would kiss him on his forehead. At the caress, Cahn would move slightly as if about to awake, whereupon the statue would flee back to its pedestal taking up its original pose. As it did so, it would slowly fade back to the colour of marble. Shortly thereafter, Sir Julien would awake and feigning a puzzled expression would go back to the statue, examine it, and pick it up once again and carry it back through the audience.

The Brass Box was Cahn's most famous trick. It was a beautifully presented brass box, about 6in by 1ft, solid brass and with a hinged lid. A member of the audience would be invited to come up to observe and blindfold Cahn. Then one of Cahn's assistants would go into the audience to collect things from people's pockets such as bus tickets, coins, and other easily identifiable small objects. These items would be put on a tray and then, in front of the viewer from the audience, put into the brass box that was then locked, with sealing wax being put on the lock for extra security. Finally the box would be put on a stand that was on a pedestal so the audience could see underneath it. A small screen, also on a pedestal, was put in front of the box. The witness was sent back to the audience. Julien would position himself to the side of the box – halfway between the box and the wing – and then would begin to describe exactly what was inside the box with his magic eyes.

For example, he would describe a return ticket to Loughborough, no. 5364 dated 7 March or the markings on a bracelet. After he had described about five different objects that the audience confirmed was correct, the witness from the audience would come up again to confirm that the box was still sealed and locked. Magic! Julien had never seen or touched any of the objects and the audience were utterly mystified.

Some months after the theatre had been completed, little Richard had one of his many bright ideas.

'Waity, can we put on a play?' he asked excitedly.

'I don't see why not,' she answered, thinking how that would keep the children busy and out of trouble for a couple of weeks.

'Let's ask Lady Cahn.'

'What an excellent idea!' Richard's mother exclaimed, clapping her hands together excitedly. 'We'll do it as a surprise for your father – you, me, Albert and Pat.'

The play had to be a farce, as not only did the genre suit the rather inexperienced cast, but it was the only type of play that Sir Julien enjoyed – indeed would even attend. Noel Coward's play *Fumed Oak* was duly selected. Albert played the part of Henry Gow which many years later was to be performed by Stanley Holloway, who was to became a good friend of Lady Cahn after Sir Julien's death. Doris Gow, the domineering wife who forced Henry into marrying her, was played by Pat. Grandma Rockett was played by Lady Cahn and Elsie the daughter was played by Richard.

Richard, acting as the little girl, started the whole performance.

'Mum, when can I put my hair up?'

'When you're old enough,' replied Doris Gow, aka Pat, who relished her role as the bossy mother.

'Alice Smith is younger than me, and she's got her hair up!'

'Never mind with Alice, you get on with your breakfast.'

If all the Cahns were involved in the preparation of something, so were the rest of the household. Various servants were called upon to assist in the lighting, costume making and stage effects. But few minded. They enjoyed the distraction, even if it meant they had to work longer hours to catch up with their regular duties. The cast and the crew practised day after day until all lines were learned.

'Listen to me mother McCree. You've had one sock on the jaw, you're not asking for another one, you're sitting up and begging for it.'

That was a line that Albert never forgot and both he and his brother Richard repeated it for years to come.

The opening (and closing) day arrived. Sir Julien sat in his customary seat at the front of the auditorium and as many seats as possible were filled up with maids and gardeners and wives and children of staff. The performance ran smoothly and the audience showed huge appreciation, clapping wildly. What they really thought of the performance would, of course, never be discussed. But most were genuinely fond of the Cahn family and it is unlikely that the performers would have been mocked even behind closed doors.

Although Cahn was the brains behind his spectacular illusions, he could not have brought them to life without his sidekick – a man by the name of Jack Chesham. Chesham was officially the estate engineer, responsible for ensuring that all the electrics in the house and around the estate worked efficiently. His workroom in the basement of Stanford Hall was a hub of activity. Fitted out with welding and cutting equipment, motors, lathes and numerous electricians', engineers' and other tools, there was always some loud noise emitting from behind the shut door. But before long his job expanded dramatically into 'principal magic maker' and he gained fame for constructing Sir Julien's stage illusions.

Much has been written about Chesham and perhaps it was his interesting role that, with hindsight, has propelled him into a position of greater importance than he really had. He stayed at Stanford Hall after Sir Julien died and continued as estate engineer when the hall passed into the Co-op's ownership, remaining there until his retirement in 1957.

A large man, with small, beady eyes, he spoke with an unfortunate lisp, caused by a missing roof of the mouth. Some say it was due to an injury sustained in the First World War, but it was more likely that he was born with it. He was brought up in Nottingham, and studied some form of engineering at evening school at Nottingham University College. After marrying, he and his wife moved to Canada where Chesham worked for Canadian Pacific Railway, followed by the motor industry and maintaining farming equipment. He left Canada for life in a Texas oil town and went to Dallas to become assistant manager and then manager of a swimming pool and ice rink. The Cheshams returned to England during the depression of the 1920s and Jack found employment with Sir Julien as estate engineer. His principal responsibilities were varied, but over the years expanded to include the overseeing of the swimming pool and the tiny sewage works that were part of the Stanford estate. But his most interesting role, and the one for which he gained notoriety, was as magician's assistant and the creator and builder of Sir Julien's stage illusions.

Chesham was not a popular member of staff, perhaps in part as a result of jealousy due to his close relationship with Sir Julien, and co-conspirator of magical secrets. But he certainly didn't endear himself to his colleagues. Many of the young housemaids were terrified of him. He tried on more than one occasion to take advantage of the naïve girls. One housemaid, then only a teenager, was sent downstairs to the basement to ask Chesham a question. Intrepidly approaching his cavernous, out of bounds domain, she became increasingly unnerved by Chesham's proximity as he talked to her. Stepping backwards to leave the room, Chesham grabbed her from behind and rubbed himself insistently against her. The young maid struggled and managed to slip out of his grasp, running in terror back to the sanctuary of the servants' quarters. While she knew what he was doing was wrong, it wasn't until some years later, when she was more worldly wise and experienced, that she fully understood and was disgusted by Chesham's behaviour. From then on, this young housemaid ensured that she was never alone in Jack Chesham's company.

This 'king of the underworld' reigned over a large, well-equipped workshop in the basement of Stanford Hall, known by everyone simply as Chesham's Shop. Chesham was the only member of staff permitted to lock his place of work when no one was working there. Obviously neither he nor Sir Julien wanted anyone to investigate or tamper with the illusions and magic tricks that were in development.

While Sir Julien insisted on having a copy of the key to Chesham's Shop, this nevertheless further elevated his status among the staff, certainly in his own eyes.

During the war, strange noises were to be heard emanating from Chesham's Shop. Rumour had it that Chesham was working for the Germans; perhaps he was using Sir Julien's state-of-the-art machinery, perhaps he was transmitting to the enemy! Everyone was suspicious, not least the Cahn boys, Albert and Richard. Not wanting to alert their father of their suspicions for fear of not being believed and reprimanded, they decided to investigate for themselves. The boys knew that Sir Julien kept the key to Chesham's Shop in a lapis lazuli box on his desk. Lady Cahn, who had a charming sense of humour and revelled in intrigue, gave her permission to 'borrow' the key. One night, long after Chesham had returned to his wife in their flat on another part of the Stanford estate, the boys crept downstairs into the basement and searched the workshops. Much to their disappointment and their mother's relief they found absolutely no incriminating evidence.

One of the most vivid memories of many of the staff living at Stanford Hall during the late 1930s was Richard Cahn's small petrol-powered car. It was a cream-coloured car perfectly sized for a young boy to drive. In the autumn of 1938, Sir Julien read that Atco, the suppliers of his lawnmowers, were to be launching a training car designed to improve road safety awareness in schools and colleges. He immediately rang the managing director and arranged to take delivery of the Atco training car prototype just in time for Richard's birthday on 15 December 1938. The car was simply a standard lawnmower with the handles and blades removed, a Villiers engine and simple bodywork bolted to the top. The Atco training car was officially launched in July 1939 but production was stopped just a few months later due to the outbreak of war with just 250 having been sold.

9

The Last Tour

At the beginning of 1939, Julien resigned from his position as Master for the Fernie Hunt. There were two principal reasons. Firstly, he was beginning to feel his age. Always a fearful rider, this fear had increased recently; he had had various health worries and felt that extreme physical exertion should be avoided. The second reason was that once again he would be away for many weeks of the season, and even when he was in the country, he frequently had other commitments that prevented him from hunting. Suggestions that he continue with a Joint Master to carry out duties within the countryside fell through and a proposal from Sir Julien to continue hunting only on two days a week was rejected. Eventually another Master was found and so ended Sir Julien's hunting days.

Over the years a fair amount of criticism was levelled at Sir Julien with regard to his various Masterships. Clearly there were many Masters greatly more committed to their hunts than Sir Julien ever was inclined to be. This was a hobby he enjoyed, but it was just that – a hobby. And as with all his pursuits, if he was going to be involved he wanted to be in control and do it his way. The only way to achieve this was by becoming Master and being Master of a hunt was also a social delineator. Masters were pillars of society, top of the social strata in country society. It was a considerable achievement!

By the end of the 1930s, the Cahn XI had attracted not only the best of the British players, but the best of the Commonwealth players as well. This was due in part to the role played by Alan Fairfax. Fairfax was a former Australian Test opening bowler and batsman who was, by the mid to late 1930s, living in England. He had been running a cricket school in Westminster since 1933. Sir Julien paid for Fairfax (and D.J. Knight) to coach Nottinghamshire upon the retirement of Jim Ironmonger in 1938. In addition, Fairfax was employed by Cahn to act as his Australian agent, and upon his visit to Australia in 1936 he sourced four excellent players for Cahn's team. The first to join were Harold Mudge and Jack Walsh in 1937, followed by Victor Jackson and Ginty Lush the following year.

Some years later Lush explained that the approach was carried out in a tactful and clearly thought-through manner. All four players were 'more or less caught on the rebound and the terms were too lucrative to pass up'. At the time they were paid £4 10s for a Shield match. Lush was on £5 a week as a fourth year cadet journalist. At 24 years old, Mudge had already proven himself as an excellent opening batsman and a slow bowler. He had taken seven wickets in an innings in the first match for NSW against the 1936–7 MCC team in Sydney. However, he was young and impatient, so when he was presented with a three-year contract to work for Cahn, with the option of renewal at £600 a year – he, like the others, snapped it up.

Lush remarked wryly that, 'Jack Walsh hadn't even played Sheffield Shield cricket but had shown remarkable skill in Colt's matches as a left hand chinaman bowler. He was out of a job and the attraction of a handsome contract with the English baronet was a dream come true. Vic Jackson was on the way to a fine cricketing career but was only 20 and had little chance of making the Australia touring team.'

Lush was in the same position. The four of them accepted Fairfax's offer and moved to England.

As with most of Sir Julien's team, they were officially employed within Cahn's furniture business. This preserved their amateur status as they were paid for their retail work and in return played cricket for Cahn's team 'gratuitously'. Lush requested different work. Not wanting to forgo his writing ambitions, he agreed to play for Sir Julien only so long as he was able to pursue his profession as a journalist. Although he was employed by a newspaper his first priority was to play for Cahn and cricket always came first. His wages went to Sir Julien.

After a short stay at Stanford Hall, the Australians had to find their own living accommodation. They all found digs close to Nottingham – good rooms were cheap and they were well remunerated. Walsh and Jackson lived in Leicestershire as they wanted to qualify for that county and consequently had to be domiciled there. Mudge and Lush lived in Nottingham, resigned to the fact that they could not play county cricket for Nottingham as they had not been born in the county. Besides their accommodation, all their other living expenses were paid for by Sir Julien. This included their cricket paraphernalia, laundry, food and even a wine allowance. Although he drank very little himself, Sir Julien did not mind his players consuming alcohol. However, when matches were played on his own grounds, he ensured that the opposing teams were excessively well fed and imbibed, whereas his own team had strict quotas on the amount of alcohol they were allowed to consume. Legend says that Sir Julien always provided ten girls for the opposing team after major games. When asked why he only provided ten, the answer came, 'Because the chap who got me out didn't get a girl!'

When there were no cricket matches on a Wednesday, Lady Cahn always issued invitations to the players, along with their wives or girlfriends, to visit Stanford Hall for tennis, golf or swimming. The cricketers genuinely appreciated the facilities, commenting that the lawn courts were as good as Kooyong (Melbourne's famous lawn tennis club), and the nine-hole golf course which surrounded the manor was in perfect condition. The heated swimming pool was almost Olympic size with diving stands at the deep end. Although she was relatively young, the players looked upon Lady Cahn as a mother figure rather than the boss's wife. Certainly more approachable than her husband, she also enjoyed the company of the attractive young men.

Although Sir Julien's cricketing skills may have been laughed at by opposing teams or spectators, he had the unfaltering respect of his own players. Lush explains that although he was a poor player he was a good captain, 'mainly because he had studied the game all his life and also he had very good material at his command'.

He described Cahn as, 'a very fair man, courteous – although inclined to moodiness – and capable of being charming at times. He had no objections to his players' wives travelling with the team, but they were the cricketers' responsibility and their expenses were not on him.'

During 1938 Sir Julien was invited to tour New Zealand by the New Zealand Cricket Council. On 6 January 1939 the team sailed from England on the gleaming white *Monterey*, arriving in Auckland on Thursday 9 February. Accompanying the players were Lady Cahn, her brother George Wolfe and Cyril Goodway, Sir Julien's secretary and wicket-keeper, as well as his wife and close friend of Phyllis, Betty Goodway. As normal the Cahns were accompanied by Sir Julien's barber and Lady Cahn's personal maid. Cyril Goodway was a self-employed speculative builder, building houses predominantly in

Birmingham. Although he was the reserve wicket-keeper he never played in any of the matches as Maxwell was never ill. The rest of the team comprised G.F.H. Heane, C.S. Dempster, V.E. Jackson, J.G. Lush, C.R. Maxwell, H. Mudge, J.E. Walsh, A.H. Dyson, J. Hardstaff, N. Oldfield, W.E. Phillipson, T.P.B. Smith, E.A. Watts and W.E. Astill was baggage man.

The *Monterey* was an opulent cruise liner built in 1932 by the American Matson Line. There were 360 crew caring for 472 first-class passengers and 229 cabin class. Cruising being the domain of the very rich, there was little need for many cabin class. The liner's brochure eloquently describes the ship's passage: 'As the rainbow spans the horizons . . . so Matson liners . . . cross the open seas to the wonderlands of Hawaii, Samoa, Fiji, New Zealand, and Australia, weaving island pearls into a new pattern of existence.' In the pre-war years, Matson Liners dominated the Pacific Ocean, 'capturing the essence of the lands they served, combining a sophisticated glamour with a tropical spirit'.

It was no hardship being confined to the ship for five weeks. The dining rooms were decorated in pastel greens, enriched with paintings of tropical birds and ships sailing upon vibrant seas. The first-class food was enjoyed in air-conditioned surroundings. Dances took place in a room created to look like a pavilion with trellised walls, palm trees and wicker furniture. For those people who wanted a quiet moment, the writing room was decorated to meet their demands. The *Monterey*'s brochure states:

> When exciting events stir an urge to record them, the Writing Room is an inviting retreat. Dainty desks and comfortable chairs, and paintings with narrative content encircling the walls . . . encourage one to write many a note, in a setting thoughtfully planned for that precise purpose.

Then there was the library, stocked full of books, with wood-panelled walls, rare maritime prints and luxurious leather chairs.

The de luxe suites in which Sir Julien stayed were the height of modern luxury, combining beauty, comfort and utility. Another positive by-product of this tour was the meeting of Sydney Saxe. Sir Julien was aware that his personal barber, Dubnikov, wished to retire. When Cahn met the dapper Sydney Saxe, also of small stature but with his own dark hair, on board the boat, he offered Saxe the position of personal barber and valet. Upon their return to England, Saxe, an East End Jew, moved from London with his wife, but she took a dislike to the Leicestershire countryside and returned to the smog of the city. It is said that Saxe had to prove his prowess as a barber by shaving a balloon without popping it!

En route to New Zealand the boat stopped off at the beautiful island of Fiji. In the early 1980s Philip Snow wrote a detailed account of events that took place on Fiji during Cahn's visit for John Lucas and Basil Haynes, two Nottingham-based professors. This story was also recounted in Snow's book, *Years of Hope: Cambridge, Colonial Administrator in the South Seas, and Cricket*. The following pages tell his wonderful story.

In 1938 Snow was playing cricket for the Gentlemen of Leicestershire against Cahn's XI at Stanford Hall. Julien asked Snow what he did for a living, and he explained that he was shortly to depart England for a career as an administrator in the Fiji Islands. As he was in the process of planning the tour to New Zealand, Sir Julien mentioned that they would probably call in for a day at Suva, the capital of Fiji, en route, and hoped to see Snow there. In fact, Philip Snow found himself stationed on the Rewa River as Assistant District Commissioner, just 12 miles out of Suva, and regularly went into the city to play cricket.

At the beginning of 1939, the Governor of Fiji, Sir Harry Luke, announced to Snow that he had had a dispatch from the Secretary of State for the Colonies announcing an impending visit from Sir Julien and Lady Cahn and that the Cahns had requested that Snow be permitted to spend a day with them. Aware of the high standard of Fijian cricket, Snow asked the Governor if he would authorise an afternoon's leave for twenty-two Fijian Government Civil Servants of Snow's choice to put on a match for Sir Julien.

Things were soon to get personal. The Governor asked what Cahn was like. Snow explained,

> I told him that I got on well with him and that he was patently Jewish of presumably distant Asiatic origin who, for the most part, aimed to pass as the complete Englishman – a hunting, conservative, land-owning, cricket-patronising aristocrat. I added that he had a rather rasping voice but so far as I could judge his bark was worse than his bite.

Snow comments that Sir Harry Luke had changed his name from Lukach as he advanced in the Colonial Service and, although he was also Jewish, in his pursuit to become the ultimate Englishman he gave 'much personal attention to the Anglican Church'. Luke was not pleased at having to 'arrange the honours for Cahn'.

Snow met the *Monterey* as it sailed into Suva Wharf and outlined his proposed itinerary to Sir Julien who was thrilled at the prospect of a bonus cricket game. The party was driven in the number two Government House limousine to the Government Station on the Rewa River. Snow was particularly impressed by Sir Julien's cine camera, a rare commodity in those days, and particularly unusual as he used colour film. Cahn took constant footage of everything he saw. Alice, Phyllis Cahn's personal maid, was responsible for carrying Sir Julien's cameras – equipment that went everywhere with them. Sir Julien adored photography and had the very latest cine-kodak movie cameras, a zeiss contaflex camera and other photographic equipment. He even had a Vivex tri-colour process camera by Colour Photos Ltd with spare slides and accessories.

Vivex was an exciting new photographic process sold between 1931 and 1939. Unlike previous methods of exposure that required different shots for each colour, resulting in blurred images should the subject have moved, the Vivex tri-colour camera used a single shot, so that the three colour plates were exposed simultaneously. The three negative plates were processed separately to produce the separations required for printing. Then the three images were printed one on top of the other by hand to produce the final print. This unique method allowed the photographer to produce high-quality, intense colour prints.

Always aware of the latest technologies, Sir Julien admired the work of Walter Bird and Madame Yevonde – leading photographers of the era who pioneered this colour technique. In 1933 Madame Yevonde was operating out of 28 Berkeley Square, close to Claridge's Hotel where Sir Julien kept a suite. He was inspired by her colour portrait work and the colour she used in her advertising work. Yevonde's most famous colour portraits were of a number of high society ladies dressed as Roman and Greek gods and goddesses. Ahead of his time as usual, Sir Julien's attitude was quite contrary to that of the general public and indeed many photographers, who were averse to the colour process, perceiving it as gaudy and bizarre in comparison to the black-and-white pictures they were used to. Julien took huge amounts of cine-film footage and copious photographs, but tragically none of these survived the sale of Stanford Hall after his death.

Back in Fiji, Snow noted that Cahn was particularly interested in the native inhabitants and feudal aspects of Fijian village life. Even though he would have seen the majority of first-class cricket grounds in the world, Sir Julien considered Albert Park, Suva,

[one of the] most beautiful . . . spacious and green, as it is fringed by coconut palms, weeping fig trees, spreading acacias (rain trees), flame trees, pink and golden showers through which a view emerges of the lagoon, itself all the possible shades of blues and greens and on the horizon white foaming crashing reef breakers.

The party returned through lush greenery, giant fern trees and liana creepers dripping moisture in the steamy temperature. For the English party, several of whom had never ventured to such tropical lands, it was awe-inspiring.

As they drove through the capital before taking lunch at Government House, Sir Julien became entranced by watching a traffic policeman. This was two decades before the introduction of traffic lights, so the policeman was standing under a kind of concrete mushroom in the middle of the traffic junction. He had a huge head of Afro-style hair especially encouraged in the police force. Standing barefoot he wore a scallop-edged white *sulu* (knee-length skirt), blue tunic, white cuffs and red cummerbund. Sir Julien told the driver to slow down so he could film the policeman. As he was putting the camera away, the policeman held out his hand for a tip. Astonished and appalled, Snow told Sir Julien not to give him any money.

Upon the party's arrival at Government House they were greeted by an unenthusiastic Sir Luke. The luncheon conversation was, as Snow eloquently puts it, 'a little jerky, mostly initiated by Cahn who had enjoyed his expedition to the Rewa River'.

Then to Snow's dismay, Cahn said to the Governor, 'Your police are wonderful. The only thing is that they seem to know it.' Asked by the Governor to explain, Cahn referred to the soliciting of the tip. Snow recalls that Luke was instantly irate and he himself, having decided to keep the incident to himself, was deeply concerned as to what would happen next. Sure enough, Luke decided to take immediate action to show off his importance. He immediately demanded that his aide-de-camp telephone the Commissioner of Police and there and then, to the horror of the guests and Snow, ordered the instant dismissal of the policeman.

After the awkward lunch, Cahn asked to be allowed to return the hospitality, inviting the Governor to tea at 4 p.m. on the *Monterey*, prior to its departure at 5.30 p.m. Luke accepted unenthusiastically. The Cahn party, accompanied by Snow, left Government House for the cricket match that Snow had organised on Albert Park which was separated from Government House by the Botanical Gardens. A group photograph was taken with Cahn, dressed in a Palm Beach suit, standing in the middle of the team.

Julien was staggered to see 'eleven be-skirted, bare-footed, bushy-haired Fijians fielding briskly and bowling their damnedest (slow bowling was unknown, and, if seen exhibited by Europeans and Indians, judged to be due to physical frailty) against pairs of hurricane-force hitters'.

Julien turned to Snow and asked him to captain the Fijian team and bring them to England upon Snow's first leave in 1942, at Cahn's expense. Later in 1939, at a lunch to welcome the West Indian team at the British Sportsmen's Club at the Savoy Hotel, Sir Julien informed the distinguished company, including the Rt Hon. Malcolm Macdonald PC, then Secretary of State for the Colonies, that he hoped a representative Fijian team would visit England on tour shortly. Sadly, due to the war and Sir Julien's subsequent death, this never happened.

The party returned to the *Monterey* at the wharf for 3.30 and after a moment's rest in the palatial suite on the liner, Cyril Goodway and Snow made their way up on deck to greet the Governor and ADC at the top of the gangway. Unfortunately they had not anticipated the swarms of passengers returning from shore with their guests. They struggled to push through the passageways and the surging crowds and by the time they reached the gangway it was a couple of minutes after 4 p.m. Although the Governor was nowhere to be seen, his limousine was parked below the gangway. They hurried back to Cahn's suite arriving there at 4.20 p.m.

Snow describes the atmosphere as of 'not air-conditioned chill but human iciness'. Luke and the ADC were sitting at one end, the Cahns, Wolfe and Mrs Goodway at the other. There was complete silence; no one uttered a word. Snow and Goodway apologised for missing His Excellency due to the crowds, only to be greeted with a look of extreme *froideur*. Tea was barely sipped, nothing was eaten. At 4.45 p.m., after thirty minutes of excruciating, frosty silence, the Governor announced that he was leaving. Goodway and Snow accompanied them back to the gangway whereupon the ADC turned to Snow and whispered, 'You are in deep trouble'.

Snow telephoned the ADC as soon as he could. Unfortunately for him, the telephone at Government House was not switched as usual through to the ADC but was picked up by Luke himself. With a livid fury he dismissed Snow's explanations that as a guest he had not been responsible for the duty of meeting the King's representative, and ordered Snow to 'draft a letter for me to sign and send to Cahn to demand an apology for his lamentable lack of courtesy'. Snow recounts that it took him two weeks to draft the letter, each version a little more moderate than the previous. By the time he presented a couple of drafts to the Governor, he had calmed down and decided not to write at all.

Snow was appalled by Luke's reaction to Cahn. Julien Cahn clearly reminded Luke of his roots, stirring up so much distaste in Luke that he was unable to control his manners. Snow explained that, as he never saw Sir Julien again he could not know what his reaction had been. As we have no letters or diaries capturing Cahn's view of the events of that day, we can only surmise that he was equally disgusted by the bad manners of the Governor. Snow described Cahn as, in his opinion, 'a tolerant, perhaps hard-suffering man'.

Upon arriving in New Zealand, the Cahn XI's first match was played on Saturday 11 February against Auckland Colleges. It was a packed tour. They left Auckland on Tuesday 14 February, travelling by car through the magnificent New Zealand scenery, lunching in Hamilton, and then arriving in Rotorua, the town of the bubbling if rather pungent natural hot springs, by late afternoon. On 15 and 16 February they played matches against Waikato at Hamilton, then taking the sleeper train and car they arrived at Wanganui the next morning. Their third match was against Wanganui. On Sunday 19th they travelled to Palmerton North, playing their fourth match on 20 and 21 February against Combined Minor Associations. On the 22nd they left by train, arriving in Wellington in time for dinner at the Empire Hotel. Later that evening they took a steamer to Christchurch arriving early the next morning. They played their fifth match, and to date most important match, over three days against Canterbury at Christchurch. The tourists were saved from collapsing by Hardstaff's innings of 180 and the match was drawn. Huge crowds watched, raising £510 in receipts. On Tuesday the 28th they again left by rail in the early hours of the morning, arriving in Oamuru later that day. The sixth match was played against South Island Colleges at Oamuru. After a three-hour car journey they arrived in Dunedin for another four-day match where the opposing side were beaten by just an innings. Their return on 7 March was by rail, arriving at Lyttleton to connect with the evening steamer to Wellington. Here they played their eighth match over three days, the 'Test Match', finally leaving Wellington by train for Auckland on 16 March. Unfortunately it was completely ruined by rain, even though about 5,000 spectators watched the only day of play.

While staying in Wellington, the Cahns were invited to spend time with The Society of Magicians at Wellington. Julien and Phyllis stayed at the home of one of its members, Douglas Saunders, and the Society held a soirée in Cahn's honour. Unfortunately he did not have enough time to accept an invitation from the Auckland Magical Society, although he did accept honorary membership and was presented with their badge. He sent a photograph of the Wellington function to Will Goldston, telling him that he hoped to be in London the first week in May some eight weeks later, and would give Goldston a call.

Many years later, in 1960, Harold Dover wrote an article in the New Zealand magical journal, *Magicana*. He described Sir Julien's visit: 'He was a magician among magicians and was very easy to listen to as he told us his experiences and anecdotes about English magicians.'

Their final important game was played over three days in Auckland. Cahn's side hit 456 and gained a large first innings lead but could not force a win when Auckland followed on.

At this time Sir Julien received a telegram. With a broad smile on his face, he entered the players' dressing rooms and paraded it in front of his team. It was an offer of £500 a week (equivalent to £20,000 today) to appear as a magician at the Palladium in London. He ripped the telegram into pieces and dropped them on the floor. Quite a touch of showmanship and a proud moment! Julien was quite aware that his conjuring skills were quietly mocked by the great magicians of the day, so he was thrilled that his potential to pull in and amaze the crowds had been recognised by the impresarios. Nevertheless, he enjoyed his 'gentleman amateur' status as a magician and had no desire to earn money from his hobby. It was much more fun spending it. Unsurprisingly, even though the homeward journey was delayed due to a shipping strike, when they finally departed New Zealand on 24 March, Julien was in fine spirits.

Despite some bad weather, he considered the tour to have been a great success and he was pleased to be able to donate the £155 profits made to the New Zealand Cricket Council.

1939 was the Cahn XI's final cricketing season and the trip to New Zealand was Cahn's last overseas tour. When war broke out, all contracts were terminated and the players joined the Army. Those from abroad returned to their home countries for war service. Although the occasional game was still played on the ground at Stanford Hall, the Sir Julien Cahn XI never played again.

Shortly after they returned from the tour to New Zealand, Julien visited Queen Charlotte's Hopsital to witness the culmination of much of his hard work for the National Birthday Trust. He had missed the official opening, on 1 March 1939, of the first milk bank in Britain, 'The Human Milk Bureau' which was opened by The National Birthday Trust at Queen Charlotte's Hospital.

Julien had devised the plan to set it up after becoming interested in the idea of a human milk bank in 1933, when he had visited the Boston milk bank during his cricketing tour to America. He personally funded Miss Edith Dare, Matron of Queen Charlotte's Hospital, to organise, direct and manage a similar project in the UK and paid for Miss Dare's trip to Boston where she studied the operation of the Boston bank. Upon her return he invited her to Stanford Hall where they discussed the logistics of setting up the UK bureau. Cahn purchased the latest type of pumping machines from America and the most modern freezing plant. The aim of the Bureau was to make human milk readily available for sick or delicate babies whose mothers were unable to provide it themselves. It was a feat of extraordinary organisation. Every morning, nurses went out on motorcycles to collect breast milk from mothers who had more milk than they needed for one child.

One of only three in the world, the Boston milk bank had achieved international fame in 1934 when its milk was credited with saving the Dionne quintuplets born prematurely in Ontario, Canada. In 1935 a set of quadruplets was born to the Miles family in St Neots, Cambridgeshire. On Sir Julien's instructions, Miss Dare organised for sterilised human milk to be sent up to them twice daily from Queen Charlotte's. The milk was diluted with water for the first month's feeds. The main problem was fetching the milk from London twice a day. A pilot offered to help and he went by road to Queen Charlotte's, back to Hanworth and then flew at 150 miles an hour to St Neots. Their physician, Dr Paterson, was so impressed with this that he wrote to Miss Dare in July 1938 urging the opening of a centre at Queen

Charlotte's for the supply of breast milk to ailing and premature babies on a large scale.

Lady Rhys Williams was of particular assistance to Cahn in setting up the milk bank. The Bureau was housed in palatial quarters in three rooms, all floored in blue marble terrazzo with an array of teak and other benching. Julien donated £1,000 to start the Bureau and a further £1,000 for the first year's expenses. The long-term responsibility for maintaining the Bureau was assumed by the National Birthday Trust Fund.

The Bureau was inspected by members of the National Birthday Trust on 11 July 1939. Although it had only been open for three months it had already dealt with 10,000oz of expressed breast milk with supplies being sent to leading hospitals all over the country. Those who took part in the tour included Lady Baldwin, Lady Rhys Williams, the Viscountess Buckmaster, Dame Beatrix Hudson Lyall, Mrs Frances Carver, Dr Alan Moncreiff, Louis Rivett, Miss Edith Dare, Lady Howard de Walden, Dr Haden Guest, Mr & Mrs Sydney Walton – the Cahn's good friends and public relations guru – and Leonard Colebrook.

The method of processing the milk was perceived as very modern and was given coverage in a full page in the *Daily Herald* on 1 March 1939, the day the Bureau opened. The milk was treated at 65 degrees for one hour. At the end of the day, unused milk was frozen into small cakes. Mary Miles was Sir Julien's personal nurse in the latter years of his life; she recalled that '[these cakes] had to be collected very quickly, you know, refrigerated; it wasn't easy in those days like it is today to do this sort of thing . . . they looked just like peppermint creams . . . I used to like peppermint creams until I saw these.'

By June 1939 Sir Julien reported to a meeting of the National Birthday Trust Fund that the Bureau was rapidly becoming an institution 'of national importance'. By then Miss Dare reckoned several hundred babies' lives had been saved. This was of particular satisfaction to both Lucy Baldwin and Julien Cahn whose interest in the survival of infants was due to the death of both their newly born first children. In fact, Mary Miles believed that Cahn continued to grieve for his first son, Roland, all of his life.

Julien was also concerned about babies who were first given expressed breast milk and then fed with ordinary cow's milk. He planned a scheme in which each baby would be kept entirely upon the milk of a single cow during that period. In order to take the scheme a step further, he proposed maintaining a farm to ensure the supply of a particular cow's milk, and hoped to make this a nation-wide scheme once peace had been restored. Mary Miles explained that Sir Julien was always interested in eccentric projects. 'To do a milk thing,' she explained, 'well, that would have interested him because it was unusual. He was on to another person in Manchester about heart disease; you see the Human Milk Bureau wasn't the only scheme.'

Over the next few years, even after the start of the war, Julien continued his campaigning for the National Birthday Trust Fund. Due to the war, Queen Charlotte's remained the only hospital with facilities to collect and distribute human milk. In 1942 Julien had lunch in a private room at Claridge's with Ernest Brown, the Minister of Health, where Cahn explained how milk banking in the USA had been proven to greatly reduce infant mortality. He impressed upon the minister the need to undertake research into methods of preserving breast milk so as to make it available on a wider scale. In the early 1940s another scheme was discussed with Cahn whereby all the big provincial hospitals were to be encouraged to start a human milk bureau of their own, with Queen Charlotte's as the training centre. Julien was thrilled with this plan but due to the difficulties of expense and the risk of bombing it was decided to wait for 'happier times'.

The happier times were elusive. Life was difficult for everyone, but particularly threatening for high-profile Jews, practising or not.

Bans on Jews were introduced in local clubs; few if any country clubs admitted Jewish members. Usually there was no rationale behind such a policy except for an intuitive dislike of people who might have achieved wealth and social status but still carried the stigma of being different. Upper-class anti-Semitism was widespread. Sir Horace Rumbold publicly stated: 'I hate Jews.'

In 1938 a memo sent to the Board of Deputies of British Jews stated, 'within three years we may be faced with anti-Jewish legislation in this country.'

Lord Melchett was called 'a hook-nosed, yellow-skinned dirty Jewish swine.'

The *Middlesex County Times* published a letter to the editor stating: 'Jews are orientals who in every country have corrupted business by introducing the methods and morals of the oriental bazaar.' He went on to accuse the Jews of controlling international finance, the media and introducing dishonest business methods.

This shocking racism was nothing new. It had already set the backdrop for a society in which Sir Julien had grown his business, raised his family and attained high social standing. With his dark hair and sallow complexion he was quite obviously of Jewish descent. Quite how he achieved all he did against this innate hatred that was brewing within English society is really quite remarkable. Jokes about things Jewish, seemingly innocuous but with unpleasant undertones, were pervasive among members of the upper and upper-middle classes. These opinions seemed to be held by both the learned – a typical example being T.S. Eliot – and the ill-educated.

By the late thirties, a considerable cross-section of British society found its innate anti-Semitism exacerbated by the belief that the Jews were responsible for the coming war. E.M. Forster's description in 1939 describes this:

> Jew-consciousness is in the air . . . To-day, the average man suspects the people he dislikes of being Jews, and is surprised when the people he likes are Jews . . . People who would not ill-treat Jews themselves, enjoy tittering over their misfortunes; they giggle when pogroms are instituted by someone else and synagogues defiled vicariously: 'Serve them right really, Jews!'

Things only got worse. By 1940 *Truth* described an article published by the *Daily Mirror* as coming from 'the Jew-controlled sink of Fleet Street'. It was blatantly anti-Semitic in its attack of Hore-Belisha when he tendered his resignation as the Secretary of State for War in January 1940.

'Germany calling, Germany calling!' The rasping, nasal drawl of Lord Haw Haw's absurdly aristocratic voice pierced the tranquillity of Sir Julien's study. Involuntarily, Cahn turned towards the wireless unable to stop himself from listening to Haw Haw's anti-Semitic diatribe, disgust clearly evident upon his face.

'Don't listen to that nonsense!' chastised Jenny Wren.

Just as he was about to answer his secretary, the disembodied voice screeched, 'We'll get you Sir Julien Cahn!'

Some say that Sir Julien never really recovered from that threat. He was certainly quite ill for several days afterwards, and for the first time it was evident that he was deeply fearful. His already acknowledged heart condition was exacerbated. Perhaps it had been wishful thinking to consider otherwise, but now there was no doubt that Sir Julien was on Hitler's hit list.

William Joyce, nicknamed Lord Haw Haw, was a Fascist. He joined the Conservative Party but left in 1931, describing it as comprising old, weak, grasping and dishonest men, who were betraying the nation to the agents of International Finance, in other words, the Jews. He loathed Jews with a vengeance and believed that a business was antisocial if Jewish names appeared in the list of shareholders. He accused Jews of being white slave traffickers, slave-driving employers and infiltrators of the British ruling class.

Joyce joined Sir Oswald Mosley in the British Union of Fascists and quickly made a name for himself as a dedicated activist and a good speaker. He made no effort to hide his admiration for Adolf Hitler and praised him whenever possible. Joyce believed that the Second World War was the result of provocation by Jewry and International Finance. After a tip-off that he was to be interned in the UK, he fled to Berlin. Two weeks after the outbreak of war he was appointed editor and speaker for the German transmitters for Europe in Berlin. His infamous wartime broadcasts to England became popular, even though it was illegal to listen to them. They always began with the words 'Germany calling, Germany calling', which because of Joyce's broken nose sounded like: 'Jarmany calling, Jarmany calling'.

Towards the end of 1940, after the Battle of Britain, Joyce's broadcasts lost more and more listeners in Britain – but he still remained the number one broadcaster in Berlin and his anti-Semitism never faded in its virulence. After the war, he was eventually captured, flown back to Britain and executed. By then, Sir Julien was dead.

In 1939, with the grim inevitability of war so imminent, Julien was determined to put his private theatre to good use, bringing escapism and enjoyment to as many as he could. Those months were particularly fruitful in the acquisition and development of new magic tricks and illusions. During the year, Sir Julien had welcomed 100 children from the families of the unemployed, the event being arranged with the Civil Service Motoring Association and the Civil Service Car Club. On the last weekend of peace, at the end of August 1939, Cahn even entertained a conference of incorporated accountants, providing them with tea on the lawns, a performance by the sea lions and an organ recital in the theatre.

On 16 March 1939 the *Daily Sketch* reported Cahn's latest magical masterpiece:

> Here is Sir Julien Cahn's latest trick, which I saw him do two months ago in his new Theatre at Stanford Hall. A gramophone is placed on the stage. You can examine the legs of the case and stand under the stage if you think there is trickery. On the machine there is one metal 78 rpm record, handed round for the audience to see. Returning it to the machine, the conjurer then comes into the audience and asks them to whisper the name of any Opera that has ever been recorded (there are about a hundred, I believe). Within five seconds the machine starts to play an excerpt from that Opera, continuing until the next person has chosen another Opera. If the same Opera is chosen again, the machine trots out a different portion of it. How is it done?

According to Goldston's *Who's Who*, Sir Julien was the first magician to introduce a wireless receiving set in connection with 'thought transference'. In Gordon Collin's *History of the Leicester Magic Circle* he notes that in Cahn's two-hour show he could perform sixteen illusions and twelve smaller effects. For the debut of Julien's opera trick, Bizet's *Carmen* was the opera chosen and continued to be one of the most popular selections. The trick was made possible through the use of a tiny wireless, one of the first in the UK. In a room at the rear of the stage sat Waity, the Cahn children's governess, along with wireless equipment and Julien's collection of gramophone records, carefully filed alphabetically. As the member of the audience whispered the name of the opera into Sir Julien's ear, his small radio microphone tucked under his lapel picked up the words and transmitted them to Waity, who quickly had to find the correct record and place it on the gramophone. The sound was then projected into the auditorium. Another trick using the radio link used a talking skull, whose eyes would light up in answer to questions. Today it is difficult to transpose ourselves to a world without technology, and a world where such an illusion would have appeared truly magical.

Another favourite trick involved Sunshine the budgerigar. Sir Julien was not Sunshine's first owner. He had been trained by and performed with another magician. Cahn was so impressed by the bird that he persuaded the magician to part with him in exchange for £200 (equivalent to £8,500 in today's money!) and the right to perform the trick. Whether or not the bird had been for sale or whether the sum of £200 had been just too attractive an offer to refuse can only be speculated. Even so, Sir Julien still had to spend time patiently training the bird.

Sunshine was let out of his golden cage and sat on a white perch on stage. On cue he would fly to the stick that Sir Julien held out, sitting on it quietly. In his other hand, Cahn held a pack of cards. He would ask a member of the audience to shout out the name of a card.

'Give me the Jack of Hearts Sunshine!' his owner would command, fanning out the pack in his hand.

On cue, Sunshine would pick out the correct card. As is always the case when dealing with children or animals, Sunshine would sometimes make a mistake. But Sir Julien was a kind owner.

'Naughty Sunshine!' he would chastise, 'Have another go!'

And sure enough, Sunshine would deliver the correct card. Whether the mistake was attributable to the human operator or his avian assistant was debated for many years.

Garbo was Cahn's other bird assistant. A yellow canary, she performed a different trick. She was placed in front of a mirror that she pecked at to prove it was really a mirror. Then Sir Julien put a semicircular cover in front of the mirror that just covered the bird. Upon removing the cover Garbo had disappeared. Seconds later she magically reappeared on the other side of the mirror, seemingly having walked straight through the glass.

'The most popular trick', as described by the local press, involved a flow of cocktails and liqueurs from a conventional water jug. Sir Julien would stand on stage holding a tray and empty glasses with a large jug of clear water. Members of the audience were asked to select which liqueur they would like to drink. Sir Julien held the jug up high, so that the audience could see the water going down into the clear glass and then magically, the glass would fill up according to the colour of the liqueur that the member of the audience had requested. The member of the audience would then be given the glass, and would confirm that it was indeed the liqueur requested.

Phyllis Cahn's birthday was on 15 June, and in 1939 it was she who was the recipient of an unusual animal present. Julien purchased some penguins. They lived in a small pond visible from the house. Unfortunately, they did not remain long at Stanford Hall. During

1940, due to rationing restrictions, the Cahns were no longer able to feed them. So, along with the sea lions, the penguins were sent back to London Zoo.

In August 1939, Julien and Phyllis took a car journey with the children to visit two houses that Julien had recently bought as bolt-holes, should they need to escape Stanford Hall. In fact, the houses were never used, and were sold off in 1945. The nearest was an attractive country house located in a beautiful location outside Betws-y-Coed in Snowdonia, North Wales. The house was managed by a Finnish housekeeper, a woman who fuelled suspicion among the locals. She used to lie outside naked to sunbathe. Even worse than that, during the war she sometimes forgot to put up the blackout curtains so rumours spread that she was on the side of the Germans.

The other house was Bank House at Howtown, Penrith. The family only visited this house once, and Albert and Richard's sole memory is the name of the butler, a man called Fooks!

This was the last trip that the family took together in the Rolls Royce. On 3 September 1939 the Government announced that petrol and oil was to be rationed, allowing about 200 miles of motoring per month per motorist. By 1942 petrol rationing for the private motorist was cut altogether. Although fuel production continued in Britain throughout the war, much of it was reserved for war use. This was not going to discourage Sir Julien who immediately obtained dispensation for travelling and set about investigating alternative energy sources for his cars. He had the Wolesey's engine converted to run on gas, similar to many public buses. It had a large inflatable balloon connected to its roof that blew up to about the same size as the car itself, and held enough gas to get from Stanford Hall to his office on Talbot Street, Nottingham. It was a most comical sight and probably the only car on the road with such a conspicuous attachment. One of the Rolls Royces was converted to run on a burner that was located in a trailer attached to the car, and had to be continually stoked up with solid fuel to create the gas to operate the engine.

By Christmas 1939, the hall and grounds of Stanford Hall had been requisitioned for use as an Army transport supply centre and home to the 12th Battalion Royal Army Ordnance Corps. The vehicle dispersal unit took over much of the grounds, particularly the area lying to the front of the Hall. The new wing of rooms above the theatre were adapted for use by the military. This became a military medical unit, part of the City Hospital of Nottingham, housing recuperating soldiers who had been wounded in France and overseen by Dr Crow. Only commissioned officers were permitted to enter the Hall via the main entrance. However, Lady Cahn, dressed in her YMCA uniform, decided to provide a canteen for the lower ranks, accessible via a side entrance. The only occasions that the main rooms of Stanford Hall were used were when the officers from the parent Army unit at Old Dalby held their dances in the drawing room. Dancing was not a pursuit Julien Cahn had ever enjoyed, with one exception – the tango. He danced the tango to perfection.

The service men and women stationed in the area were regularly entertained at the Stanford Hall theatre, often by Sir Julien performing magic. Captain Alec Bell, otherwise known as Peter Warlock, was based at a War Office depot in Loughborough. He received an invitation from Sir Julien to visit Stanford Hall for a buffet supper. Peter's company included his own magic and a good band with a piano accordion. Over a buffet supper after a show at the Hall, Peter mentioned that he wanted to perform the Bullet Catch. Sir Julien invited him to come over for tea in the near future to discuss the project and shortly afterwards Peter Warlock presented the Bullet Catch at Stanford Hall.

The Bullet Catch is one of the most famous and potentially lethal magic tricks. It has actually claimed the lives of at least fifteen magicians. The most famous fatality was Chung Ling Soo (William Robinson – oriental names gave magicians mystery) who was shot on stage in 1918. Rumours persisted that his death was not an accident, but was a murder committed by another magician, motivated by jealousy. A bullet is fired directly at the performer, who catches the bullet in his teeth. Those who perform this stunt invite disaster and although Warlock's experience can not be classified as a disaster, he probably felt it was at the time.

To Peter Warlock's dismay, the firing of the bullet created a small hole in Sir Julien's magnificent cyclorama. The cyclorama was the nineteenth-century version of virtual reality! Artists tried to give viewers a 3D surround effect by painting a large-scale realistic scene on the inside of a cylinder. Standing inside, one would get the feeling of seeing a distant place. By the beginning of the twentieth century, projectors were used to display images on a surrounding screen. Cycloramas for the stage were seamless pieces of fabric used for creating the illusion of an infinite background. Images were projected on to the cyclorama to give fabulous effects. Stanford Hall's cyclorama was used for creating a sunrise scene, creating the illusion of slowly moving from night to bright sunlight. A hole in the cyclorama would completely ruin all such effects.

The next morning Capt Bell sent a lance corporal surreptitiously onto the stage to paper over the hole to hide it. Whether or not Sir Julien ever discovered the hole is not recorded, but if he had, Peter Warlock would have had little to fear. Sir Julien is unlikely to have lost his temper; he probably would have found the 'hole' escapade rather amusing, during a time when there was little else to chuckle about.

Both Albert and Richard inherited their father's interest in magic. At the start of the war Albert had acquired about seven or eight of the tricks for his own amusement. Eventually he became quite proficient at executing this magic and he built up a professional show.

At the age of 20 Albert was working as an apprentice engineer (a reserved occupation) at the Brush Electrical Company in Loughborough, but he volunteered to go into the Army and joined the REME. Just prior to the outbreak of war, George Black had put a large number of musicals on the London stage. Upon joining the Army as a captain, he became appalled by the low standard of entertainment offered to the troops by ENSA. Typically this organisation consisted of rather ancient and retired artists who were too old to serve their country in the Army. Consequently, Capt George Black formed a unit called 'Stars in Battledress'. They invited volunteers to make up shows that were then sent to various camps at home and abroad in order to entertain the troops at a much higher standard.

Albert, who was in the Army as an acting unpaid lance corporal, volunteered and was selected to perform his magic. The show he joined was headed by Bruce Trent (Bill Butters' real name) who was a star in a large musical production prior to the outbreak of war. Small tricks abandoned by Sir Julien became the nucleus of Albert's performance, supplemented by a psychic act that he invented. This act was watched every night by the rest of the cast who never worked out how it was done.

Meanwhile, Richard had been too young to join the Army upon the outbreak of war, so Sir Julien decided to send him to work down the coalmines. As soon as he turned 17, Richard also joined the Army. He developed his own magic act and was able to join Albert in the same unit and the same show. Richard called himself 'Professor Memorino' and gave a performance demonstrating his extraordinary feats of memory.

10

An Untimely End

In 1942 Sir Julien decided that he had had enough of his business. Although Jays and Campbells was still enormously profitable, despite the country being at war, the business was proving to be an untenable mental and emotional burden to Julien. The problems and worries weighed him down, made him feel physically unwell and far outweighed any financial rewards. In previous years he had found work exciting, challenging and stimulating. Now he dreaded going to the office. He even began to fear reading the newspapers in case there were more unfavourable reports on his companies.

The Government had introduced numerous laws and regulations relating to hire purchase. Julien's best staff had been called up, and most of the shops were being run by second-rate managers. It seemed to Julien that every week one or other of his managers was breaking the law, taking advantage of the public, getting involved in rationing irregularities and price control overcharges, disregarding the controls imposed by head office. Travel was restricted and it was proving impossible to visit most of the stores, stores that were located all over the country. Whenever his managers got into trouble, Sir Julien's name was quoted in the newspapers. He dreaded the bad publicity and simply could not bear for his name to be besmirched any longer. His sons were too young to take over the business. The business he had created was rapidly turning into an uncontrollable monster and Julien was becoming increasingly desperate to be rid of its clutches.

Over the next few months, Sir Isaac Wolfson was a frequent visitor to Talbot House. A small, chubby fellow, his face became well known. The staff thought that he was a friend of Sir Julien's. In fact, he was visiting to tie up the deal of Sir Julien's life.

On 5 October 1943, in the boardroom of Talbot House, Sir Julien signed a contract and sold his business to Great Universal Stores, of

197

which Sir Isaac Wolfson was Managing Director. The *Nottingham Guardian* stated that GUS 'purchased 3,500,000 ordinary shares of 10 shillings each in Jays & Campbells constituting the whole of the ordinary share capital'.

As they signed the deal there were various accountants and solicitors around the table, representing both sides. George Brereton was a tax accountant with Hubart, Durose and Payne, Sir Julien's Nottingham-based accountants. He recalled the stunned silence of all the advisors when Wolfson and Cahn started to argue about who would keep the two jade ashtrays that were placed in the centre of the boardroom table. How bizarrely inappropriate it seemed for Wolfson to want two ashtrays when he had just completed a deal to buy the largest furniture business in the country. And why would Cahn care when he had enough money to buy anything he should ever want? Brereton then recalled a visit he had made to Wolfson's London head office, when he had been taken to an underground room, lined with shelves stashed full of jade objects. Wolfson was an avid collector of jade artefacts. Eventually, much to the relief of all present, the men agreed to keep one each.

Sir Julien was relieved to be out of the business; at long last he could relax. When he read in the newspapers about the troubles facing his previous company he just smiled wryly and set the paper down gently.

Just weeks later, in the House of Commons, a Mr Robertson asked the President of the Board of Trade if he would take immediate steps to apply to the court for an order to close the Jays and Campbells group of retail furniture stores. Apparently the stores had been convicted of a long series of price control overcharges, resulting in fines ranging from £50 to £3,500 that had had no effect on the company due to the large profits derived from 'illegal trading'. The President of the Board of Trade replied that between April and November 1943, five convictions under the Goods and Services Price Control Act were obtained against one firm and four convictions against another in the group of furniture dealers. He stated that until proceedings were instituted or further convictions obtained under the 1941 Act he could not make a closing order. During those latter few months, things had clearly spun out of Sir Julien's control.

Although Jays & Campbells may have had problems in the latter months of Sir Julien's ownership, things were to get much worse without him. Five years later, in June 1948, Eastbourne County Court heard the case of Mrs Bennett who was being sued by the Gosford Furniture Company (part of Jays) for the return of furniture obtained under a hire-purchase agreement.

Mrs Bennet stated that the bedroom suite that had cost her £118 was found to be made of old wooden Tate and Lyle sugar boxes. When the judge asked the manager of Jays if this was true, he said that it was almost true, although he could not swear that the boxes were actually Tate and Lyle! The judge commented that it seemed a ridiculous price for a collection of sugar boxes. The manager of Jays replied that the Board of Trade fixed the price. The judge was forced to give judgement for the return of the furniture, but pronounced that, 'a disgusting outrage has been perpetrated in selling such low-quality goods for such a high price. It seems particularly unfair as Mrs Bennett had already repaid £68 of the debt.' Sir Julien would have been appalled that the company he once owned was selling such shoddy stock.

Those first few weeks of retirement were extremely difficult for Sir Julien. He was cantankerous and restless. He had little to do and think about other than the dreadful war. Even his charitable activities were curtailed and the only public duty that he was still able to undertake was that of a magistrate in Nottingham. He only sat in the Family Courts.

Julien allowed rationing to affect him and the Stanford Hall household as little as possible. There were some foodstuffs that he simply could not do without, in particular cherry brandy chocolates. Sir Julien was well known to the staff at Fortnum & Mason in London as he had purchased numerous hampers and luxury foods over the years. In early December of 1940, Miss Honey, who was in charge of the Fortnum's chocolate department, received a gift of fine black lace underwear. She knew exactly what was required of her. A couple of weeks later Sir Julien arrived in store. She handed him a large box, surreptitiously wrapped in brown paper. Inside lay a very large quantity of cherry brandy chocolates.

Health, well-being and medical complaints were always high on Sir Julien's agenda. Whenever he had the slightest worry about his health he had no hesitation in chartering a special train to bring Lord Horder, extra physician to King George VI, from London at short notice. His fascination with medicine was evident through his charitable works and went back to the early 1920s when he first set up the sun-ray clinic. When he built Stanford Hall he installed all his own equipment. There were three rooms in the basement that were managed by a resident nurse. In the early thirties this role was undertaken by a physiotherapist or masseuse. These women were responsible for operating the array of medical contraptions at Stanford Hall, including the sun-ray machine, enema chair and medical baths. Of course they also attended to any minor medical ailments of the family and staff. It was said that Rhoda, the senior housemaid, spent too many hours in the sauna at Stanford Hall and damaged her liver as a result.

The combination of Sir Julien's obsession with health and an excess of money resulted in Cahn kitting out a laboratory in the basement, complete with test tubes, stands, beakers, measures, funnels, string rods, chemicals, scales, an automatically operated bacteria incubator, a hellige comparator with coloured disks that was used to analyse blood and urine, and many other contraptions one might have expected to find in a well-equipped 1930s laboratory. If it could be measured, Sir Julien wanted to measure it. If equipment was needed for relief or cure, then the latest model would be installed post haste. Whether there was anyone with the skills to use this equipment is debateable.

Three nurses were employed in succession: a lady called Sheila believed to be of Malaysian extraction, Sister Warner and finally Mary Miles.

Kitty Hill took on the role of masseuse and physiotherapist and was employed at the same time as Mary Miles. During the war Kitty and Mary helped Lady Cahn run the mobile canteen at Stanford Hall for the benefit of the soldiers stationed in the park. Eventually the commanding officer, Captain John Mundy, married Kitty Hill.

Contrary to the medical wisdom of today, Sir Julien was advised to be as inactive as possible to minimise the stress on his heart. All exercise was forbidden. A common sight, particularly at weekends, was to see Sir Julien scuttling from the house to the cricket field or down to the tennis court in his specially commissioned electrically powered wheelchair. It was a chair with three wheels, steered with a long handle. Buttons on the handle allowed the user to select several different speeds. Big car batteries that emitted a loud whine were located on the side of the chair. They were charged every day without fail. It was certainly not a vehicle of stealth and when the Cahn boys 'borrowed' it, they were extremely lucky not to have been caught in the strictly out-of-bounds vehicle.

The main surgery located in the basement of Stanford Hall had a number of machines, some of which would be considered quite bizarre today, along with others that are still in use. There was the 'Studa Room' that housed the Studa chair complete with a tank, drainage fittings and various chromium pipes, tubes, taps and stops. This was an early contraption for colonic irrigation. The 'Vichey Room' housed a douche bed – a rubber bed upon which the patient would lie and be showered with jets of water. A 'Meridian' diathermi apparatus on chromium stand and castors, an ultraviolet-ray machine and a Hanovia sollex lamp lived in the sun-ray room. Quite what the Beresford self-rising pump with Donovan automatic float control (20 gallons per minute), complete with switches, radiant heat bridge, vibrator, nitrous-oxide machine (presented by National British and Trust Fund) and all the various other bizarre-sounding contraptions did, are not known.

Around 1937, when Sir Julien had first become concerned about his failing health, he installed a lift that rose from the basement all the way up to the third floor. No one was allowed to use it except Sir Julien, although his children used to ride up and down in the lift when they were sure that their father was far away ensconced in work.

Always prone to hypochondria, by the middle of the 1930s when Sir Julien was diagnosed with a heart condition, his concern for his own health began to preoccupy his thoughts. As a result of these concerns, combined with a genuine decline in his health, he employed his own fully qualified nurse, Mary Miles.

The arrival at Stanford Hall of Mary Miles was a great relief to Sir Julien. She was an educated lady bringing up a young daughter, Pat, by herself. Her husband had been a Japanese prisoner of war, who, upon his release, tragically committed suicide. Mary Miles took on the role as carer to Sir Julien on a freelance basis, ensuring that she was available to look after her daughter as well. Whenever Sir Julien felt unwell, or perhaps just wanted someone to share his worries with, Mary Miles, in a completely professional capacity, came to his assistance. She was never merely a member of staff but rapidly became one of Sir Julien's closest confidantes.

She took her role so seriously that she would never divulge any of the personal thoughts her employer shared with her, even when she was well into her nineties, over fifty years after Sir Julien had died.

Mary Miles had an easy-going relationship with Sir Julien, and was sufficiently confident to tease him and not be afraid of him as so many of the staff were. Mary was treated as a member of the family, eating with both the family and guests when people came over for meals. She never forgot Sir Julien's kindness towards her – incidents such as when Pat Miles' school telephoned to say she wasn't well, and Sir Julien immediately arranged for the chauffeur to collect her from school, take her to a specialist who immediately transferred her to hospital for treatment of appendicitis.

Julien Cahn spent the morning of Tuesday 26 September 1944 sitting as a magistrate in the Family Courts in Nottingham. As normal, Robson drove him home, where he spent a quiet afternoon followed by an early supper. He retired to his study to smoke a cigar. Suddenly he felt unwell. Just moments later he died of a massive heart attack. There was nothing that anyone could do to save him. The most auspicious day in the Jewish calendar, 26 September was the start of Yom Kippur, the Day of Atonement, a day when even lapsed Jews attend synagogue. Not Sir Julien. He spent his last day just like any other, doing charitable works, eating a light meal and reading journals. There was nothing to suggest that that day was to signify the end of an era.

Julien's death was the most terrible shock to Phyllis, who at the age of 48 was now a widow. She had spent the twenty-eight years of their marriage indulging in bridge, sports, shopping and the occasional charitable affair; she had no knowledge of business or financial management. Theirs had been an unconventional marriage by twenty-first-century standards. The couple had little in common and to a considerable degree had led their own lives within it. Phyllis' relationship with her husband had been far from easy. It had never been a marriage of great friendship or meeting of minds, more a marriage of companionship and convenience. The shock for Phyllis was of a practical kind rather than the loss of her soulmate. The luxurious edifice that propped up her life started crumbling the instant that her husband passed away.

On 28 September, Sir Julien Cahn was cremated at Wilford Crematorium. The only people present were Phyllis, Pat, Albert and Richard Cahn, accompanied by Sir Robert Doncaster and Mr and Mrs Gershon, Cahn's cousin and friend. In accordance with his wishes, Julien's ashes were scattered over the principal cricket ground at Stanford Hall.

Over the next few days, Cahn's death was reported in the obituary sections of all the local and most of the national newspapers. Most recounted his achievements in some detail. *The Times* was typical, describing him as a 'philanthropist and sportsman' and listing all of the causes he had supported and the successes achieved with his cricket team. Despite the fact that success in business was probably his greatest achievement, and was the facilitator for all his other notable work, the Nottingham Furniture Company was scantily mentioned at the end of the obituary.

The *Weekly Guardian* stated: 'No man was more liberal with his wealth for deserving causes and his many benefactions included considerable help to various hospitals and maternity homes.'

The *Nottingham Guardian* actually described Sir Julien, the man: 'Sir Julien Cahn never seemed to be ruffled or in a hurry, and he was always notably polite and good humoured, though he could be acidly witty when occasion arose.'

The implications of Sir Julien's death were profound, affecting his immediate family, staff and all of the organisations that he had supported. Using his wealth, connections and nouse, Cahn had managed to buffer those closest to him from the harshest affects of the war. His demise brought an immediate end to such comfort.

11

After Effects

Albert Cahn was the principal heir to his father's fortune and inherited his title, the baronetcy. At the time of Julien Cahn's death, Albert was serving in the Royal Electrical and Mechanical Engineers. He was granted compassionate leave for the funeral and for some time afterwards to sort out the family affairs. Such time off was unusual, particularly as he was only a lowly lance corporal. Upon his return Albert received a most severe reprimand from his colonel. Uncomfortable with his newly acquired title, he omitted to call himself 'Sir Albert' when filling out official Army forms and faced accusations of using a false name.

The contents of Julien's will held no surprises for Phyllis, with the exception of one clause. Should she remarry at any time in the future, she would be restricted to a very small annual income from the Cahn estate. The majority of his effects were left to Phyllis and the children; however, Sir Julien made specific requests for £1,000 to be given to the National Secular Society, the Rationalist Press Association and Imperial Cancer Research.

It quickly became apparent that Phyllis could not afford to stay at Stanford Hall. Death duties were prohibitive and Sir Robert Doncaster, her co-executor, advised her to start selling off as much of the contents of the house as she could bear to part with. The vultures swooped quickly. Many were previous friends of the Cahns, who, aware of Phyllis' naïvity and the phenomenal bargains to be had, offered derisory sums for the Cahns' priceless collections. Within months of Sir Julien's death the contents of Stanford Hall were dessimated.

Julien's two major collections – cricket memorabilia and magic equipment – necessitated their own specialist auctions. Both were fiascos and recorded in detail by various attendees. The first was the cricket sale.

Sir Julien had acquired what was probably the greatest collection of cricketing books and pictures, including almost every book ever written on the subject as well as a notable collection of bats and cricketing memorabilia. The library was really quite magnificent. The centrepieces of the collection were two sets of scores and biographies – *Arthur Haygarth's Cricket Scores and Biographies* that incorporated many valuable documents attached to the books, and F.S. Ashley-Cooper's library that was annotated with important data. Ashley-Cooper was a very distinguished and well-known cricket historian who died in 1932. His collection, numbering several thousand books, was purchased by Sir Julien in 1930. The following year, a catalogue of the books was privately published unambiguously entitled 'Sir Julien Cahn's catalogue of cricket literature as purchased from FS Ashley-Cooper'. Decades later, in 1972 the *Sunday Telegraph* described the collection as 'the best cricket library ever collected'.

Haygarth, who died in 1903, was an English cricketer who achieved fame as a cricket writer, historian and biographer. He compiled the *Frederick Lillywhite's Cricket Scores and Biographies* in which he recorded all key scores dating back to 1744 running to a staggering 14 volumes.

Upon Cahn's death in 1944, the library became the centre of a controversial mystery. Lady Cahn offered the Marylebone Cricket Club (MCC) the opportunity to select any item in the Cahn library that they did not already possess. As it was wartime they were unable to send a representative from Lord's to Stanford Hall and instead chose a local Nottingham firm to act on their behalf.

It was Ashley-Cooper's set of books that was chosen by the MCC. Unfortunately, due to the haste with which the selection was carried out, it was later discovered that the Lord's collection contained about half of the Haygarth and half of the Ashley-Cooper sets, substantially diminishing the value of the gift. Somewhere, a private collector had the balance. E.E. Snow, writing in 1964, pointed out that ownership of the Ashley-Cooper set morally resided with the MCC and it was to be hoped that the collector in question would honour this in due course. Unfortunately this was never to be the case.

The rest of the library went to auction, together with another important collection that was to precede it in the sale. Unfortunately, at the last moment the other collection was withdrawn and the sale commenced with the Cahn library. Most of the important bidders had planned their arrival based upon the originally advertised time of the Cahn collection sale. By the time they arrived much of it had been sold off at ridiculously low prices to disinterested buyers or those lucky bidders who had perchance turned up early. Eric Pensen and Gil Vamplew of East Leake planned to attend the auction. Vamplew had a collection of about 400 cricket books at the time. However, when he arrived, early, he was horrified to find furniture under the hammer, all of the cricketing lots having been already sold. Some of the most important and valuable pamphlets, annuals and brochures were dispersed in this way. The Charing Cross Road dealer, a man called Jackson, initially refused all offers from interested cricket dealers and then apparently died before disposing of them. Much later Mrs Jackson did dispose of some of the material but sadly only about one-third of the known collection has reappeared and the whereabouts of the remainder is still a mystery that intrigues collectors of cricket books to this day.

Sir Julien also had a fine collection of cricket bats of historical interest. After his death, some were purchased by the Nottinghamshire County Cricket Club. The collection is intact and housed at the Trent Bridge ground. However, controversy surrounded a collecton of historical bats that were acquired by Redmayne & Todd Ltd, a Nottingham-based sports shop. These were offered for sale in July 1947 but it is clear that no consent was given for their sale. In a letter to George Wolfe, Lady Cahn's brother, from Sir Robert Doncaster, Sir Julien's right-hand man and executor, written in July 1947, Doncaster comments on the list of bats belonging to Cahn now for sale. 'I don't like it and I am of the opinion that no consent to the sale was given. However perhaps it is better to let it alone.'

Lady Cahn did not want to rock the boat and so, yet another priceless collection was let go for a pittance.

A couple of months after Sir Julien's death, Jack Chesham approached Lady Cahn and offered £600 in return for all the magic equipment.

'It'th no good to anyone without my inthructionsth,' he explained cunningly to Lady Cahn with his customary lisp. 'I'll take it off your handth.'

'Very well!' agreed Phyllis, relieved that Chesham was dealing with some of Sir Julien's effects.

Having acquired the collection, Chesham then advertised a 'Magical auction' to be held in the theatre at Stanford Hall on Sunday

18 February 1945. Whether the Cahn family were aware of this event is unknown, but it seems rather brazen to have held the sale at his former master's home. It proved to be a farcical occasion that those present would never forget.

The sale was reported by the late Harry Bosworth in the February 1945 issue of *The Budget*, and subsequently, in 1966, Bayard Grimshaw, who was also present, provided a splendid account in *The World's Fair*. The following description of this unique event leans heavily on both these sources and on Peter Warlock's recollections.

The magnitude of Sir Julien's collection was renowned, so despite the difficulties of wartime travel, the sale was extremely well attended by both professional and amateur magicians. Attendees included members of the Leicester Magic Circle and The Magician's Club, as well as other famous magicians including Cecil Lyle and his wife Lucille Lafarge, Sirdani, Cingalee, Edmund Younger, Walter Wandman, Peter Warlock, Richard Ritson, Eric Lewis, Archie Tear, Cyraldo, Max Andrews, Chris Van Bern and most of the Davenport family. A few had been guests at Stanford Hall in previous years, but for most it was their first visit. Len Sturgess of the Leicester Magic Circle acted as the auctioneer.

The proceedings began at 1 p.m. with Chesham announcing that he was presenting Sir Julien's Magic Skull – the bizarre skull that answered questions by its eyes lighting up – to the Leicester Magic Circle in recognition of 'Sir Julien's long and cordial association with the club'. Perhaps this gesture was to ease Chesham's conscience as the thought of his master's skull presiding over the auction cannot have been a comfortable one. The auction comprised the impressive collection of illusions, props and stage effects as well as plenty of smaller items. The illusions were demonstrated by Chesham with the help of a group of young ladies especially recruited for the occasion. Either Sir Julien's regular stage hands had already left the employ of the Cahn family or they did not want to participate in the sale. The assistants were ill-prepared and many of the illusions were clumsily presented. Some were just displayed and the effect described. In between the sale of the large illusions, the small items were auctioned off.

The main drama of the afternoon occurred just after Cecil Lyle, Britian's leading illusionist from 1940 until his death in 1955, had bought the illusion Million Dollar Mystery invented by Selbit (a box from which an extraordinary number of objects or people appear to come out of) together with backcloth for £100.

The next lot was the mental mystery, The Brass Box, that had been Sir Julien's favourite trick. Chesham presented this illusion but then announced that it used the same principle as the former illusion. Therefore, a duplicate of the 'necessary' (in other words, the mirror tunnel that enabled both effects) would have to be constructed for the purchaser. Lyle, known for his volatile temper, immediately objected on the grounds that he had just bought what was offered as an exclusive item. An argument ensued involving Lewis and George Davenport, Sirdani and Cingalee. It was finally agreed that Lyle should have the first opportunity of securing The Brass Box. It was put up again and, to the consternation of everyone, not least Chesham, Lyle bid just £1. Due to the unpleasant atmosphere, no other bid was forthcoming and The Brass Box was sold to Lyle for that paltry sum. Lyle also bought The Elastic Lady for £47, a contortionist illusion where a lady's arms are stretched beyond belief.

Ted Younger was an eager buyer and acquired most of the scenic effect from the theatre. Since Ted's own Theatre of Magic at Woolsington was significantly smaller than the Stanford Hall Theatre, it was correctly assumed that he was bidding on behalf of Edgar Benyon. Younger acquired a Palace set for £75, the Card Scene (massive cards) for £55 and the Garden Scene, including a profusion of feather darts and bouquets as well as the girls' dresses used with it, for £170. Selbit's other illusions were sold at very reasonable prices. An original version of Sawing Through a Woman went for £21 10s, the Spirit Paintings for £40, Through the Eye of a Needle for £26 and The Village Pump for £25.

The amusing illusion The Slimming Machine, which involved a stout girl being placed in an outsize cabinet which was then rotated and from which she emerged exceedingly slim, sold for £15. This huge piece of equipment had been commissioned by Will Goldston, Harry Bosworth built it for £80, and Goldston sold it to Cahn for £240. The Mene-Tekel illusion apparently suffered from a poor presentation yet this did not deter eager bidders and it finally realised £44. The old Sphinx illusion proved to be not so popular and reached only £13. But amidst all these large stage items there were plenty of smaller tricks, and there were many bargains to be had.

There seems to be no record of the total sum realised by the dispersal of Sir Julien's extensive collection of magic equipment, although Peter Warlock said he would be surprised if it exceeded £2,500, which must have represented just a fraction of its original cost.

There was much discussion and speculation due to neither The Maids of the Mist illusion or the Magical Opera Gramophone being offered for sale in the auction. Presumably Chesham kept these effects for his own personal use, although no one is aware of him having performed with either after Sir Julien's death.

A couple of months after her husband had died, Phyllis Cahn found a pile of estate agent's brochures featuring properties on the south coast of England. Sir Julien had mentioned his desire to retire to the south of England after the war had ended, but Phyllis had not taken his comments seriously. She was amazed to discover that her husband had been very serious indeed. As she was browsing through the brochures she noticed that her deceased husband had placed two ticks against a property called 'The Thatches' in Angmering, a village that Phyllis had never heard of before. After a particularly depressing conversation with her co-executor, Sir Robert Doncaster, Phyllis realised that in order to meet the massive cost of death duties, having already disposed of most of the effects within it, she would have no choice but to sell Stanford Hall. Her previously lavish way of life had ceased due to the war. Her children had grown up and left home; the servants had left long before. There was little reason to remain in Nottinghamshire. She rang the estate agent and was pleased to discover that The Thatches was still on the market.

Some weeks later, she made the long trip down to the south coast to visit the house in Angmering, near Littlehampton in West Sussex. As she arrived at the beautiful house, considered large by most, but petite by Stanford Hall's standard, the estate agent was nowhere to be seen. She walked to the front door and to her bemusement found it open. Upon entering the house she was immediately charmed. When, at the end of 1945, Lady Cahn relocated to Angmering, she renamed the house 'Sesame' in remembrance of that first visit when she found the door wide open.

Phyllis did not move down to Sussex alone. She was accompanied by Waity, previously the children's governess, who became her companion and eventually her closest friend and confidante. Waity had never married, and while she talked about someone called Dr Twigg and there were rumours about her friendship with one of the grooms at Stanford Hall, the Cahn children were never aware of her enjoying any serious relationships. As adults, Albert and Richard bought Waity her own apartment and they cared for her as their own mother, until she died in her eighties just a couple of years after the death of Lady Cahn in 1979.

Arthur Harrup had been a senior footman at Stanford Hall before joining the Army. He also returned to Lady Cahn's employment once the war had finished, and moved down to Sussex where he spent the rest of his days. Although his sister Bess had married Cyril Firth, son of Herbert Firth, Stanford Hall's joiner, Arthur never married. It was said that Lady Cahn gave Arthur most of her deceased husband's bespoke suits and clothes. Only the shirts, shoes and coats fitted him, so he gave the rest to his father, a butcher in Rochdale. He must have been the smartest dressed butcher in the north of England.

Arthur and Waity were also joined by Mrs Bentley, the Cahns' fabulous cook. Although life was very different indeed, the standard of cuisine that Phyllis Cahn had become so used to was, thanks to Mrs Bentley, never to be compromised.

Pat Cahn's war service had initially been as an Army driver with the FANY's. She then became a nurse at Harlow Wood Orthopaedic Hospital near Mansfield, where she was extremely popular with the convalescing soldiers. A year after her father died, Pat married Flt Lt Jules Silverston, an early prisoner of war. The traditional Jewish ceremony took place in the theatre at Stanford Hall, the last memorable family occasion to be held before the Hall was sold. That same year, Silverston obtained a post working for General Electric in South Africa. The newly-weds emigrated and Pat spent the rest of her life there.

On 29 March 1945, Stanford Hall was bought by the Co-operative Society for a paltry £54,000. They rapidly converted it into a college. Over the years, the few items of value were gradually sold off, although many of the fine facilities, such as the theatre and swimming pool, were still offered for use to the general public. Eventually in 2000, the Co-op sold the Hall.

Having changed hands a couple of times, Stanford Hall was purchased for £6 million in 2007 by self-made millionaire Chek Whyte. He had big plans for the property and quickly turned it into the headquarters for his empire. He applied for planning permission to build a £60 million, 120-home retirement village in the grounds, complete with spa and shops. By the beginning of 2009 he had embarked upon major refurbishment to the ground floor of the Hall, restoring many of the larger rooms to their former glory. Unfortunately, later that year Whyte fell victim to the economic downturn and was declared bankrupt.

Once again, the future of Stanford Hall is unknown. The theatre, although still beautiful, needs rewiring and has been banned from use as the building does not comply with current health and safety regulations. The Wurlitzer organ remains in place, but despite appeals to protect it, is fast deteriorating. The upper floors of Stanford Hall are tattered wrecks, with gaping holes in the roof and ceilings. Chek Whyte certainly had every intention of bringing the Hall back to its former glory and filling it with as much colour, happiness and bon viveur as was enjoyed in Sir Julien Cahn's days. Whether he will yet achieve this remains to be seen.

***

Sir Julien Cahn was a complicated, eccentric, frequently difficult man who expected to be in control. He set the highest of standards for himself and others and invariably these standards were met. Failure was not countenanced. However, he was also charming and excessively generous and was the proponent of fun. Perhaps if he had lived beyond the Second World War, his would have become more of a household name, for his achievements across so many fields were considerable. Country house cricket never again reached such peaks of success and opulence. There were few in the twentieth century who so successfully used social chutzpah, political escapades and flamboyant acts of philanthropy to facilitate their climb up the social ladder. There were certainly few, if any, Jews who became so assimilated into the British upper-class establishment.

Thanks

I have been assisted by numerous people in the course of my research into the life of my grandfather, Sir Julien Cahn. My particular thanks go to Joy Tacey for sharing so many memories and introductions and giving me a wonderful portrait of my grandparents; to Professor John Lucas for so generously sharing his earlier research; to Professor Edwin Dawes for giving me all of the articles he has written on Cahn and magic; to Haidee Jackson and Professor John Beckett for such a warm welcome and insightful day at Newstead Abbey; to David Lazell for setting me off on the course of discovery, who sadly passed away in 2007; to Una Perbedy for bringing alive the magic of being part of the Stanford Hall staff and caste; to Peter Wynne-Thomas for giving me a crash-course in cricket and a fabulous day in the archives at Trent Bridge; and to Muriel Phenix for the warm and insightful transatlantic telephone conversations. This book would not have been possible without the agreement, support, memories and patience of my wonderful Uncle Albert, and the most inspirational father anyone could be lucky enough to have, Richard Cahn.

I hope that I have recorded everyone who has helped me in the course of my research, but if I have inadvertently left names off the following list, I extend my sincere apologies. Any mistakes within this book are my own.

With thanks to:
Roy Bingham, Helen Boynton, Diana Brammer, Jill Brereton, Gillian Brewin, S.N. Bridgeman, Robin Brodhurst, Alan Carlyle, Stephen Chalke, Frank Chambers, Jane Collard, Audrey Concannon, Michael Dobbs, Tim Dobson, Mrs Dord, Felicity Eggins, Mavis Ellis, Audrey Everest, Eric Fletcher (who sadly passed away shortly after we met), James Foulds, Mervyn Gould, Joe Green, Mike Hall, Professor Basil

Thanks

Haynes, Mr S. Haynes, Vernon Hawley, John Hodder, Patricia Holdroyd, Jean Howcroft, Gabriel Jaffé, Grenville Jennings, Mrs E. Knight, Arthur Lockwood, Gillian Lonergan of the Co-op, the *Loughborough Echo*, Pat Lund, Vera Malcolm, Christopher Martin-Jenkins, Barry Martin, Eileen Mason, Paul Mason, Daphne Pentecost, John Pitts, Mr H. Ramsay-Cox, Violet Reynolds, Glenis Rhinds, Rose Ridley, Margaret Rigley, Peter Rogan, June Rose, April Sebag Montefiore, Cybil Seger, John Sherwin, Andy Smart and the *Nottingham Evening Post*, M. Smith, David Snapper, Martin Tailby, Mrs D. Watkins, Brian Willett, Susan Williams, Ruth Wittman, Mina Whitelocks, Norman Wolfe, Colin Womble.

Bibliography

Austin, C.G.A. *The History of the Nottingham Harmonic Society*, 1955

Claridge's, 'Celebration of a Century'

Collin, G. *The History of The Leicester Magic Circle & It's Members*, 2003

Colyer, R.J. *The Welsh Plant Breeding Station: 1919–1950*, Llandysul, Gomer Press, 1970

Cullen, T. *Maundy Gregory Purveyor of Honours*, The Bodley Head, 1974

Fisher, N. *Eight Hundred Years – The Story of Nottingham's Jews*

Fountain, R. *A History of the Burton Hunt – the first 300 years*, Lincoln, Burton Hunt, 1996

Fox-Smith, V.R. *Hire Purchase Organisation and Management*, 1932

Jeffreys, J.B. *Retail Trading in Britain, 1850–1950*

Jolles, M. *Jews and the Carlton Club*, London, Jolles Publications, 2002

King-Hall, S. *Chatham House: A Brief Account of the Origins, Purposes and Methods of the Royal Institute of International Affairs*, 1937

Larwood, H. *The Larwood Story*

Lazell, D. *Sir Julien Cahn at Stanford Hall and a view from the Co-operative College*, Loughborough, Heart of Albion, 1993

Lucas, E.V. *A Hundred Years of Trent Bridge*, privately printed for Sir Julien Cahn Bart., 1938

Macmillan, G. *Honours for Sale*, The Richards Press, 1954

Macneill Weir MP, L. *The Tragedy of Ramsay Macdonald*, Secker and Warburg

Marquand, D. *Ramsay Macdonald*, Jonathan Cape, 1997

Martin-Jenkins, C. *The Cricketer Book of Cricket Eccentrics and Eccentric Benhaviour*, Century Publishing, 1985

Reddick, T. *Never Cross a Bat*, Cape Town, Don Nelson, 1979

Snow, E.E. *Sir Julien Cahn's XI*

Snow, P. *The Years of Hope: Cambridge, Colonial Adminstrator in the South Seas and Cricket*, Radcliffe Press, 1997

Swanton, E.W. *Follow On*, Collins, 1977

Thompson, G. *History of the Fernie Hunt 1856–1987*, 1987

The Antique Collector Magazine 5/84, p. 64

Walker, J. *The Queen Has Been Pleased: the British Honours System*, London, Sidgwick & Jackson Ltd, 1986

Williams, J.A. *Cricket and Race*, Berg, 2001

Williams, Susan A. *Women & Childbirth in the Twentieth Century: a History of the National Birthday Trust Fund 1928–1993*, Stroud, Sutton Publishing, 1997

Wynne-Thomas, P. *Sir Julien Cahn's Team 1923–1941*

Index

217